Crime and Justice

Crime and Justice
An Annual Review of Research

Edited by Michael Tonry and Norval Morris
with the Support of The National Institute of Justice

VOLUME 6

The University of Chicago Press, Chicago and London

This volume was prepared under Grant Number 83-IJ-CX-0040(S2) awarded to the Castine Research Corporation by the National Institute of Justice, U.S. Department of Justice, under the Omnibus Crime Control and Safe Streets Act of 1968 as amended. Points of view or opinions expressed in this volume are those of the editors or authors and do not necessarily represent the official position or policies of the U.S. Department of Justice. Additional support was provided by The German Marshall Fund of the United States under Grant Number 1-31536.

The University of Chicago Press, Chicago 60637
The University of Chicago Press, Ltd., London

ISSN: 0192-3234
ISBN: 0-226-80800-9

LCN: 80-642217

Contents

Introduction

One effect of the 1967 report of the President's Crime Commission, "The Challenge of Crime in a Free Society," and the institutional arrangements that brought the federal government into the funding of criminological research, has been the emergence of new relationships between policymakers, administrators, and researchers. In the main, it has been one of the healthiest and most promising developments of those nearly two decades; but there have also been tensions and difficulties that should be recognized. Researchers have learned about the realities of the problems they study and have been given access to data previously denied them, and, on the other side, administrators have learned that the scholars can be of practical value to them.

A number of recent publications bear witness to this emerging recognition of the utility of research. A pamphlet published by the National Institute of Justice under the title "Putting Research to Work: Tools for the Criminal Justice Professional" is a guide for the administrator to assistance he can gain from the slow accumulation of knowledge in this field. The excellent series of research briefs, bulletins, and special reports published by the National Institute of Justice and the Bureau of Justice Statistics are further testaments of governmental recognition of the value of research data to the practitioner, as is the *Report to the Nation*, a comprehensive statistical picture of crime and criminal justice in the United States that was recently issued by the Bureau of Justice Statistics.

In the private sector, the four-volume "Encyclopedia of Crime and Justice," published by Macmillan/Free Press, is an excellent collection of basic knowledge in this field.

Twenty years ago such publications would have held little interest for the administrator; today the ambitious administrator knows that in the long run he will be lost without them.

This volume and the five that preceded it in this series are products of that new relationship. It is subsidized by the main federal funding agency for criminal justice research, the National Institute of Justice, and it is greatly encouraged by the close and continuing interest of the senior staff of that Institute; it is fashioned by an editorial board composed mainly of researchers but with a valuable leavening of experienced practitioners; and the essays are planned to meet the needs both of the scholar, who wants to be advised of what is known about a problem in the criminal justice system, and of the administrator, who wants to be informed of the policy implications of that knowledge.

To this extent, the relationships between practice and theory refashioned in the past two decades hold nothing but promise of advantage for the future. What, then, is the down side of these new relationships? Overclaiming by the researchers; overreliance by the administrators. Let us offer just three examples—you can multiply them for yourself.

"Nothing works," said Martinson. Actually, he didn't say quite that, but that is what was heard, and he didn't take enough trouble to quell the flood of misunderstanding and thoughtless popularization of his work, so that a great deal of damage was done to many correctional systems and funds were curtailed for humane programs that adhered to American values of equality of opportunity and respect for self-development.

Or, take a more recent important experiment, itself the product of collaboration between police administrators and a research institution—the Minnesota Domestic Violence Experiment. The thrust of this experiment was to suggest that, for certain acts of domestic violence, arrest followed by a night in jail was a more effective deterrent to later violence than were two other common police reactions to these situations—temporarily separating the parties or counseling them. It is an important and creative research experiment, but it has been received by too many—understandably eager for promising solutions to intractable problems—as if it were ultimate truth. The word has gone out: arrest is the preferred option for *all* situations of domestic violence. This research, and its findings, however, are subject to alternative explanations and require further analysis and replication before programs are implemented. The National Institute of Justice is considering replication of the Minneapolis experiment in a variety of jurisdictions in order to test both the experiment's basic findings and its applicability in different settings.

Selective incapacitation offers the third example. Major efforts are under way to investigate criminal careers and to test the promise and limitations of incapacitative crime control strategies—important public policy issues, considerable funds, and talented researchers are involved. Yet it will take time with justice and precision to define policies of selective incapacitation responsive to the community's legitimate demands for better social protection and yet respectful of important values of liberty and justice. Volume 5 in this series contained a major essay by Jacqueline Cohen reviewing incapacitation research, and this volume contains essays on the identification of "high-rate" offenders and on the legal and ethical limits of efforts to predict dangerousness. Still, much more needs to be learned than is known. Researchers must be modest in their claims, administrators realistic in their expectations.

It is the hope of the editors that this series may represent the best in this relationship—that it should be responsive to social needs and not be preoccupied with scholarly conflicts; that it should neither exaggerate what we know nor seek to advocate policy on weak factual foundations. The new relationships of the past two decades demand much of those who support scholarly research and those who pursue it; there are temptations on both sides; but it is a much healthier situation than obtained when the scholars and the practitioners were pursuing divergent interests, as they still are in most other countries.

This volume reflects again a commitment to scholarship about topics of contemporary importance—including essays on ethical limits on the use of predictions of dangerousness, on the identification of high-rate offenders, on the effects on inmates of prison crowding, and on accumulating knowledge about community service orders—an alternative sanction with which other countries, notably Great Britain, have had more experience than has the United States. One essay reviews major recent shifts in thinking about the insanity defense. Another, on the organization of criminological research in the Scandinavian countries, continues a series begun in volume 5. The final essay in this volume, by the director of the Home Office Research Unit and a colleague, concerns efforts to develop frameworks for deploying research findings in ways that contribute both to policy formulation and to the incremental accumulation of knowledge.

Norval Morris and Marc Miller

Predictions of Dangerousness

ABSTRACT

Long-term predictions of future dangerousness are used throughout the criminal law in investigation, pretrial detention, bail, sentencing, prison administration, parole, and early release decisions. Explicit use of such predictions by courts and legislatures is increasing. Reliance on predictions of dangerousness raises questions about the definition of dangerousness, the ethical limits on the use of such predictions, and the practical difficulties in proving dangerousness. The use of short-term predictions of dangerousness is much more widely acknowledged and accepted than the use of long-term predictions considered in this essay. Lawyers have relegated predictions of dangerousness to the psychiatric professions, leaving the moral and evidentiary issues untouched. The appropriate application of predictions of dangerousness is not a technical question of how well a prediction can be made, nor is it a question of the burden of proof required to prove elements of a criminal or civil charge. The use of predictions of dangerousness requires a political judgment balancing the risk and harm to society with the intrusion on the liberty of each member of a preventatively detained group. Not all types of prediction are equally satisfactory. Actuarial predictions are preferable to predictions that rely on an intuitive judgment by psychiatric professionals. The use of predictions of dangerousness to alter individual dispositions should be allowed only to the extent that such dispositions would be justified as deserved independent of those predictions. Within the range of punishment or control not undeserved, relative predictions of dangerousness may properly influence dispositional decisions. These prin-

Norval Morris is Julius Kreeger Professor of Law and Criminology at The University of Chicago Law School. Marc Miller is a 1984 graduate of The University of Chicago Law School and Law Clerk to Chief Judge John C. Godbold of the United States Court of Appeals for the Eleventh Circuit (1984–85). We are grateful for the assistance of Albert Alschuler, Alfred Blumstein, Steve Gilles, Edward Levi, John Monahan, Howard Miller, Geoffrey Stone, Michael Tonry, and Franklin Zimring with successive drafts of this essay.

1

ciples strike a balance between individual autonomy and state authority. In the paradigm context of sentencing, the controlling principle for the use of predictions of dangerousness is that the base expectancy rate of violence for the criminal predicted as dangerous must be shown by reliable evidence to be substantially higher than the base expectancy rate of another criminal with a closely similar record, convicted of a closely similar crime, but not predicted to be unusually dangerous, before the greater dangerousness of the former may be relied on to intensify or extend his punishment.

This essay considers the definitional, moral, and evidentiary problems in the application of the concept of "dangerousness" in the criminal justice system.

Predictions of dangerousness have played a role in decision making throughout the criminal justice system. Indeed, their explicit use has recently been approved in two decisions of the United States Supreme Court, *Jones v. United States*, 103 S. Ct. 3043 (1983), and *Barefoot v. Estelle*, 103 S. Ct. 3383 (1983). And, of course, predictions of dangerousness also underlie the civil commitment of those mentally ill or retarded persons who are thought likely to be a danger to themselves or others.

In *Barefoot v. Estelle* the Court was faced with the constitutionality of the Texas death penalty statute, which, in effect, allows a finding of future dangerousness to justify a capital sentence, and considered the constitutionality of testimony given under that statute. The Court upheld both the statute and the testimony given under it in Barefoot's case. *Jones v. United States* presented the question of the constitutionality of committing on grounds of future dangerousness one who had pleaded not guilty by reason of insanity to a term that might continue beyond the possible sentence for which he could have been held as a prisoner or for which he could have been held as a patient on grounds applicable to civil commitment.

We propose to get the dragon out onto the plain. We will not focus on how well dangerousness can be predicted. We are primarily concerned here with long-term predictions concerning behavior over months or years, since the use of short-term predictions of dangerousness in the criminal justice system, while less controversial than the use of long-term predictions, does not raise the same moral questions.[1] We

---

[1] The distinct issues raised by the use of short-term predictions of dangerousness appear in the recent Supreme Court decision in Schall v. Martin, 104 S. Ct. 2403 (1984). In *Martin*, the Court upheld a New York statute that allowed pretrial detention of

assume, for purposes of this essay, that present predictive capacities will prove to be the best we have for several decades. Suppose that, even among those with a high risk of committing a future crime of violence, to be sure of preventing one such crime we would have to detain three of those at risk. We submit that it is still ethically appropriate and socially desirable to take such predictions into account in many police, prosecutorial, judicial, correctional, and legislative decisions.

There is much opposition to such a view. That the future criminal violence of any one individual can be predicted with no better odds than one in three leads many commentators to reject, root and branch, reliance on any such predictions as a ground for any interference with individual liberty; but that is an impossible position to maintain. The reality of this element in many decisions about individual liberty cannot be denied and should be confronted by those who care about freedom under law. In making the case for selective incapacitation as a sentencing strategy, James Q. Wilson (1983) puts this point with force: "It is not enough to say, in opposition to selective incapacitation, that it involves predicting behavior, as if that were intolerable and never done. The entire criminal justice system is shot through at every stage (bail, probation, sentencing, and parole) with efforts at prediction, and neces-

---

juveniles accused of delinquency if there was "serious risk" that the juvenile would commit another delinquent act during the time before trial. The statute was attacked as fatally vague because "it is virtually impossible to predict future criminal conduct with any accuracy." *Id.* at 2417. The majority responded by noting that "from a legal point of view there is nothing inherently unattainable about a prediction of future criminal conduct." *Id.* The majority realized that "[s]uch a judgment forms an important element in many decisions, and we have specifically rejected the contention . . . that it is impossible to predict future behavior and that the question is so vague as to be meaningless." *Id.* at 2418 (citing Jurek v. Texas, 428 U.S. 262, 274 [1976]). *Martin* is distinguishable from the predictions of dangerousness discussed in this paper because in *Martin* "the detention [was] strictly limited in time." *Id.* at 2413. The maximum detention was seventeen days for juveniles accused of a serious crime and six days for those accused of a major crime. Such short-term predictions invoke different interests for both the state and the individual from those invoked by the use of long-term predictions. *Martin* involved the sui generis element of the state's *parens patriae* interest in the juvenile, and the majority seemed to turn the decision on the belief that juveniles "are always in some form of custody." *Id.* at 2410; see also In re Gault, 387 U.S. 1, 17 (1966). The Court used this special state interest to justify detention for juveniles that might not be constitutional for adults. We wonder about the validity of characterizing the guiding hand of a parent and the guiding hand of the state in the same benign manner. The majority also failed to distinguish different types of predictions of future criminal behavior, assuming the prediction under the New York statute to be based on a "host" of variables "which cannot be readily codified." *Id.* at 2418. It is here, we suggest, that the discretion vested in the decision maker may indeed be unacceptable. The use of predictions of future behavior does not require unbounded discretion on the part of the decision maker, and all predictions of dangerous or criminal behavior are not as uneasily based as the Court seems to imply.

sarily so; if we did not try to predict, we would release on bail or on probation either many more or many fewer persons, and make some sentences either much longer or much shorter" (p. 79).

A jurisprudence that pretends to exclude such concepts is self-deceptive; they figure frequently and prominently in decision making throughout the criminal law, whether or not they are spelled out in the case law.[2] If such predictions are in fact made and relied on—if they cannot be banished from the criminal law—that is one reason for acknowledging them, for studying them, and for trying to improve their accuracy. But the justification is larger than this response to the inevitable; there is a positive justification for developing a jurisprudence of such predictions. We must, indeed, develop such a jurisprudence if we are, with appreciation of our modest store of knowledge of human behavior, justly to allocate our properly limited punitive powers under the criminal law. A merciful and just system of punishment presupposes leniency toward those who least threaten social injury; and this, in turn, inexorably involves predictions of dangerousness.

At the extremes, the reality of such predictions as appropriate guides to the exercise of discretion under the criminal law is obvious. In deciding whether to arrest in a situation of matrimonial dispute, the policeman would be failing in his duty were he not to take into account his best estimate of the risk of injury to the wife if he does not make an arrest; in deciding whether to indict, and for what, the prosecutor will and should consider the danger to others if he does not go forward with a charge. We are not claiming for a moment that other factors may not outweigh these considerations of future risk—merely that they are properly and inevitably considered. At the sentencing level the role of

<hr>

[2] Federal and state cases recognize this fact. United States v. Glover, 725 F.2d 120 (D.C. Cir. 1984) (police decision to arrest); Toussaint v. Yockey, 722 F.2d 1490 (9th Cir. 1984) (prison movement); Wyler v. United States, 725 F.2d 156 (2d Cir. 1983) (police search); United States v. Cox, 719 F.2d 285 (8th Cir. 1983) (bail and sentencing); United States v. Davis, 710 F.2d 104 (3d Cir. 1983) ("district judges routinely determine whether a defendant is dangerous for the purposes of regular sentencing and setting bail"); Inmates of B-Block v. Jeffes, 470 A.2d 176 (Penn. 1983) (prison control); Illinois v. Carmack, 103 Ill. App. 3d 1027 (1982) (police action); Gammage v. State, 630 S.W.2d 309 (Tex. App. 1982) (constitutionality of manacling defendant during trial). Predictions of dangerousness play a central role in the Model Penal Code's (MPC's) provision on attempt, focusing on the dangerousness of the actor and not the dangerousness of his conduct. American Law Institute (1960). The MPC's attempt provision has been adopted by some of the circuits. See, e.g., United States v. Mandujano, 499 F.2d 370 (5th Cir. 1974) (Rives, J.), cert. denied 419 U.S. 1114 (1975). The Harvard Dangerous Offender Project (Moore et al. 1983) presents many examples showing the pervasive role of predictions of dangerousness throughout the criminal law.

predictions of dangerousness has authoritatively been recognized: all current members of the United States Supreme Court have expressed their agreement with Justice Stevens's statement in *Jurek v. Texas*, 428 U.S. 262 (1976), that "[a]ny sentencing authority must predict a convicted person's probable future conduct when it engages in the process of determining what punishment to impose." And the point holds true for the exercise of discretion by correctional and parole agencies—the extension of leniency to the nonthreatening increases the likelihood of a prediction of relative dangerousness to the remainder. That we are often compelled to such predictions though guided by inadequate knowledge—that our prediction capacities are poor—is a regrettable truth. Many important decisions have to be taken on the basis of inadequate knowledge, and such is the case with predictions of dangerousness in the application of both criminal and mental health law.

It is, of course, sensible to take careful stock of our predictive capacities if they are to figure, implicitly or expressly, in sentencing decisions and in the exercise of other discretions under the criminal law. We are fortified in that task by the recent publication of two books, one in this country, one in England, which excellently survey and summarize what is now known about the prediction of dangerousness. John Monahan, in *The Clinical Prediction of Violent Behavior* (1981), focuses on the state of the art in predicting violence. Monahan's work has become a standard resource in this country, and his general conclusions about the present limits on predictive accuracy were expressly accepted by both the majority and the dissentients in the recent Supreme Court case of *Barefoot v. Estelle*. The second work, *Dangerousness and Criminal Justice* by Jean Floud and Warren Young (1981), has attracted extensive commentary in the United Kingdom but less in this country.[3] Floud and Young consider the use of explicit predictions of dangerousness for "protective sentencing"—the lengthening of sentences for offenders identified as "dangerous"—and make a major contribution to previously unexamined questions of how and when predictions of dangerousness can justly be used in the criminal law. In other papers (1978, 1982, 1984) Monahan offers his view on the appropriate application of such predictions in the criminal law. In

---

[3] The book has generated extensive debate among English criminologists, including "Dangerousness and Criminal Justice" (1982); see also "Predicting Dangerousness" (1983). Excellent and reasonably current bibliographies of the relevant literature concerning both the empirical and the jurisprudential aspects of dangerousness are supplied by Floud and Young (1981, pp.203–34), and Monahan (1981, pp. 124–34).

this essay we rely on Floud and Young and on Monahan (1981) for the empirical assessments of predictive capacities relevant to our analysis, and we have been greatly assisted by their reflections on the jurisprudential issues.

We must stress that we do not advocate the extended application of predictions of dangerousness as a tool for achieving more effective crime control: we would indeed be highly skeptical of such a program and would see it as likely to achieve only grave injustice. Our effort is rather to define the proper and modest use of a concept necessary to the operation of the criminal law. Many values other than the hope of preventing future injuries determine criminal sanctions; a theory of criminal justice is vastly broader than a theory of crime prevention by controlling those who threaten criminal injuries. But predictions of dangerousness are one basis on which punishment resources are in fact allocated, and if we are to be guided by that consideration in justly differentiating among individuals, the relevant principles for such differentiation must be enunciated.

Lest we be mistaken for advocates of an extension of preemptive sentencing, let us mention some of the limiting principles we shall develop in this essay. We argue that punishment should not be extended or imposed on the basis of predictions of dangerousness beyond what would be justified independent of that prediction. Thus, concepts of "desert" define the upper limits of allowable punishment.[4] Within these limits, however, predictions of dangerousness may properly influence sentencing and punishment decisions, broadly defined, based on the balancing principles developed in this essay. Defining a proper role for predictive sentencing should certainly not be mistaken for advocacy of its present extension; indeed, one may reasonably hope that defining a proper role for express predictions would reduce the present pervasive reliance on implicit predictions, which are often based on erroneous assumptions.

The preemptive strike—capturing the criminal before the crime—has great attraction, and efforts at such anticipatory interventions are growing throughout the criminal law, although both the jurisprudential justifications for such interventions and knowledge of their efficacy are lacking. It is not our purpose in this essay to focus on how well

[4]There may be additional considerations in setting the corresponding lower limits of just punishment, but this is the subject for another essay.

dangerousness can be predicted; our aim is to enunciate principles under which preemptive strikes on the basis of predictions of dangerousness would be jurisprudentially acceptable.

In the first part of this essay we deal with definitions, limit the scope of our inquiry, and suggest some present and likely future applications of predictions of dangerousness. In the second part we discuss the limits of present capacities to predict dangerousness. The third part deals with common conceptual problems regarding prediction of violent behavior and what is involved in shifting risk between individuals and society. In the fourth part we review the development of judicial doctrines of dangerousness and strike at what we see as the fundamental imprecisions in the present judicial consideration of this concept. The fifth part contains our general theory of the appropriate use of such predictions. In the sixth part we consider some objections to our general theory.

I. Predictions of Dangerousness

There is nothing alien about using predictions of the future behavior of others to guide our conduct; it is hard to imagine life without such assumptions both of the continuities and discontinuities of the behavior of others and without reliance on such assumptions. It would certainly be difficult to cross a city street; driving a car would be unthinkable.

In this essay we concentrate on the use of explicit predictions of dangerousness, whether spelled out in statutes or articulated by judges in decisions, but we stress the pervasive importance of the implicit predictions we are not discussing. They play a fundamental role in the operation of the criminal law, even though they may never be articulated or even recognized as such by those relying on them.

There is a lengthy history of reliance on explicit predictions of dangerousness, dating at least from the sixteenth century, and of applying express predictions of dangerousness as a ground for invocation of criminal sanctions. Here is a brief catalog:

1. With the enclosures of the commons and the Elizabethan Poor Laws came the Vagrancy Acts, providing sanctions against sturdy rogues and vagabonds, those wandering abroad without lawful or visible means of support, those loitering with intent, and those falling within similar arcane phraseology which still underpins the disorderly conduct statutes, regulations, and ordinances of many states, cities, and counties in the United States. These sanctions are plainly preemptive

strikes against those seen as likely to be disturbing, disruptive, or dangerous. Included in this group would be "suspicious persons" ordinances, "stop and frisk," and public drunkenness laws.

2. Habitual Offender Laws and "third-time loser" laws all have a long and checkered history in England and this country. Their quality of being in part based on predictions of future criminal acts was most manifest in what was called the "dual track" system of punishment in some European habitual-criminal statutes that had their analogues in this country. Under English habitual-criminal legislation for many years, when the habitual criminal had finished the term of imprisonment for his last offense he would then be held as a habitual criminal, the conditions of his detention being ameliorated and more recreational facilities and comforts extended to him, since he was now not being "punished" but rather detained because of his high likelihood of future criminality.

3. For persistent but less serious habitual offenders, unredeemable nuisances rather than serious threats, many states devised and applied Habitual Petty Offender Laws, jurisprudentially akin to the previous category.

4. Sexual Psychopath Laws are perhaps the best known example of sentences statutorily based on predictions of dangerousness. They disgraced our jurisprudence, grossly misapplying what little knowledge we have about the sexual offender, achieving injustice without social protection.

5. Special Dangerous Offender statutes were recommended by the American Law Institute in its Model Penal Code and have found diverse ways into the statute books of most states. Such statutes often rely expressly on the alleged capacity of psychologists to assist juries or the sentencing judge in predicting the greater future dangerousness of certain categories of offenders and therefore the propriety of imposing increased sanctions on them. There are related federal Special Dangerous Offender statutory provisions enacted to limit unprincipled Sexual Psychopath statutes (18 U.S.C. § 3575).

6. Sentencing generally: Setting aside those situations where the legislature has provided a mandatory sentence without allowing the sentencing judge discretion in its imposition, it is clear that predictions of dangerousness influence a wide swath of criminal sanctions. The judge's view of the gravity of the harm, the seriousness of the criminal's past record, and the likelihood of his future criminality has frequently been shown to be important in the determination of the sentence im-

posed within the discretion statutorily available to the judge. In those many statutes that specify what are aggravating and what are mitigating circumstances, to be taken into account in fixing sentences, the likely future dangerousness of the offender is frequently expressly included in the list of aggravating factors. The specification that the offender does not present a threat of future injury, and the approval therefore of a penalty—say probation—less severe than the imprisonment that otherwise might be ordered may itself function as a prediction of relative dangerousness to those not so selected as "safe."

7. Sentencing of young offenders in juvenile courts seems even more clearly than that of adult offenders to be largely based on predictions of their likely criminality—on the likely pattern of their lives if they are not detained.

8. Parole is widespread. Those less likely to commit crime during the parole period may be released; those more likely may be held. In the federal system and several states these predictions are quantified into parole prediction tables. Many criticize this whole development, but rarely on the ground that it is usurpation of power based on mistaken predictions.

9. Recent prison crowding combined with judicial orders limiting overcrowding have compelled the early release of prisoners in several states before the completion of their prison terms, less time off for good behavior. In every instance, efforts were made—and publicized—to insure that the less dangerous were being selected for earlier release and the more dangerous detained to complete their terms.

10. Bail practice is another excellent example of express predictions of dangerousness. The received doctrine is that bail is adjusted to the prediction of the accused's likelihood of appearance for trial—not a prediction of dangerousness—but it is the common knowledge of the profession that judges do take into account the likelihood of criminality, particularly serious criminality, prior to trial. Elsewhere, in both common law and civil law countries, the fiction of the nonconsideration of the likely dangerousness of the offender prior to trial has been abandoned, and there is strong pressure in this country for its attenuation and eventual abandonment, provided speedy trials can be arranged for those detained as dangerous.

11. A grim conclusion to this catalog: Recent initiatives for the reinstatement of capital punishment have led in several states to the possibility of the application of that punishment instead of protracted imprisonment because, as the Texas Criminal Code (§ 37.071), for

example, states, "there is a probability that the defendant would commit criminal acts of violence that would constitute a continuing threat to society."

Recently the stakes of these types of predictions have been raised in the criminal law, with career criminal projects being applied at the police and prosecutorial levels and policies of selective incapacitation at the sentencing level under the apparent belief that legislators, police, prosecutors, judges, and juries are able to select the most dangerous criminals for swifter and more determined prosecution and for more protracted incarceration. James Q. Wilson (1983) summarizes the thrust of these policy recommendations as follows: "Prosecutors would screen all arrested persons . . . and give priority to those who, whatever their crime, were predicted to be high-rate offenders. . . . If found guilty, the offender's sentence would be shaped . . . by an informed judgment as to whether he committed crimes at a high or low rate when free on the street. . . . Scarce prison space would be conserved by keeping the terms of low-rate offenders very short and by reserving the longer terms for the minority of violent predators" (pp. 286–87).

Policies of selective law enforcement, selective prosecution, and selective incapacitation attract increasing support; they are paradigms of efforts to predict dangerousness and to apply the preemptive strike in the criminal justice system.

Though in this essay we focus on problems in the application of the criminal law, parallel developments in the law relating to the civil commitment of the mentally ill merit mention. The law has shifted steadily over the past twenty years toward reliance on predictions of dangerousness to the patient or to others, as well as on his mental illness or retardation, as preconditions to civil commitment. Efforts to improve the validity of these predictions by requiring proof of an overt act of injury or threatened injury have been litigated,[5] the argument reaching constitutional proportions, and, as we shall later discuss, a great deal of judicial attention has been devoted to the standard of proof of dangerousness necessary for such a commitment.

One point of importance to criminal law predictions of dangerousness arises from the burgeoning experience with these predictions as a

---

[5] Here is another dragon that needs to be brought out on the plain: the misuse of alleged predictions of dangerousness to conceal commitments under the civil law based in fact on the person's need for treatment or on a substituted or proxy judgment of what is good for him. See Lessard v. Schmidt, 349 F. Supp. 1078 (E.D. Wis. 1972), vacated on separate grounds, 414 U.S. 473 (1974).

basis for civil commitment. Short-term predictions, made in times of impending crisis and limited in effect, prove to have much higher levels of reliability than longer-term predictions that the patient if released will be a danger to himself or others.

The necessity of acting upon short-term predictions of harm, for example, the threats of an angry husband in a domestic relations dispute or the threat of suicide by one severely depressed, seems obvious. While ready acceptance of the use of predictions of dangerousness in such situations supports our general point that predictions of dangerousness are a necessary factor in regulating the relationship between individual and state, we are more concerned with the moral problems raised by the use of long-term predictions of violent behavior—predictions concerning months and years, not hours and days.

In the discussion so far, "dangerousness" itself has been left vague and undefined. But if we are considering predictions, we must seek agreement, if not precision, on the meaning of "dangerousness." The key elements in defining the term are the type and magnitude of harm predicted and the predicted level of risk or the rate of that harm, the product of these variables being a measure of total harm that at some point many in our society would agree constitutes dangerousness. The level at which society determines which risks are unacceptable and the justified effect of such a determination are suggested later in this essay.

Defining dangerousness for the purposes of our inquiry involves more than simply assessing the risk of injury involved in a given situation. With equanimity—at least without the same sort of fear that is inspired by criminal violence—we all accept more substantial risks of injury than those that flow from criminals. The hazards of industrial accidents, of fire, and of movement in traffic inflict far more physical injury than does violent crime. Yet these are not the types of injury anyone would include for analysis in this essay. The risk from the car is high, the risk from the knife is low; yet we fear the latter more than the former as we move out of doors at night.

Hence we confine "dangerousness" in this essay to intentional behavior that is physically dangerous to the person or threatens a person or persons other than the perpetrator—in effect, to assaultive criminality. We do not mean to depreciate the significance of the threats to social welfare of predatory theft and many other types of crime.[6] And gener-

[6] We also exclude considerations of self-injury as a ground for civil commitment of the mentally ill, the danger to others from a patient, as distinct from the danger to the

ally we are thinking of the graver types of assaultive criminality, since it
is our view that serious physical injury to the person or the threat of
such injury is what emotionally fuels the whole movement toward the
use of predictions of dangerousness in the criminal law, and that it is
therefore appropriate to develop our thesis around those harms.[7] A
tough case for exclusion is home burglary, since it is an offense that
sometimes involves injury to the person or the threat of such injury and
generally creates fear of such injury. In sum, we are considering the
prediction of what would colloquially be called the behavior of "a
violent criminal."

The psychological reality involved in this narrowing of the definition
of dangerousness to the behavior of the assaultive criminal is that harms
intentionally inflicted on the person generate higher levels of fear than
injuries accidentally caused to the person or intentionally caused to
property.[8] Be that as it may, this essay is confined to the prediction of
violent criminality, though it is hoped that the analysis may be applicable to other harms.

II. Empirical Knowledge

Psychologists and psychiatrists have long considered the predictability
of "dangerousness" (Floud and Young 1981; Monahan 1981, pp. 124–
34), but only recently have scholars outside those fields explored the
limits and uses of predictions of dangerousness. Criminologists interested in parole prediction have also been considering these questions for
more than two decades, but legal commentators seem to have avoided
until recently the difficult jurisprudential issues involved in taking

---

patient, providing the analogy to the criminal's threat to the physical safety of others. It
should be noted that predictions of suicidal attempts can for some disturbed persons be
made with higher likelihoods than any predictions of violence to others; similarly, predictions of predatory theft can often be made with higher likelihoods than can predictions of
criminal violence.

[7] Though it is a question left for other authors whether predictions of lesser harms at a
higher rate might similarly justify the preemptive strike as do larger harms at a lower
rate, we suggest that there may well be additional limiting considerations.

[8] William Lowrance (1976) lists an array of considerations influencing safety judgments (pp. 87–94) (Lowrance's discussion is in the context of dangerous products but the
considerations are identical). The extreme fear and dread of assaultive criminality follow
from a number of these: such violence is a risk borne involuntarily; the effect is immediate; the risk is unknown to people operating in society; the risk is encountered
"nonoccupationally" (in the sense that people rarely choose to live in high crime areas and
because we set aside intimate violence); the hazards are "dread"; the harms affect virtually
everybody; and the consequences are often irreversible (i.e., the harms are often very
severe).

power over an individual based on his dangerousness. Assumptions about the legal relevance of such predictions often turned on perceptions of the accuracy of prediction, the assumption being that until psychologists could predict with a 50 percent base expectancy rate of serious violence or of a threat of violence to the person over some relevant time period that the member of the high-risk group is at large, there was nothing for the lawyer to discuss.[9]

By conceiving of predictions of dangerousness as "the province of psychiatry,"[10] lawyers foreclosed appropriate jurisprudential consideration of the use of predictions. Recently, the tables have turned: the psychiatric literature and the official statements of the organized profession of psychiatry, paradoxically, stress the unreliability of psychiatric predictions (American Psychiatric Association 1982), while the courts increasingly rely on predictions by individual psychiatrists and psychologists. Courts and the psychological professionals each affirm the prediction of dangerousness to be the province of the other. The courts, including the Supreme Court in *Jones* and *Barefoot*, thus allow much greater reliance to be placed on psychological predictions of dangerousness than do the organized professions of psychiatry and psychology.

It is important to determine which types of predictions are appropriate to use. This involves two inquiries. The present discussion will consider practical problems with the various types of predictions and, in particular, the problem with clinical assessments of future dangerousness when used to extend sentences. We later briefly discuss which aspects of a person's life are socially or legally unacceptable as factors in prediction, the paradigm problem being constitutional and moral questions about the use of race as a variable in prediction.

Classifications are often arbitrary, and the classification that follows is not necessarily compelling. Nevertheless, we see three basic paths to the prediction of future behavior.

First, the *anamnestic* prediction: This is how he behaved in the past

[9] This assumption arises from confusion between the minimal standard of proof generally required to find a fact to a legally persuasive degree, and the level of prediction necessary to justify the use of predictions of dangerousness. This error is extensively discussed in Sec. IV below.

[10] "The idea is deeply rooted that identifying 'dangerous' persons for legal purposes is a matter of diagnosing pathological attributes of character and this is nowadays thought to be the province of psychiatry; 'dangerousness' is presumed to be something for students of abnormal psychology, even when it is not clearly associated with mental illness" (Floud and Young 1981, p. 22).

when circumstances were similar. It is likely that he will behave in the same way now.

Second, the *actuarial* prediction: This is how people like him, situated as he is, behaved in the past. It is likely that he will behave as they did. Actuarial prediction is the basis of all insurance and of a great many of our efforts to share and shift risk in the community.

Third, the *clinical* prediction, which is harder to state: "From my experience of the world, from my professional training, from what I know about mental illness and mental health, from my observations of this patient and efforts to diagnose him, I think he will behave in the following fashion in the future." Clinical prediction has elements of the first two, but it includes professional judgments that the psychological literature treats as distinct from the others.[11]

Anamnestic and actuarial predictions are linear in the sense that historical facts to justify the prediction can be produced and adduced, weighed and weighted. Clinical predictions are not like that. They are immune from evidentiary examination except in relation to the reputation, experience, and past success or failure of the predictor. Floud and Young rightly refer to "the *art* of making clinical (individualized) assessments of 'dangerousness' " (p. 29; emphasis added).[12]

Actuarial predictions are often reliable. Anamnestic predictions also are often very reliable. Indeed they reach the highest levels of validity.

---

[11] Of course, predictions, especially clinical predictions, tend to be blended from different sources and elements. And if an actuarial prediction has a clinical element, it falls prey, in part, to the more general criticism of clinical predictions. Our model for actuarial prediction presumes elements that do not require clinical identification. Thus the categorization—the identification of an individual as a member of an actuarially defined group—would not require the expertise of psychologists or psychiatrists. The use of such professionals to provide information otherwise obtainable about the subject might well be found inadmissible in the judge's discretion because of overpersuasiveness. Perhaps there is a fourth category encompassing predictions based on the expressed intentions of the potential actor, which we might call *promissory* predictions, whose impact will vary with their content and with their relationship to other anamnestic and actuarial predictors. When such predictions take the form of threats, they themselves constitute a ground for preemptive intervention.

[12] The psychologist or psychiatrist may present evidence underlying a clinical judgment: this just moves the prediction to one of the testable and therefore acceptable categories. It is not predictions made by psychiatrists or psychologists that we oppose; it is predictions made by such people on an intuitive, untested, and unverifiable basis. If such a professional made a prediction based on validated actuarial evidence, it would be acceptable evidence within our principles. Further, it is worth emphasizing that our skepticism about clinical predictions of dangerousness, in which we find support from the organized profession of psychiatry, does not in any way reflect an underlying skepticism about the great value and importance of psychiatrists and psychologists in many areas.

He has taken out the old raincoat and exposed his rampant self to the young girls in the park every Friday for the past year. Here he is, this Friday, wearing his raincoat though the weather be fine and he is heading again for the park.

Who says a prediction of only one in three is all you can make in such a situation? Of course you can make a higher prediction. The fact that you can make a higher prediction in this situation does not controvert what we said earlier; it is a short-term prediction and it does not concern a crime of violence.

Clinical predictions are of a different order. They are intuitive rather than verifiable, except in the result. It seems that the best predictions of human behavior would be based on a combination of all three types of prediction. Such an ideal prediction would observe the pattern of behavior of the person under consideration, would be advised by how others like him behaved in the past, and would also be guided by a total clinical consideration of his case, which would improve on the prediction from the first two categories by taking into account what was distinctive in him. It would individualize the prediction to his particular circumstances. Regrettably, this is not workable for the prediction of violent behavior at the present level of our knowledge. Floud and Young, like Monahan, conclude that "[p]sychological theory is not as effective as statistical theory in selecting what is relevant and important" (p. 27). There have been no demonstrations and no claims to demonstrate that the addition of a clinical element in predictions can improve upon actuarial and anamnestic predictions (see Farrington and Tarling 1983).

This is not to argue that reliance should never be placed on expert clinical or even intuitive lay predictions of violence. In emergency situations, such as the short-term commitment of a mentally ill husband threatening injury to his wife, there is little choice. But where a longer and more significant deprivation of liberty, such as extended incarceration, may result from the determination of dangerousness, clinical predictions must find their validity and reliability in data concerning the nearest like group.

We accept completely the conclusions of Floud and Young, and of Monahan, on the limits of predictive capacity. With our present knowledge, with the best possible long-term predictions of violent behavior we can expect to make one true positive prediction of violence to the person for every two false positive predictions.[13] The body of research supporting this modest conclusion is not extensive, but there are no acceptable studies reaching a contrary result. We know of only eight serious prospective studies, and retrospective studies are a different matter—only the first steps on which predictions might be built. These eight prospective studies are excellently summarized in John Monahan (1978).

The assumption that three individuals must be controlled if the violent crime of one (no one knowing which one) is to be prevented is important and necessary to our thesis, since it forces us to confront issues that our current verbal manipulations of imprecise burdens of proof and of unquantified articulations of risk allow us to finesse. And when that confrontation occurs, the problem shifts from one of language and statutory interpretation to one of morality—of the proper balance between state authority and personal autonomy. The assumption on which we will lay out our theory of the proper use of long-term predictions is that no research on this topic, in this country or in Western Europe, claims a capacity to select a group of persons, no matter what their criminal records, who have a 50 percent base expectancy rate of serious violence or of a threat of violence to the person over the next five years they are at large. The Supreme Court in *Barefoot*, both the majority and the minority, accepted that proposition. "The 'best' clinical research currently in existence indicates that *psychiatrists and psychologists are accurate in no more than one out of three predictions of violent behavior over a several year period among institutionalized populations that had both committed violence in the past . . . and who are diagnosed as mentally ill*" (*Barefoot v. Estelle*, 103 S. Ct. 3383, 3398 n.7; emphasis in original [citing Monahan at 47–49]).

It is partly because predictive capacity is at this level that it has been neglected by legal commentators. There is a tendency to dismiss it as so low, so unreliable, as not to merit consideration. But that is a serious

---

[13] Among the most obvious problems with such statistics in predicting a rare event such as severely violent conduct is that researchers may not be aware of some violent occurrences, and thus the predictions may be understated. To the extent that this is true, any reliance on the lower known figure is not made *less* acceptable. Two points should be made: first, the "dark figures" for crimes of violence against the person are lower than for crimes against property or for an amorphous notion of general "recidivism"; and second, prospective studies which follow a group of individuals will be particularly sensitive to events which might not otherwise be noted by the criminal justice system. We reject the use of *any* assumptions made about unreported crime to boost reliance upon predictions.

error. Given the relative rarity of the event to be predicted—violent criminality—a base expectancy rate of one in three is not a low rate of prediction: it is a very high rate of prediction. The relationships among personal characteristics and social circumstances—among character, personality, and chance—are obviously of extreme complexity and thus most difficult to predict; but a group of three people, one of whom within a few months will commit a crime of extreme personal violence, is a very dangerous group indeed.

It should be recognized that these studies analyzing the limits of our predictive capacities leave out of account a few very rare individuals so disturbed and dangerous that no one considers them likely candidates for freedom. There are exceptional, gravely psychotic, extremely and repetitively violent persons whose likely future criminality does not merit study since it is so obvious.[14] And, of course, there are extreme cases of repetitive murder where the ordinary processes of the criminal law preclude consideration of the offender's future dangerousness. But these extreme cases should be excluded from our consideration. They throw no light on the reality of the problem we confront, which is the propriety of restricting the freedom of those who are not such clear cases and yet have characteristics, histories, and social circumstances that indicate their high levels of dangerousness.

One last point on the question of our capacity to predict future criminal violence: the epistemology of prediction provides no grounds for predictions of individual behavior; it refers by nature to predictions of the behavior of defined groups of individuals. It is a common and confusing mistake to think of our problem as one of individual prediction. The individual in question always belongs, by virtue of certain stated and previously tested characteristics and circumstances, to a

---

[14] There is, of course, the question how proof would be taken about such exceptional individuals. Usually their records will foreclose the lurking difficulties in this question. In a letter commenting on an earlier draft of this essay, Monahan provided a pungent story to explicate this point. He wrote of speaking to a federal judicial sentencing conference: "I gave my stock speech about the probability of violence never being higher than 1-in-3 in the research. A judge raised his hand and said that he recently had a case of a murderer with a large number of prior violent offenses who, when asked if he had anything to say before sentence was imposed, stated 'if I get out, the first thing I am going to do is murder the prosecutor, the second thing I am going to do is murder you, Your Honor, the third thing I am going to do is murder every witness who testified against me and the fourth thing I am going to do is murder each member of the jury.' The judge asked if I thought that this person's probability of violence was no greater than 1-in-3. I called for a coffee break" (letter from John Monahan to Norval Morris, February 27, 1984).

group with a given likelihood of violent criminality. It is the justice of applying to each individual powers influenced by his membership in that group that is at issue.

III. Prediction and Risk Shifting

It is widely recognized that "statistical predictions are made for groups and not for individuals" (Farrington and Tarling 1983, p. 20); yet, as Floud and Young observe, critics of the use of predictions often make the mistake of "identifying statistical entities . . . with particular, mis-judged individuals" (1981, p. 21). A statistical prediction of dangerous-ness, based on membership in a group for which a consistent and tested pattern of conduct has been shown, is the statement of a *condition* (membership in a defined group with possession of certain attributes) and not the prediction of a *result* (of future violent acts in each individual case). This is not reflected in the language of "false positives" and "false negatives," which imply the total absence of the predicted condi-tion: here dangerousness. Floud and Young (1981) point out that "[e]rrors of prediction do not represent determinable individuals. . . . *But the fact that if we were to set them at liberty, only half of those we are at any time detaining as dangerous would do further serious harm, does not mean that the other half are all in this sense innocent*" (p. 48, emphasis added).[15]

Analogies to dangerous objects rather than to dangerous persons may help clarify these points. If the event or result being predicted were fixed a priori, and the result did not involve an interaction between the object and circumstance, then given a prediction of dangerousness, false positives could correctly be viewed ex post as never having been dangerous in fact (even if, by definition, they were not so identified originally).

In contrast—and we will give this example some historical perspec-tive to make it easier to appreciate, think of the postwar days in Lon-don. For some time after the war unexploded bombs would be found and would have to be moved and rendered safe. Death and severe

---

[15] The theoretical model of the behavior being predicted has a critical impact on the meaning of the terms "false positive" and "true positive." As a simple, initial question, it matters whether the predicted event exists in only two states—pregnant or not preg-nant—as contrasted with a degree of dangerousness. If the latter is the case, then any two state model imposed on a continuum ("dangerous" or "not dangerous") must be arbitrary and will force the person defining the point at which the two states change to recognize some justification for choosing that line. The difference between, e.g., predicting recidi-vism and predicting dangerousness is that, given a precise definition of recidivism, a person either will or will not have committed an offense at a particular point in time. Recidivism is an event; dangerousness is a condition—a "probabilistic condition."

injuries were very rare; the base expectancy rate was very low; there were large numbers of "false positives" for every "true positive"— bombs that did not go off, as distinguished from those that did. Yet assuming that all or virtually all of the bombs did have the *potential* to detonate, no one would say that because it proved to be a "false positive" it was not dangerous. That is not how words are used when the focus is dangerous objects as distinct from dangerous people, yet where the eventuality of the predicted event is a product of a range of characteristics inherent in the object and chance, the similarities of risk and analysis are great. Floud and Young refer to this as "the dynamic interaction of the individual's character and circumstance" (p. 57).[16]

We do not mean to suggest that all members of a group predicted to be dangerous are necessarily violent by nature. It is not necessarily true that each member of a group predicted to be highly dangerous will be dangerous even in some small degree: some eternally docile individual with bad luck might fulfill all of the requirements of membership in a particular high-risk group; there really is a "road to Damascus"; and people do grow older and burn out. We believe the distribution of violent tendencies within groups predicted to be highly dangerous will be narrow, yet we must, of course, recognize that some of the individuals so predicted may not have much potential for violence. Yet our justification for using predictions of dangerousness in the criminal law does not rely solely on our conception of human nature.

Conversely, of course, some people are dangerous though not predicted to be dangerous (the social scientist's "false negative"); the likelihood of potential violence is distributed within the group predicted not to be dangerous in the same sense that it is distributed in the group predicted to be dangerous. The *prediction* of dangerousness is usually an all-or-nothing, two-state prediction, but dangerousness itself is distributed over a range of levels even within a fairly narrow group. The tension and problems arising from such artificial modeling must be recognized.

The conceptual difficulty in viewing a prediction of dangerousness as the identification of membership in a group with a certain likelihood of harm stems in part from the language of prediction, and especially the language of true and false positives, which seem to point to the *outcome*

---

[16] Floud and Young (1981) think that the element of chance "must be very large" even when there is an optimal prediction of an individual's character. Perhaps the randomness, the element of circumstance and chance, is as large as two in three for certain types of extreme and rare behavior.

in each individual case. Considering the use of the terms "prediction" and "dangerousness," Monahan observes that dangerous behavior "may be thought of as a prediction in itself." It might be preferable, as Monahan suggests, to refer not to predictions of "dangerous behavior" but to predictions of "violence" (1981, p. 5). We suggest that the same clarity would come out of focusing on the identification of individuals as members of groups which exhibit high levels of violence rather than on predictions of individual dangerousness. Similar precision would come from referring to the "assessment" or "evaluation" of the potential for violence; yet the language of predictions of dangerousness is so entrenched in the writings of courts and scholars that we do not seriously propose a change in usage. We seek only conceptual clarity.

Concern about requiring the innocent to pay for the violent[17]— viewing the false positives as people who were a priori not dangerous but who must pay for the individuals who became true positives and hence were a priori the only "dangerous" members of the group—arises as an analogy to the principle of the criminal trial, that it is better that nine guilty men be acquitted than that one innocent man be found guilty. This line of reasoning, though it has persuaded many commentators and some judges, is deeply flawed.

If one truly read a statistical prediction of one in three to mean that one person was "bad" or "guilty" and the other two "innocent" or "harmless," then under no circumstances would statistical predictions of dangerousness be acceptable grounds on which to restrict any person's liberty. The analogy to the criminal trial would hold true, and even if we could predict nine in ten, we would not be justified in detaining the tenth, "innocent" member of the group. And, of course, we could never civilly commit anyone, except for very short periods, as there would be no justification for detention under present theory. It seems odd that we are more willing to use predictions of dangerousness to detain those whom we think of as less culpable for their acts.

A statement of a prediction of dangerousness, then, is a statement of a present condition, not the prediction of a particular result; and further, within our limiting principles, we must act on the condition independently of the result. The belief that it is the prediction of a result is an error that is constantly made and leads many astray. In

---

[17] Innocence here meaning only a false positive. See the discussion at Sec. IV below, of the evidentiary considerations surrounding Addington v. United States, 441 U.S. 418 (1979).

sum, that the person predicted as dangerous does no future injury does not mean that the classification was erroneous even though the prediction itself was wrong.

A prediction of the likelihood of harm does not and cannot in itself explain how such predictions should be used in the criminal law. The just application of predictions of dangerousness involves a societal determination of what levels of risk and harm are unacceptable. In looking at any risk imposed on society there is the question who should bear that risk. In the case of the risks and harms imposed by the use of certain pesticides and fertilizers, a social determination must be made of who will bear the risk: consumers (through the harms caused by the chemical), farmers (through reduced productivity if these substances are banned), taxpayers (through the government), or industry. In the case of the danger from violent criminals, the determination that must be made is whether society or members of the group predicted to be violent should bear the costs of their threat. Floud and Young, in the context of justifying extended sentences for offenders predicted as dangerous, note that the analogy to the criminal trial

> misrepresents the moral choice that has to be made in considering whether protective measures may be justly imposed. The question is not "how many innocent persons are to sacrifice their liberty for the extra protection that special sentences for dangerous offenders will provide?" but "what is the moral choice between the alternative risks: the risk of harm to potential victims or the risk of unnecessarily detaining offenders judged to be dangerous. . . ."
>
> The problem is to make a just redistribution of risk in circumstances that do not permit of its being reduced. [P. 49]

Floud and Young are correct. The societal decision, the moral decision, is not whether to place the burden of avoiding the risk on the false positives, but how to balance the risk of harm to society and the certain intrusion on the liberty of each member of the preventively detained group. At some level of predicted harm from the group, the intrusions on each individual's liberty may be justified. Thus, again in the context of extending sentences, the goal is "a just redistribution of certain risks of grave harm: the grave harm that potentially recidivist offenders may do to their unknown victims and the grave harm which is suffered by offenders if they are subjected to the hardship of preventive measures which risk being unnecessary because they depend on predictive judgments of their conduct which are inherently uncertain" (Floud and

Young 1981, p. xvii). This assumption presupposes that the risk can be quantified as a base expectancy rate and the harm defined with some precision and, further, that it can be substantially shifted from the community, the cost of the shift being paid by the individual by his being controlled in one or another fashion, usually by detaining him in custody.

Let us assume a properly convicted criminal, criminal X, with a one-in-three base expectancy rate of violence (as we have defined it) and another criminal, criminal Y, also properly convicted of the identical offense, but with a very much lower base expectancy rate—same record, same offense. Unlike X, Y was not a school dropout, and he has a job to which he may return and a supportive family who will take him back if he is not imprisoned, or after his release from prison. May criminal X be sent to prison while criminal Y is not? Or may criminal X be sent to prison for a longer term than criminal Y, despite the same record and the same gravity of offense, the longer sentence being justified by the utilitarian advantages of selective incapacitation? Our answer to both questions is that he may.

To justify protective sentencing, the level of prediction must be high and the threatened harm severe, whereas a much lower level of risk may properly be relied on to justify a lesser deprivation of liberty. It is sometimes suggested that it is improper to restrict liberty at all on weak predictions of future harm. Confining ourselves to predictions of future violence to the person, we shall suggest situations in which it would be entirely proper to exercise state power to restrict individual autonomy on the basis of such a prediction. A somewhat frivolous example may make the point. At the 1983 annual meeting of the National Rifle Association (NRA), when President Reagan undertook the heavy burden of persuading the NRA membership of the virtues of the handgun, all those attending had to pass through metal detectors as they entered the auditorium to insure that they were not entering the president's presence in their usual heavily armed condition. The authorities responsible for the president's security had properly formed the view that the audience presented a higher base expectancy rate of an assassination attempt than another audience of similar size—since not all the president's audiences are so tested (though it would not matter to the thrust of this example if they were). We do not know what the base expectancy rate of an assassination attempt is; let us guess at one in a hundred million. Is it reasonable to impose the obligation of passing through a metal detector on the basis of such a low prediction? Of course it is.

Similarly, if someone about to board an airplane matches the risk profile for a hijacker, it is probably an appropriate interference with that person's freedom to ask him to step aside and answer a few questions and, if some ground warrants it, to search him.[18] Always the base expectancy rate—the relationship between the true positive predictions (one in a hundred million) and false positive predictions—must be balanced by two further considerations: How serious is the interference with liberty involved in preventing the possibility of that prediction coming true, and how serious is the injury if it does come true?

Take the NRA convention case another step. Should anyone with a past record of threatening the president be excluded from the auditorium? Of course. A very slight risk of a most serious injury without any grave interference is a justification in our view for invocation of state authority. So dangerousness should be balanced in relation to the extent of the harm risked, the likelihood of its occurrence, and the extent of individual autonomy to be invaded to avoid the harm. It is important to recognize that determinations of what levels of risk and harm are unacceptable are inherently policy determinations. Defining unacceptable levels of dangerousness thus emerges as a social and political rather than an empirical task (Flood and Young 1981, pp. 4–5, 9).[19]

The distinction between the determination of risk and harm and the political decision as to when the risk and harm are unacceptable and justify certain action—is made clear in the parallel context of societal hazards brilliantly discussed by Lowrance (1976). After outlining the measurement of risk from various objects and activities, Lowrance notes that he has avoided the term "measuring safety," because safety is not measured but determined by weighing social values. In Lowrance's definition, "a thing is safe if its attendant risks are judged to be acceptable."[20] While Lowrance does not include the risk of harm from human beings, the parallels with our discussion are clear. Measuring the probability and severity of harm from a group "is an empirical, scientific

[18] See United States v. Lopez, 328 F. Supp. 1077 (E.D.N.Y. 1971) (Weinstein, J.) (discussing the ethics of hijacker screening and upholding the constitutionality of such a system).

[19] "It is a truism that the selection of certain kinds of conduct as making a man eligible to be treated as 'dangerous' . . . is essentially a political process" (Flood and Young 1981). The critical role of social judgment has been more generally recognized in the context of civil commitment. See also State v. Krol, 68 N.J. 236, 260–62; 344 A.2d 289, 302 (1975).

[20] Courts have had more luck comprehending the scope of the social policy determinations involved in dealing with the risk from things as opposed to people. See, e.g., Dalerko v. Heil Co., 681 F.2d 445 (5th Cir. 1982).

activity." Determining dangerousness—"judging the [un]acceptability of risks—is a normative, political activity."

Isolating this element of balance, and the corresponding social determination inherent in any use of predictions of dangerousness in criminal law, makes clear that judgments about the use of dangerousness are relativistic and judgmental, not absolute. The relative nature of predictions can be clarified in a rhetorical fashion by noting that a law that extended the term of any felon "found to be 20 times as likely to be violent over the course of the next five years as the average criminal," however unjust, would not seem unacceptable or illogical on its face even if the base expectancy rate of violence for the felons identified as "20 times more dangerous" were at a predicted level of one in three, a level many deem absolutely unacceptable.

That predictions are most valuable as a way of distinguishing between individuals in similar situations is not hard to understand. An individual is most readily understood to be dangerous compared with other persons, and the aim of isolating dangerous criminals makes sense only if we recognize that there are other criminals who are less dangerous. The appropriate use of predictions thus requires that before we attach the label of "dangerous" to any person, or criminal, we must identify the group in reference to which the claim of dangerousness is made. In part, this determination must be practical. If the group is made up of individuals identical in all respects, it is not possible to distinguish between them on any relevant grounds. Comparing all felons with the general population would be likely to lead to felons' being identified as a more dangerous group. The need to establish a category for a meaningful judgment about dangerousness is often intuitively apparent to inmates: when asked whether there are dangerous criminals, many inmates laugh, or reply jokingly, "We are all dangerous," while the answer to the question "Are there some inmates who are more dangerous then others?" is often precise and certain—the smiles disappear, and the inmates describe who of their colleagues they perceive to be more dangerous than others and why. We later present a theory defining groups within which it is, in our view, appropriate to use predictions of dangerousness to distinguish between individuals in making determinations about detention, prosecution, bail, sentencing, and release.

We will also present our theory of how predictions should appropriately and justly be used. As an approach to suggesting how the notion of risk shifting should be applied, consider the hypothetical case of a sixteen-year-old black youth who has just dropped out of school and who has no employment, whose mother was herself a child on welfare when he was born, who does not know his father, who runs with a street gang, and who lives in a destroyed inner-city neighborhood. Assume that we can assess the risk of his being involved in the next six months in a crime of personal violence. Let us give him a base expectancy rate of violence of one in twenty, to be conservative. That risk now rests on the community in which he lives. May we, without further justification, at this one-in-twenty level, shift that risk from the community and make him bear the cost of the shift in the coinage of institutional detention until we can do something to reduce the risk, by retraining him or by allowing time to pass while the threat he presents diminishes? Clearly not. But let him be involved in a nonviolent crime, say, shoplifting, and even if that conviction makes no difference to his base expectancy rate of a crime of violence there is no doubt that in practice we would then take into account the risk of a crime of violence in deciding what to do about him and for how long. Within our sentencing discretions we would take into account the risk of violence he presents.

The balance of risk to the community and the restriction of individual liberty is a policy question to be determined by the legislature. If a legislative enactment does not make clear what levels of dangerousness are acceptable, however, it falls on the courts to determine the balance between the likelihood of injury—the extent of potential harm—and the extent of the restriction on individual liberty that is justified in decreasing the risk and related harm.

That a judge has the power to take individual factors into account in sentencing—including factors presented to the judge that would violate the "rigid rules of evidence"—is unquestionable under the modern sentencing theory developed by Justice Black in *Williams v. New York*, 337 U.S. 241 (1948). Justice Black observed that "modern concepts individualizing punishment" require access to information not relevant or admissible in a trial: "The belief no longer prevails that every offense in a like legal category calls for an identical punishment without regard to the past life and habits of a particular offender" and "punishment should fit the offender and not merely the crime" (337 U.S. at 247).[21]

---

[21] The doctrine remains vital—see, e.g., Roberts v. Louisiana, 420 U.S. 325, 333 (1976)—and has been adopted in many states. Elson v. Alaska, 659 P.2d 1195 (Alas. 1983); Arizona v. Connecticut, 669 P.2d 581, 137 Ariz. 148 (Ariz. 1983) (en banc). Justice Black recognized the potential for abuse by judges with such broad discretion and sources

Thus, the sentencing judge has the clear power to operate in a principled fashion regarding predictions of dangerousness, even in the absence of legislative guidance.

IV. Dangerousness: Evidence and Proof

The greatest bar to a sensitive judicial consideration of the appropriate role of dangerousness at various stages in the criminal and mental health law has been the confusion between the standards of proof required to find criminal guilt, or to identify those subject to the state's powers under the mental health law, and the level of confidence required for the proper use of predictions of dangerousness. This confusion has been entrenched by the Supreme Court. Evidentiary problems concerning the proper role of psychologists in predicting dangerousness stem from this basic error. We will examine judicial consideration of the concept of dangerousness in the criminal law in recent Supreme Court cases.[22] Recall for these purposes our discussion of the meaning of a prediction of dangerousness—not an outcome in an individual case, but the condition of having the attributes of membership in a group with a defined level of expected violence.

In *Addington v. Texas*, 441 U.S. 418 (1979), the Supreme Court held without dissent that in a civil commitment hearing the due process clause of the Fourteenth Amendment requires a standard of proof on the issues of the patient's mental illness and of his danger to himself or to others equal to or greater than "clear and convincing" evidence. The Court recognized the difficulty of quantifying, even of clearly stating, the differences among the usual three standards of proof—balance of probabilities, beyond reasonable doubt, and an intermediate standard of clear and convincing evidence—but saw the distinctions as "more than an empty semantic exercise" (441 U.S. 418, 425; citation omitted) and in fact an expression of "the degree of confidence our society thinks. . . [the fact finder] should have in the correctness of factual

---

of information. "Leaving a sentencing judge free to avail himself of out-of-court information in making such a fateful choice of sentences does secure to him a broad discretionary power, one susceptible of abuse" (337 U.S. 241, 251). We believe that the principled use of predictions of dangerousness would limit possible abuses by judges in sentencing.

[22] The concept of dangerousness in the criminal law is a relatively recent addition to Supreme Court jurisprudence. The Court has considered the use of predictions of dangerousness in only twenty cases, ten in the past three years, and never before 1972. Of all of these cases, civil and criminal, only seven involved extended discussions of dangerousness.

conclusions for a particular type of adjudication" (441 U.S. at 423; citing *In re Winship*, 397 U.S. 358, 370 [1970]; Harlan, J., concurring).

One of the reasons the Court was satisfied by the "clear and convincing" standard in an issue involving deprivation of individual liberty, rejecting the need, as a constitutional matter, for proof beyond reasonable doubt,[23] was that "*[g]iven the lack of certainty and the fallibility of psychiatric diagnosis there is a serious question as to whether a state could ever prove beyond a reasonable doubt that an individual is both mentally ill and likely to be dangerous*" (441 U.S. at 429; emphasis added).[24] In explaining this statement Chief Justice Burger noted that "[t]he subtleties and nuances of psychiatric diagnosis render certainties virtually beyond reach in most situations." The end result of requiring the highest standard of proof for findings of dangerousness, in Chief Justice Burger's view, would be that jurors and judges "could be forced by the criminal law standard of proof to reject commitment for many patients desperately in need of institutionalized psychiatric care" (441 U.S. at 430).

The Court must be wrong. That an individual is likely to be dangerous *can* be proved at any level required, provided "likely to be dangerous" is given careful construction. If that phrase is defined as "belonging to a group with a risk of dangerous behavior unacceptable in relation to its gravity, if the harm occurs, balanced against the reduction of individual freedom involved in its avoidance," then the existence of the likelihood of injury can be proved at the same level as many other facts. It is a fact in the same sense that a broken bone is a fact. By contrast, if the phrase "likely to be dangerous" is defined as requiring proof on a balance of probability that *this* patient will injure himself or others, or that he is more likely to do so than not, then it cannot be proved at any level of confidence, since it is very rarely so. In the latter perspective, in practice, it can never be proved, since at present our best predictive capacities fall far below the requisite level of proof.

The confusion lies in the admixture of ideas about the probability of future events and the degrees of confidence in facts required by the usual three standards of proof. The existence of dangerousness is not a

---

[23] Many state civil commitment statutes continue to require proof beyond reasonable doubt in this context. See *Addington*, 441 U.S. 418, 431 n.5 (fourteen states requiring proof beyond a reasonable doubt when *Addington* was decided in 1979).

[24] As we noted earlier, the language of predictions can be very awkward. Here, the Court writes of an individual who is "likely to be dangerous," yet "dangerous" itself means likely to be violent or do something harmful in the future.

question of the weight of the burden of proof to be placed on the affirmant of a risk, and it is a mistake to decide the balance between the risk to the community and the restrictions on the individual in terms of the burden of proof. As we have stressed in identifying the elements that lead to a justified use of predictions of dangerousness, the determination of acceptable and unacceptable levels of risk is an entirely distinct policy question to be decided by a legislature or deduced by a judge interpreting a statute that vests sentencing discretion in the judge; the answer is not capable of expression solely as a problem of evidence. Once the risk is defined, the elements that go to prove the existence of that risk can be made subject to different burdens of proof, but not the risk itself.[25] Thus two quite separate issues emerge: the weight of the burden of proof and the degree of probability of the injurious event sought to be avoided by the statute. Blending the two, as if they were susceptible to a single conclusion, has caused confusion.[26]

In one sense—a sense not encompassed within the Court's decision in *Addington*—a requirement of clear and convincing evidence of "dangerousness," or even of proof beyond reasonable doubt of "dangerousness," is achievable and may be appropriate. Assume that a one-in-three base rate sufficiently defines that condition; proof that the disturbed patient belongs to that group—has the attributes that define his membership—may be required under whatever burden of proof policy dictates. Proof that he is correctly classified is clearly distinguishable from proof that he as an individual will injure himself or others; that he has a base expectancy rate of one in three and not of one in ten is susceptible of precise proof.

Assume, following *Addington*, that the risk of serious injury to another person, if the patient is not civilly committed, is one in three. Does *Addington*'s constitutional requirement of clear and convincing evidence of dangerousness preclude the civil commitment of this pa-

---

[25] We reject on logical grounds any tie between standard of proof and the level of prediction necessary to justify preventive detention or any lesser intrusion on the individual's liberty. We do not deny that standards of proof have a role in applying predictions of dangerousness: that role, which can be satisfied at whatever level of proof is desired, is to insure the correct categorization of the individual. The confusion of the standard of proof with levels of prediction has been the greatest barrier to a sensitive consideration of the jurisprudence of dangerousness in American courts. It is not only the courts, but social scientists as well who have made this error (see Monahan and Wexler 1978).

[26] The decision in *Addington* may well be supported by other considerations, but it is not justified by the impossibility of proving risk beyond a reasonable doubt.

tient? Clearly not. If it did, few indeed could be constitutionally committed. What *Addington* should be read to require is a larger degree of confidence than a preponderance of the evidence by the trier of facts, judge or jury, of the definition of the group. This higher degree of confidence would apply as well to proof of the base expectancy rate of violence for the group, which one hopes has been validly assessed and shown to be relatively stable, and to proof that this patient indeed falls within that group.

For the use of predictions of dangerousness in the criminal as opposed to mental health law, the problem is identical. Thus the elements of "dangerousness" capable of proof in the case of the hypothetical young offender, posed earlier, include not only his personal circumstances—the historical facts of his mother and his absent father, his truancy, his school and employment records, and his gang membership—but also his base expectancy rate of violence. The scientific work necessary to define a group and to assess its base expectancy rate of criminal violence within a given period has or has not been done, or has only been partially done. Its stability over time and in different regions has been tested, partially tested, or not tested.[27] If the facts of the future criminal behavior of the group to which our hypothetical offender is said to belong have been found actuarially, then the question of his risk to the community is not properly related to the different burdens of proof of those actuarial facts. Proof of the base expectancy rate is not inherently more difficult than proof of the historical facts on which the rate was calculated. It makes little difference whether the burden of their proof is on a balance of probabilities, or by clear and convincing evidence, or beyond reasonable doubt.

It is a mistake to confuse the sufficiency of proof of dangerousness with a decision whether to require proof beyond a reasonable doubt, or

---

[27] This essay sets out our conception of an ideal—the requirements for the proper use of predictions of dangerousness—which we acknowledge cannot presently be attained. We leave for another time the extended development of a "practical" jurisprudence of dangerousness. See Sec. IV below for interim "practical" suggestions. Courts faced with inadequate, imperfect, or incomplete evidence will have to decide whether to consider the evidence and what weight that evidence—whether from actuarial studies or clinical predictions—should be given. This problem will become more complex before it becomes less so, as new initial actuarial studies of relevant groups become available. Perhaps courts should recognize "good enough" science, for those times (almost always) when "perfect" science does not exist. Recognizing and utilizing good enough science would properly reward efforts at producing perfect science. It would also reward the principled use of predictions of dangerousness; judges could take the imperfections in the available studies and predictions into account when using such predictions.

by clear and convincing evidence, or on a balance of probability. The decision by the Supreme Court in *Addington* has entrenched this error and has impeded rational analysis.

Addington figured prominently in the recent case of *Jones v. United States*, 103 S. Ct. 3034 (1983). The defendant, Michael Jones, had pleaded not guilty by reason of insanity to attempted petty larceny. The issue in the case was the constitutionality of committing Jones on grounds of future dangerousness to a term that might continue beyond the possible sentence for which he could have been held as a prisoner or for which he could have been held as a patient on grounds applicable to civil commitment.

Justice Powell for the Court found a continuing presumption both of mental illness and of dangerousness based on the commission of the criminal act for which Jones had pleaded not guilty by reason of insanity. The expiration of the "hypothetical" maximum sentence, had Jones been convicted of the criminal act in question, was held to be irrelevant. Regarding mental illness, Justice Powell wrote that "[i]t comports with common sense to conclude that someone whose mental illness was sufficient to lead him to commit a criminal act is likely to remain ill and in need of treatment" (103 S. Ct. 3043, at 3050). As far as Jones's continued dangerousness, Justice Powell wrote in *Barefoot* that "[t]he fact that a person has been found beyond a reasonable doubt to have committed a criminal act certainly indicates dangerousness" (103 S. Ct. 3383, 3044).[28] Thus, the Court held that Jones could be detained even without a finding by clear and convincing evidence that he remained dangerous and mentally ill. His dangerousness was presumed on the basis of the earlier plea.

The presumptions of continuing mental illness and dangerousness were found by the majority even though Jones had committed an offense that, in commonsense terms, was nonviolent. The Court suggested a definition of dangerousness that would remove all sense from the term; when attempted petty larceny of a jacket is included as a "dangerous" act, the type and extent of predicted harm justifying the use of a prediction of dangerousness grows enormous.

Justice Brennan's dissent observed that "[n]one of the available evidence that criminal behavior by the mentally ill is likely to repeat itself

---

[28] One must wonder if there is any limit on the extent of this presumption of dangerousness other than the possibility that at some point in his indefinite commitment Jones may be able to prove that he is no longer mentally ill or dangerous. Recall, too, that Jones's criminal act carrying this powerful and continuing diagnostic consequence for five Justices of the Supreme Court was attempted petit larceny of a jacket.

distinguishes between behaviors that were 'the product' of mental illness and those that were not. *It is completely unlikely that persons acquitted by reason of insanity display a rate of future 'dangerous' activity higher than civil committees with similar arrest records, or than persons convicted of crimes who were later found to be mentally ill*" (103 S. Ct. 3043, 3058; emphasis added).[29]

The willingness of the majority to presume dangerousness on the basis of the plea of insanity, especially absent any supporting evidence of the defendant's continued dangerousness, is, as the dissent notes, groundless. The same paradox noted earlier holds: the Court seems more willing to find or assume dangerousness when mental illness is involved, without further analysis, even though the civil committee or, here, the defendant who pleads not guilty by reason of insanity, is in theory less culpable than those convicted of violating the criminal law.

Confusion about dangerousness is painfully evident in the opinion of the Court in *Barefoot v. Estelle*, 103 S. Ct. 3383 (1983), particularly in discussing the admissibility of psychiatric testimony of dangerousness. Such testimony was admitted under the Texas death penalty statute, which allows capital punishment under a finding that "there is a probability that the defendant would commit criminal acts of violence that would constitute a continuing threat to society" (Texas Code Crim. Proc. § 37.071). The decision by the same five-member majority as in *Jones* was delivered by Justice White, who began by stating that "[t]he suggestion that no psychiatrist's testimony may be presented with respect to a defendant's future dangerousness is somewhat like asking us to disinvent the wheel" (103 S. Ct. 3383, 3396). The Court then expressly approved Justice Stevens's statement in *Jurek* that "[a]ny sentencing authority must predict a convicted person's probable future conduct when it engages in the process of determining what punishment to impose" (103 S. Ct. at 3396).

The Court confused the question whether predictions of dangerousness should be allowed at all with the entirely separate issue of what evidence of prediction—in other words, what types of predictions— should be admissible in evidence. Having recognized that predictions of dangerousness cannot be removed from the criminal law, the Court then seemed to assume that the testimony of psychiatrists regarding the defendant's dangerousness could not be excluded on any constitutional

[29] Justice Brennan is supported here by the work of Monahan and Steadman (1983*a*, 1983*b*).

grounds, no matter how unfounded or prejudicial the specific testimony in any given case.[30] While we agree that predictions of dangerousness are a necessary and even critical element in sentencing and related decisions in the criminal law, we cannot accept the Court's conclusion that all evidence of future dangerousness is admissible. As we discussed earlier in this essay, all predictions are not created equal—and clinical predictions are less equal than actuarial or anamnestic predictions.

Justice Blackmun, in his powerful dissent, correctly found the testimony of the *Barefoot* psychiatrists so highly prejudicial and overpersuasive that such evidence should not have been admitted on evidentiary grounds. One psychiatrist for the State, Dr. Grigson, testified that he could "give a medical opinion within reasonable psychiatric certainty as to [the] psychological or psychiatric makeup of an individual." Dr. Grigson thought he could predict that Barefoot "most certainly would" commit future acts of criminal violence, and claimed that the degree of probability that Barefoot would commit criminal acts of violence that would constitute a continuing threat to society was "one hundred percent and absolute." Dr. Holbrook, without the benefit of a personal interview or clinical examination of Barefoot, testified that it was "within [his] capacity as a doctor of psychiatry to predict the future dangerousness of an individual within a reasonable medical certainty," and that "within reasonable psychiatric certainty" there was "a probability that Thomas A. Barefoot . . . will commit criminal acts of violence in the future that would constitute a continuing threat to society" (103 S. Ct. 3383, 3407).[31]

Such statements, impossible of proof and rejected by the American Psychiatric Association (APA),[32] rely for their probative force on the

---

[30] Of course, there may be eighth amendment or fourteenth amendment due process objections to the admission of such highly prejudicial "expert" testimony regarding such a serious determination (as Justice Blackmun suggests in his dissent at 103 S. Ct. 3383, 3410–11). The constitutional limits on federal review of state statutes and testimony given under state statutes may have raised a smaller constitutional hurdle than a federal statute would, but we do not see how the testimony actually given by Grigson and Holbrook in *Barefoot*, at least, could get over even the most deferential constitutional hurdle.

[31] The record indicates that Barefoot did not fit into the category of people so exceptional as to overcome our principles of the just use of predictions of dangerousness. Barefoot had not previously been convicted of a violent offense, but had been convicted of drug offenses and possession of an unregistered firearm. The conviction leading to the capital sentence was for the killing of a police officer. Barefoot was executed in late 1984.

[32] The *Barefoot* brief for the APA as amicus curiae concluded that: "The forecast of future violent conduct on the part of a defendant in a capital case is, at bottom, a lay determination, not an expert psychiatric determination. To the extent such predictions

title attached to the witnesses.[33] Pointing to the absurdity of the witnesses' statements and their express reliance on professional expertise in making their predictions, Justice Blackmun argued in dissent that such testimony cannot justly be allowed. This does not mean, in our view, that all predictions of dangerousness are inadmissible, nor is the ground of our disagreement with the *Barefoot* majority the fact that long-term predictions of dangerousness can be made at best only at a level of one in three. We later suggest how predictions may appropriately be applied even to support the unpleasant application of a capital sentence, if a finding of greater dangerousness is a constitutionally allowable or a constitutionally mandated means of identifying those liable to such punishment. *Barefoot* provides an example of why clinical predictions should not be allowed, and yet the Court upheld the admittance of the proffered testimony on both constitutional and evidentiary grounds. Even if clinical predictions are accepted in court, as under current practice, the trial judge must exercise some judgment about the reliability of witnesses and the potentially prejudicial effect of the evidence. Here the trial judge allowed improper testimony with little doubt of the resulting prejudice. Given the inevitable potential for prejudice with such testimony, perhaps the judge should always hear the evidence first and should not allow testimony of great prejudice and lacking competence, such as that given in *Barefoot*.

The issue whether predictions of dangerousness could be made based on a hypothetical case, without benefit of any actual clinical probing, is spurious. Clinical predictions of dangerousness naturally lose much of their probative force without personal examination, since the psychiatrist should be making a judgment based on all he or she knows or has observed about the individual. In our view clinical predictions should never be used in the criminal law when stakes are this high because they are inherently suspect and untestable.[34] On the other hand, an actuarial prediction could be made based on a hypothetical case in

---

have any validity, they can only be made on the basis of essentially actuarial data to which psychiatrists, *qua* psychiatrists, can bring no special interpretive skills. On the other hand, the use of psychiatric testimony on this issue causes serious prejudice to the defendant. By dressing up the actuarial data with an 'expert' opinion, the psychiatrist's testimony is likely to receive undue weight. In addition, it permits the jury to avoid the difficult actuarial questions by seeking refuge in a medical diagnosis that provides a false aura of certainty. For these reasons, psychiatric testimony of future dangerousness impermissibly distorts the factfinding process in capital cases" (brief of Amicus Curiae, American Psychiatric Association at 9, Barefoot v. Estelle, 103 S. Ct 3383 [1983]).

[33] Restraints on such testimony by members of the psychiatric and psychological professions have been suggested as well (see, e.g., Ewing 1982).

[34] See the discussion at Sec. II above.

which all of the relevant elements had been proven at whatever level of proof is required.

Let us offer an example of the Court's misunderstanding of the notion of dangerousness through the incorrect analogy to predictions of dangerousness in the Court's recent decision of *California v. Ramos*, 103 S. Ct. 3446 (1983). The majority in that case incorrectly analogized predictions of dangerousness such as those upheld in *Jurek v. Texas*, 428 U.S. 262 (1976), and *Barefoot* to California's "Briggs instruction," which requires that the trial judge in a death case inform the jury that a sentence of life imprisonment without the possibility of parole may be commuted by the governor to a sentence that includes the possibility of parole. The Court observed that

> bringing to the jury's attention the possibility that the defendant may be returned to society, the Briggs Instruction invites the jury to assess whether the defendant is someone whose probable future behavior makes it undesirable that he be permitted to return to society. Like [the use of predictions of dangerousness in *Jurek* and *Barefoot*] the Briggs Instruction focuses the jury on the defendant's probable future dangerousness. The approval in *Jurek* of explicit consideration of this factor in the capital sentencing decision defeats [the] contention that, because of the speculativeness involved, the State of California may not constitutionally permit consideration *of commutation.* [103 S. Ct. 3446, 3454; emphasis added; citations excluded]

This analogy shows fundamental misunderstanding of predictions of dangerousness. *Ramos* concerned the prediction of the future governor's behavior rather than the prediction of the offender's future behavior. A commutation of a sentence by a governor would be a near-random event based wholly on individual factors which are essentially unpredictable (e.g., new evidence showing that the defendant is innocent; or a highly public response to a trial; or as an act of random but no doubt carefully chosen clemency, as a sign of forgiveness and compassion on the part of the executive). In other words, the probability of such an occurrence is so near to zero and the factors so unrelated to any prediction of *group* behavior that the majority's analogy to predictions of dangerousness is indeed an "intellectual sleight of hand" (103 S. Ct. 3446, 3467; Blackmun, J., dissenting).[35] The majority seemed to think that dangerousness could be evaluated by the trier on an intuitive,

---

[35] On remand from the Supreme Court, the California Supreme Court, in The People v. Ramos (November 1, 1984), held the Briggs instruction unconstitutional under the

unstructured, and individualized basis, as shown by the misleading reference to "lay" testimony.[36]

Thus, the Court has not carefully considered the meaning of predictions of dangerousness. Such consideration has been avoided because of the confusion with burdens of proof so evident in *Addington*, obscured by groundless presumptions in *Jones*, and ignored by the majority in *Barefoot*, in which admittedly meaningless and overpersuasive accusations of future dangerousness by psychiatrists were allowed to justify the imposition of capital punishment where a finding of likely future dangerousness was required by statute.[37]

V. The Proper Use of Predictions

In this part we offer three principles for the just invocation of predictions of dangerousness under the criminal law. We assume, for this purpose, validly established base expectancy rates of dangerousness for defined groups of offenders, though we recognize that such an assumption tends to exaggerate present knowledge. We shall present our three principles, state what we mean by them, and then offer some examples of how they might with justice be applied in various areas of the criminal law.

Our first submission concerning the proper use of predictions of dangerousness under the aegis of the criminal law—as distinct from the mental health law or immigration law or the law relating to quarantine or to spies—is this:

Punishment should not be imposed, nor the term of punishment extended, by virtue of a prediction of dangerousness, beyond that which would be justified as a deserved punishment independently of that prediction.

California constitution "because it is seriously and prejudicially misleading and because it invites the jury to be influenced by speculative and improper considerations." *Ramos* suggests the important and independent role the state courts can play in developing a jurisprudence of dangerousness.

[36] Justice Blackmun appears to be correct on the use of the term "lay" testimony in *Jurek* and Estelle v. Smith, 451 U.S. 454, 472–73 (1981). See *Barefoot*, 103 S. Ct. 3383, 3416–17 (Blackmun, J., dissenting). It does not mean testimony by persons off the street, but testimony by social scientists armed with statistical predictions.

[37] That the statute in Texas may have indicated unrealistic assumptions by the legislature about the present ability to predict future dangerousness, and thus may have suggested to the psychiatrists that they testify in the terms they did, does not absolve the error in placing such testimony before a jury. The legislature may have demanded an impossible finding (in trying to satisfy the current constitutional doctrine regarding the death penalty) in which case our analysis would not apply, but we later suggest a possible interpretation of the Texas statute which would give it a sensible and operational meaning.

It will be noted that this submission speaks both to the assumption of predictive power and to the limitation of that power. Floud and Young, in their book on this subject, fail to make this helpful distinction. They consider, as our first principle does, the initial point at which such predictions can justly be made, though they lapse into overstatement, but they do not carefully isolate the proper limitations on the application of such predictions thereafter. They write of the "dangerousness of dangerousness" and are perceptive of the risk of a "slippery slope" to "universal preventive confinement," where predictive judgments would be used to incapacitate individuals predicted to be dangerous whether or not they had committed an offense. They argue that a "right to be presumed harmless, like the right to be presumed innocent, is fundamental to a free society" (1981, p. 44). The rhetoric is overblown, but the point has merit, as does their conclusion that a "man must justly forfeit his right to be presumed innocent before his right to be presumed harmless can be brought into question" (p. 46).

We would agree with this conclusion, but with this important qualification. Powers under the criminal law are sometimes properly and necessarily exercised prior to findings of guilt by a judicial authority—powers of arrest, of bail, of search and seizure, and so on. We agree with the thrust of the point made by Floud and Young but would modify it to this extent: a prediction of dangerousness can never alone justify the invocation of authority over the individual under the criminal law that would not exist without such a prediction.

Floud and Young would even further confine the application of predictions of dangerousness, which they suggest should not be applied to first offenders. Again, we have to broaden the base. A sensitive means of distinguishing between first offenders (especially those convicted of serious crimes) who present a high risk of future serious criminality and those who do not is of great practical importance if it can be done within proper ethical limits.

Our second submission is:

Provided the previous limitation is respected, predictions of dangerousness may properly influence sentencing decisions and other decisions under the criminal law.

The first submission prevents utilitarian values from justifying the exercise of state authority over individuals merely because of a prediction, here assumed to be valid and stable, of their membership in a group with a high risk of future dangerousness. To this extent the first submission is deontological, expressing adherence to values enshrined in the criminal law that seek to strike a just balance between individual autonomy and state authority.

The second submission moves into the utilitarian. It suggests that, if there are otherwise existing justifications for the exercise of state authority over the individual, it is entirely proper to take into account his membership in such a group. And this leads to the third and limiting principle, which defines the jurisprudence we offer in this field—that of the "limiting retributivist."

The third principle is:

> The base expectancy rate of violence for the criminal predicted as dangerous must be shown by reliable evidence to be substantially higher than the base expectancy rate of another criminal with a closely similar criminal record and convicted of a closely similar crime but not predicted as unusually dangerous, before the greater dangerousness of the former may be relied on to intensify or extend his punishment.

It is our general submission that these three principles enunciate a jurisprudence of predictions of dangerousness that would achieve both individual justice and better community protection than at present.

Our view depends on the recognition that there is a range of just punishments for a given offense; that we lack the moral calipers to say with precision of a given punishment, "That was a just punishment." All we can with precision say is: "As we know our community and its values, that does not seem an unjust punishment." It therefore seems entirely proper to us, within a range of not unjust punishments, to take account of different levels of dangerousness of those to be punished; but the concept of the deserved, or rather the not undeserved, punishment properly limits the range within which utilitarian values may operate.

The injustice of a punishment, assuming proper proof of guilt, is thus defined in part deontologically, in limited retributivist terms and not solely in utilitarian terms. The upper and lower limits of "deserved" punishment set the range within which utilitarian values, including values of mercy and human understanding, may properly fix the punishment to be imposed.

There is often a range of "not-unjust" punishments, measured in relation to the gravity of the offense and the offender's criminal record. And when punishment systems fail to appreciate the need for such a range and set up mandatory sentences, as occasionally happens, they always get into trouble. Such systems either are circumvented, or achieve gross injustice, or both. Punishments and a scale of just punishments should always allow for discretion to be exercised, under proper legislative guidance, by the judicial officer of the state.

Justifying the application of predictions of dangerousness to an individual within this range of just punishments also helps determine the appropriate group in comparison with which his relative dangerousness should be determined. This is a group with a similar criminal record, who have committed crimes of similar gravity to that of the offender being sentenced, since universally these are the two leading determinants of what are seen as just punishments. Hence the structure of our three principles, allowing room for predictions in sentencing within the concept of the not unjust sentence, and using gravity of crime and criminal record to determine the comparison group against which an offender's higher base expectancy rate of violence must be established. Once criminal record and severity of the current offense are included, the definition of groups with higher base expectancy rates than those with similar crimes and similar criminal records becomes very much more difficult of proof—but it is a prerequisite to justice in sentencing.

It may help give substance to these submissions to suggest how our theory of just predictions of dangerousness might operate in various areas of the criminal law of particular present concern. Overall, the principles we offer would have a dramatically restrictive effect on the acceptability of predictions of dangerousness in the criminal law, but our principles would also allow room for the future development of an enlarged capacity to apply such predictions with justice.

Let us try to give operational perspective to these principles by considering their application in four areas of the criminal law: First, in relation to sentencing under such systems as that first established in Minnesota, further developed in Pennsylvania, and now finding increasing acceptance in other states and also under other systems of sentencing;[38] second, in relation to the problem of early release under pressure of prison overcrowding; third, in relation to the problem of release on bail or on the accused's own recognizance; and, finally, in relation to the difficult problem that confronted the Supreme Court in *Barefoot v. Estelle*. In none of these will we do more than suggest the basis of a just invocation of predictions of dangerousness.

A. Sentencing: Minnesota and Pennsylvania and Other Systems

As we have seen, predictions of dangerousness are in fact taken into account in sentencing, and there is Supreme Court authority expressly

[38] See Minnesota Sentencing Guidelines Commission (1980), Pennsylvania Commission on Sentencing (1982), and Washington Sentencing Guidelines Commission (1983).

approving that practice. Given discretion in sentencing, that result is inevitable. Nevertheless how should it properly operate? Let us assume a Minnesota/Pennsylvania-type sentencing system by which the gravity of the offense and the convicted person's criminal record define both whether he should be imprisoned and, if so, the range of months within which the term should be set. These guidelines bind or, in Pennsylvania, guide the sentencing judge unless he wishes to impose a more lenient or more severe sentence than the guidelines provide (of course within his statutory powers), in which case he must give reasons for his "departure" from the guidelines.

Our principles would not justify a "departure" on the grounds of the offender's predicted dangerousness; they would justify the judge's setting a sentence at the top of the range set by the guidelines[39] provided the criminal being sentenced had been shown on a valid basis to have a higher base expectancy rate of dangerousness than other criminals falling within those same guidelines. Let us put the matter colloquially for those who are acquainted with the "boxes" of the Minnesota/Pennsylvania-type sentencing system: the boxes would both set the limits and define the comparison group for the extension of punishment on the basis of an offender's predicted greater dangerousness.

The Minnesota/Pennsylvania system of sentencing narrows the discretion of the judge. How should our principles operate when the upper limit on the judge's sentencing power is the maximum provided by statute? Presumably, that maximum is statutorily intended to apply to the "worst case–worst record" offender. We are not suggesting, in such a situation, that predictions of dangerousness justify increments of sentencing up to that maximum. The operating maximum in such a case must be what the judge would think not undeserved for such an offender as he has before him, and with a similar record (those factors would fix his estimate of the not-undeserved maximum for such an offender, which would set the upper limit of an increment of sentence on the basis of dangerousness). The advantage of considering the application of our principles in a Minnesota/Pennsylvania-type sentencing system is that such a system gives some operative and ascertainable meaning to the upper limit of desert in the individual case, which other sentencing systems tend to conceal.

---

[39] A series of Minnesota cases have made clear that dangerousness cannot justify a durational departure by a judge on the grounds that the legislature specifically accounted for future dangerousness in setting the sentencing guidelines. See, e.g., Minnesota v. Dietz, No. co-83-384 (Minn. Feb. 17, 1984); Minnesota v. Ott, 341 N.W.2d 883 (1984); Minnesota v. Gardner, 328 N.W.2d 159 (1983).

B. Early Release

Assume a state prison system so crowded that in response to legislatively approved powers some prisoners must be released prior to the termination of their sentences, less time off for good behavior, and apart from the state's parole system. This situation has recently occurred in several states, sometimes under legislative authority, sometimes pursuant to gubernatorial powers of clemency, and sometimes under court order.

How are prisoners to be selected for early release? Should the state release all those with only, say, three months to serve, or four months, or whatever period will produce the necessary reduction of population? Early release is never carried out in that way. Invariably, an effort is made to select a group with a lower rate of likely dangerousness, particularly for the period during which they will now be at large when they would otherwise have been in custody. The political pressures to this end are compelling, and if it be assumed that the sentences on all were just, then no injustice is caused by extending this clemency to a few. That this involves predictions of dangerousness is obvious, and they are exactly the predictions of dangerousness that have been used by those who have developed and applied parole prediction tables for several decades—efforts to assess actuarially the likelihood that various categories of prisoners will commit crimes during their parole periods. It will be seen that our three principles have application here. To the extent that predictions of dangerousness retain less validity at the far end of a prison term, distant from the critical acts which supported any original prediction, given the problems of fairness in distributing early release among otherwise noncomparable inmates, and given the paucity of data, the release decision really becomes, and should be recognized as, a wholly political decision.

We are not, of course, seeking to justify the parole system or current practices of early release. Rather, if a parole system, giving some discretion to the releasing authority, is itself a just system, then predictions of dangerousness, if valid and based on the comparison groups we have suggested, are ethically justifiable. And in the case of early release, the categories for the comparison groups and for the selection are also obvious. Some prisoners convicted of particularly heinous crimes, whose early release would stir public anxiety, will be excluded, and the remaining and proper comparison group will be those with a defined time to serve. Within that group, base expectancy rates of dangerousness may justly be considered.

C. Bail and Release

Let us pursue another example, one that both severely tests our principles and reveals their potential for application outside the area of sentencing on which we have concentrated. The questions of bail or release on the accused's own recognizance, of appearance for trial and of crimes committed during such release, are of great public concern and have generated various proposals for preventive detention prior to trial. Such proposals all involve, in one way or another, efforts to predict those either less likely to appear for trial or more likely to commit a crime if left at large pending trial.

We wish to avoid becoming involved in the heated constitutional and policy conflicts attending those bail reform proposals; they are serious issues, but our concern is narrower. If release on bail is to be denied to those having a higher base expectancy rate of not appearing or of committing a crime prior to trial, what are the limiting principles, akin to the concept of a deserved punishment, that can set bounds to the imposition of these disadvantages on our unknown arrested "false positives"?

None of the arrested but untried deserve punishment in the same sense that the convicted offender being sentenced, or the sentenced offender being considered for early release, have a deserved, applicable maximum sanction. Can "probable cause" for the arrest substitute for a "deserved maximum punishment" as a limiting principle? It would seem not. No punishment is "deserved" by the arrested person, whether or not there is probable cause for the arrest. But the analogy is close in this sense: predictions of dangerousness properly function only within discretions otherwise lawfully justified.

Current bail reform proposals are restrictive of liberty, but let us start with the converse case to explain this point. Consider a bail reform proposal that suggested that release pending trial of those charged with capital crimes should cease to be governed by an unfettered judicial discretion, but should be made subject to defined prediction processes by which only those accused of capital crimes, and with a stated high base expectancy rate of flight, should be detained, the predictive criteria being stated. None would, we suggest, object on grounds of civil liberty that the "false positives" with high base expectancy rates would as a consequence not be at large pending trial while others accused of capital crimes would be free on bail. The point is that the detention of all is justified on grounds other than their predicted dangerousness and is not constitutionally objectionable; hence neither is the detention of a few, provided the base expectancy rates are validly established and proved. Here the greater does include the lesser.

Now consider the reverse and more likely "reform." Bail may be denied to those who, for example, have previously jumped bail or committed a crime while on bail, or are charged with a crime of serious personal violence and had previously been convicted of such a crime, or have a record of drug abuse. If it is legislatively accepted and passes constitutional muster, no matter what its wisdom as social policy, it seems to us that it is entirely proper to apply here exactly the same principles for exercising discretion based on predictions of dangerousness as in the sentencing situation, the early release situation, or other areas of the criminal law where powers are lawfully taken over defined groups of citizens, the exercise of those powers being modulated by predictions of dangerousness.

By contrast, and to drive home the point, we would regard as wholly unprincipled a bail "reform" statute which provided simpliciter that arrested persons with a base expectancy rate of, say, one in three of not appearing for trial or one in four of committing a crime of a certain gravity while at large pending trial, may be denied bail. What it comes to is that the legislature must, within its constitutional powers, address the reality of false positives for the group; that difficult balance cannot be left to the judge in the individual case.

As conviction of a crime is the nonutilitarian justification for the application of the prediction of dangerousness in sentencing, so the existence of probable cause for an arrest and of legislative authority to deny bail—or to set it beyond the reach of the arrested person—are the preconditions for consideration of the likely dangerousness of the arrested person in this situation. Who will then form the comparison group against which one arrested person's higher base expectancy rate of dangerousness justifies his detention? Other persons arrested for a crime of similar gravity and with similar records.

D. Barefoot v. Estelle

As our fourth example of how the principles we offer in this essay would properly limit, and yet allow room for reliance on, predictions of dangerousness, let us build on the case of *Barefoot v. Estelle*, earlier discussed, in which the testimony of two psychiatrists was in our view improperly allowed to go to the jury on the prisoner's future dangerousness and therefore fitness for capital punishment. *Barefoot* provides a paradigm for the application of our offered principles.

The Texas psychiatrists testified as expert witnesses that the murderer, Barefoot, was a sociopath (a meaningless though profoundly pejorative diagnosis) and that he was highly likely to be a danger to the community if released and to other prisoners if detained. The applicable Texas statute authorized Barefoot's execution if "there is a probability that the defendant would commit criminal acts of violence that would constitute a continuing threat to society."

Again, it is not our purpose to defend such a statute—far from it. Rather, our purpose is to suggest how predictions of dangerousness can with justice be applied within such a statute, reluctantly, for the moment, assuming its ethical validity.

In the case itself, the two witnesses greatly exaggerated their predictive powers, and the suggestion by the majority in the Supreme Court that the jury was capable of distinguishing "the wheat from the chaff" in that testimony, to use the majority's own metaphor—to separate the good prediction from the bad prediction—is at best ingenuous, since the majority also agreed that there was no wheat there—just chaff! And chaff with a powerful prejudicial effect. But, however that may be, what would be proper proof under this statute?

If our principles are correct, the two psychiatrists should have been asked something like the following: If Barefoot's murder is compared with murders of similar gravity by men with a similar record to Barefoot's, does the fact that you diagnose him as a sociopath mean, when added to the other diagnostic information you have about him, that he has a higher likelihood than those other similar murderers with similar records of being injurious to others if not executed? The point is not that Barefoot has a high likelihood of injuring others in the future—we will assume that. What we have to know is whether he has a *higher* likelihood than those with whom we are comparing him. Otherwise we must execute them all or not execute Barefoot. He must be distinguished validly from them by his greater dangerousness if we are with justice to select him for this greater punishment. We must have a comparison group against whom to establish his greater dangerousness. Who should constitute that comparison group? They must be murderers of similar record, whose killings were of similar gravity, whom you do not call sociopaths and do not otherwise selectively diagnose. Very well, doctors, give us the evidence on which you based this diagnostic category "sociopath" and found that this sociopath, Barefoot, has a higher base expectancy rate than those others.

Of course, there is no such evidence. But that, we submit, is the proper thrust of the inquiry. Only with such evidence could one defend a selection under which one might with justice increase a punishment by virtue of a prediction of future violent behavior—and not otherwise.

VI. Some Objections

In this section we recognize some of the objections that have been made to the use of predictions of dangerousness, usually in the context of sentencing, and we conclude that none of these objections carry much weight.[40] Most of these objections have been dealt with in the earlier sections of this essay. An objection which has not been widely suggested, but which poses a little more difficulty, is that making determinations based on predictions of future dangerousness would violate the prohibition against "status offenses" suggested in such cases as *Robinson v. California*, 370 U.S. 660 (1962). The final consideration, which poses the most serious dilemma, is the racially biased effect of predictions of dangerousness in the criminal justice system. We conclude that the impact of such predictions will not be biased against blacks at any point beyond the determination of guilt or innocence, and that possible biases in prosecution or at other selective stages of the criminal law will be minimized and controlled by the use of such predictions.

The most common objections to the use of predictions of dangerousness include the claim that predictions have not yet been made at a sufficient level of accuracy to be reliable, that the use of predictions is unfair to those who would be false positives in any given predicted group (that predictions are of groups yet we use them "against" individuals), and that predictions of dangerousness do not help (i.e., that such predictions, if valid, carry so little weight as to make them not worth the effort). These claims have already been dealt with in this essay: the notion of "convicting the innocent" has been shown to be misguided, based on incorrect assumptions about the nature of the prediction of violent behavior; and we have argued that a prediction of dangerousness for some groups at a level of one in three is not a low prediction at all, given the rarity and severity of behavior being predicted. Finally, the argument that predictions of dangerousness just do not help is surely wrong: it is fundamental that the criminal justice system must constantly distinguish among people similarly situated in some relevant respect, because of limited resources, to minimize poten-

[40] For a catalog of some objections and some suggested responses, see Walker (1982). See also Von Hirsch (1972, 1976); Floud and Young (1981, pp. 38–49).

Predictions of Dangerousness   45

tial and actual harms to society, and out of a sense of justice to those incorrectly *assumed* to be dangerous by sentencing authorities that make implicit and ungrounded predictions of future behavior.

One argument frequently made is that using predictions of dangerousness is "unjust" because a person is being "punished, not for what he has done, but for what it is believed he may do in the future" (Swedish National Council for Crime Prevention 1978; Von Hirsch 1983). Walker (1982) responds to this argument by attacking the underlying assumption that the only justifiable aim of a sentence must be retributive punishment.

A similar argument could be made based on the doctrine in American jurisprudence that forbids punishment for a "status offense": thus any punishment added to a sentence, or a decision earlier in the criminal process to prosecute an individual, based on the status of being predicted to be dangerous, would be unjustified (see, e.g., *Robinson v. California*, 370 U.S. 660 [1962]; *Lambert v. California*, 355 U.S. 225 [1957]).

We counter both of these arguments by noting that we suggest the use of predictions of dangerousness as a verifiable, scientific tool to distinguish between people already subject to the state's power on other grounds. Thus, a person convicted of a crime is being sentenced or punished for that offense, and we offer the predictions as a way of justly and efficiently determining which sentence in a range of possible sentences is appropriate. We have expressly limited the use of such predictions in the criminal law so as to deny them an independent force in justifying a deprivation of liberty.

Our argument here holds true even for those who believe that there is a single appropriate punishment for a given offense (e.g., a "strict" retributivist). If the state narrows the range of options justified by a given act of the individual, the possible effect of a prediction of dangerousness or nondangerousness will likewise be narrowed.[41]

The most difficult objection to the use of predictions, even within our limiting principles, is the suggestion that they will have a biased impact in terms of race. We believe this is largely incorrect for all uses of predictions subsequent to the guilt determination stage of the crimi-

[41] The difficult case here, akin to that of bail, is the decision to prosecute or to observe specific individuals because they fall in a higher risk group. Our response in this case is that the individual can be observed at present without any higher suspicion, but that an actuarial prediction of dangerousness would not justify, e.g., the issuance of a search or arrest warrant without independent probable cause.

nal process. This conclusion is based on studies which find little or no difference between races in so far as the future behavior of convicted criminals is concerned (see, e.g., Petersilia 1983). These studies are bolstered by the recent theoretical and statistical work of Blumstein and Graddy (1981/82), whose initial findings indicate that "the large differences between races in aggregate arrest statistics are primarily a consequence of differences in participation rather than differences in recidivism" (Blumstein and Graddy 1981/82, p. 288; see also Blumstein 1982).

Blumstein and Graddy found a high consistency of rearrest probability between whites and nonwhites for those who are caught and convicted of index crimes. Though they are distinct, we assume that the similarity in rates of recidivism would be largely reflected in predictions of dangerousness for individuals convicted of crime, given the intertwined relationship of serious criminality and violence. Convicted defendants would already have passed through the "prevalence filter" suggested by Blumstein and Graddy because every member of both groups under consideration, black and white, would have been convicted of an offense. Thus the disparities in racial effect are likely to be minimal.

The careful use of predictions would operate to limit or eradicate bias based solely on the prejudice of the decision maker at all points in the criminal justice system. While this essay has concentrated on the explicit use of predictions of dangerousness, we have noted that implicit predictions of future behavior occur throughout the criminal law. These predictions cannot be carefully controlled or tested as they are often based on intuitive judgments. The proper use of predictions would diminish the effect of bias and stereotypes on the part of the decision maker by requiring a statistical justification to isolate any individual for greater or lesser punishment, or a greater or lesser intrusion on individual liberty. As we have stressed, the proper use of predictions of dangerousness will in fact act as a limiting principle.

To the extent that decisions in the criminal law have not passed through Blumstein and Graddy's "prevalence filter"—to the extent that preconviction decisions are made on the basis of predictions and the results are racially skewed—we only suggest that the criminal justice system cannot be used to rectify inequities in society. Even if we are wrong that the requirement of verifiable statistical predictions will limit discretion and the role prejudice plays in unbounded judgments, the criminal justice system is the wrong place, in our view, to apply notions of remedial justice to correct biases which run to the heart of the society. A racially skewed result in prosecutions, for example, should lead to a search for the causes of that skewing, not to a cover-up of the disliked result. We should not and cannot hide from the fact that racial disparities remain in the criminal justice system and in society as a whole.

We do not mean that race or any superficial substitute for race should be allowed as an express factor in making predictions of dangerousness. Predictions here raise the same problems as in other areas of the law, particularly the operation of the equal protection clause of the Fourteenth Amendment. We do not at present face the question of the justice of using factors wholly correlated with culture or race, such as the presence of a physiological trait occurring only in one race that leads to dramatically increased levels of violence for those individuals. If such a trait were proved, we believe that it would nevertheless be morally and constitutionally wrong to use race or a superficial substitute for race as a factor to distinguish between individuals or groups made subject to the state's tremendous criminal and mental health law powers. To the extent that facially neutral factors such as education, housing, and employment reflect racial inequalities, these problems should be attacked directly, and not collaterally through the alteration of neutral rules in an effort to balance their unequal racial effect. It is of the first importance that we base our predictions of dangerousness on validated knowledge and not on prejudice, particularly racial prejudice.

VII. Conclusions
Let us introduce our conclusions, summarizing the thrust of this essay, with some cautionary qualifications. Our essay is somewhat utopian, in the sense that we started by recognizing the pervasive use of predictions of dangerousness, implicit and explicit, in the criminal law and conclude by enunciating rigid principles highly restrictive of the use of such predictions. We are well aware that it is our principles and not practice that will fall in this conflict.

This does not mean that for a moment we withdraw our submissions; it means only that we recognize that the path to a responsible jurisprudence of prediction under the criminal law is neither short nor likely to be of easy passage. Hence, while a complete jurisprudence is for a later time and later authors, at this stage we suggest that judgments be made (1) in the light of these principles; (2) in the light of available studies and evidence identifying both positive and negative predictive elements; (3) in open recognition of generally limited predictive abilities; and (4) with the realization that intuition is often wrong. Finally, (5) the term "dangerousness" must be more carefully used. "Dangerousness" should not be used as a synonym for recidivism, vileness in the particular act, general disrespect for law, or criminal life-style.[42] More specifically, the type of predicted probable or potential harm underlying a prediction of dangerousness must be kept within some principled limits, and not allowed to extend to meaningless or open-ended descriptions of harm, such as the minor harm found sufficient by the majority in *Jones*.

Returning then to the utopian: As is so often the case with issues of justice, procedural and evidentiary issues become of central importance. We have argued that clinical predictions of dangerousness unsupported by actuarial studies should rarely be relied on. It is shocking that the Supreme Court relies on such statements absent validated statistical support. Clinical judgments firmly grounded on well-established base expectancy rates are a precondition, rarely fulfilled, to the just invocation of prediction of dangerousness as a ground for intensifying punishment. Our theory provides a rational process by which one can think of the just use of predictions. Unless these principles or something like them are followed, the present movement toward the overuse of predictions of dangerousness will be a threat to justice.

Developing a coherent and practical jurisprudence of dangerousness will not be an easy task. Courts have long hidden behind the wall of standards of proof and behind the white coats of psychiatrists and psychologists, so that difficult issues have been avoided. Yet predictions of dangerousness have been applied implicitly and explicitly by judges and parole boards, hospital administrators and psychologists, police and correctional officers, victims of crime and prosecutors of criminals. Scholarship and legal analysis have failed sufficiently to recognize the danger of this untested and intuitive use of our poor capacity to predict future violent behavior. There is a danger both to liberty and to effective crime control in the concept of dangerousness, yet we cannot and should not do without it. It is wrong to extend the application of the concept of dangerousness in the criminal law and in the law of mental health without more careful evaluation of our predictive capacities than those eight prospective studies that make up our limited present knowledge and without better efforts at jurisprudential analysis of the proper role of dangerousness in those systems of social control.

---

[42] Sundeberg v. Alaska, 652 P.2d 113 (1982) (recidivism); Quintana v. Commonwealth, 224 Va. 127 (1982) (vileness in the act); United States v. Hondo, 575 F. Supp. 628 (Minn. 1978) (general disrespect for law); United States v. Jarrett, 705 F.2d 198 (7th Cir. 1983) (criminal life-style) (interpreting the federal Dangerous Special Offender Statute).

Afterword

Just before publication of this essay, the Comprehensive Crime Control Act of 1984 was signed into law: Pub. L. No. 98-473 (October 12, 1984) (codified at 98 Stat. 1837). Congress expressly supported the use of predictions of dangerousness in pretrial detention and sentencing decisions for federal offenses. See 18 U.S.C. § 3142(b) (pretrial detention) ("The judicial officer shall order the pretrial release of the person in his recognizance . . . unless the judicial officer determines that such release will . . . endanger the safety of any other person or the community."); 18 U.S.C. § 3553(a)(2)(C) (sentencing) ("The court, in determining the particular sentence to be imposed, shall consider—the need for the sentence imposed to protect the public from further crimes of the defendant . . ."). We hope that state courts and legislatures will carefully consider the application of similar principles. The bail reform, although loosely structured, is a step toward the honest administration of pretrial detention; the sentencing provision, also broadly stated, adds a realistic element to the often tortured efforts to legislate and to find just sentences.

REFERENCES

American Law Institute. 1960. *Model Penal Code* (tentative draft no. 10). Philadelphia: American Law Institute.

American Psychiatric Association. 1982. *Statement on the Insanity Defense*. Washington, D.C.: American Psychiatric Association.

Blumstein, Alfred. 1982. "On Racial Disproportionality of United States Prison Populations." *Journal of Law and Criminology* 73:1259–81.

Blumstein, Alfred, and Elizabeth Graddy. 1981/82. "Prevalence and Recidivism in Index Arrests: A Feedback Model." *Law and Society Review* 16:265–90.

"Dangerousness and Criminal Justice: A Collection of Papers." 1982. *British Journal of Criminology* 22:213–3l4.

Ewing, Charles. 1983. " 'Dr. Death' and The Case for an Ethical Ban on Psychiatric and Psychological Predictions of Dangerousness in Capital Sentencing Proceedings." *American Journal of Criminology and Medicine* 8:407–28.

Farrington, David, and Roger Tarling. 1983. *Criminological Prediction*. London: Home Office Research and Planning Unit.

Floud, Jean, and Warren Young. 1981. *Dangerousness and Criminal Justice*. London: Heinemann Educational Books.

Lowrance, William. 1976. *Of Acceptable Risk: Science and the Determination of Safety*. Los Altos, Calif.: William Kaufman.

Minnesota Sentencing Guidelines Commission. 1980. *Report to the Legislature*. Minneapolis: Minnesota Sentencing Guidelines Commission.

Monahan, John. 1978. "The Prediction of Violent Behavior: A Methodological Critique and Prospectus." In *Deterrence and Incapacitation: Estimating the Effects of Criminal Sanctions on Crime Roles*, edited by Alfred Blumstein, Jacqueline Cohen, and Daniel Nagin. Washington, D.C.: National Academy Press.

———. 1981. *The Clinical Prediction of Violent Behavior*. Rockville, Md.: U.S. Department of Health and Human Services.

———. 1982. "The Case for Prediction in the Modified Desert Model of Criminal Sentencing." *International Journal of Law and Psychiatry* 5:103–13.

———. 1984. "The Prediction of Violent Behavior: Toward a Second Generation of Theory and Policy." *American Journal of Psychiatry* 141:10–15.

Monahan, John, and Henry Steadman. 1983a. "Crime and Mental Disorder." In *Crime and Justice: An Annual Review of Research*, vol. 4, edited by Michael Tonry and Norval Morris. Chicago: University of Chicago Press.

———, eds. 1983b. *Mentally Disordered Offenders*. New York: Plenum Press.

Monahan, John, and David Wexler. 1978. "A Definite Maybe: Proof and Probability in Civil Commitment." *Law and Human Behavior* 2:37–42.

Moore, Mark H., Susan Estrich, and Daniel McGillis, with William Spelman. 1983. *Dealing with Dangerous Offenders*. Cambridge, Mass.: Harvard University, Kennedy Institute of Government.

Morse, Stephen. 1978. "Crazy Behavior, Morals and Science: An Analysis of the Mental Health Law." *Southern California Law Review* 51:527–654.

Pennsylvania Commission on Sentencing. 1982. *Report to the Legislature*. Harrisburg: Pennsylvania Commission on Sentencing.

Petersilia, Joan. 1983. *Racial Disparities in the Criminal Justice System*. Santa Monica, Calif.: Rand Corporation.

"Predicting Dangerousness." 1983. *Journal of Criminal Justice Ethics*. Symposium Issue (Winter/Spring), pp. 3–17.

Swedish National Council for Crime Prevention. 1978. *A New Penal System*. Stockholm: Swedish National Council for Crime Prevention.

Von Hirsch, Andrew. 1972. "Prediction of Criminal Conduct and Preventative Confinement of Convicted Persons." *Buffalo Law Review* 21:717–58.

———. 1976. *Doing Justice: The Choice of Punishment*. New York: Hill & Wang.

Von Hirsch, Andrew, and Don Gottfredson. 1983. "Selective Incapacitation: Some Queries about Research Designs and Equity." *New York University Review of Law and Social Change*, vol. 12.

Walker, Nigel. 1982. "Unscientific, Unwise, Unprofitable or Unjust?" *British Journal of Criminology* 22:276–84.

Washington Sentencing Guidelines Commission. 1983. *Report to the Legislature*. Olympia: Washington Sentencing Guidelines Commission.

Wilson, James Q. 1983. *Crime and Public Policy*. San Francisco: Institute for Contemporary Studies Press.

Ken Pease

Community Service Orders

ABSTRACT

Community service orders are penal sanctions in which convicted offenders are placed in unpaid positions with nonprofit or governmental agencies. Proponents typically urge the use of community service as an alternative to imprisonment. Community service programs have been established in many countries. The most extensive and most studied experience is British. Following a 1970 recommendation of the Advisory Council on the Penal System, enabling legislation was passed in 1972 and pilot programs were initiated in 1973 in six probation districts. By the late seventies, community service programs were in place throughout the United Kingdom. In 1982, more than 30,000 orders were imposed on 8 percent of offenders sentenced for serious crimes. A major Home Office evaluation of the British system used four different methods to calculate the extent to which those sentenced to community service would otherwise have been imprisoned. By every method, it appeared that no more than half would have been imprisoned. Research in Great Britain and in several other countries confirms this finding. For community service to be justified as an alternative to incarceration but used as a supplement to nonincarcerative sentences is hypocritical. Offenders who would not have been imprisoned in the absence of orders may find themselves later imprisoned for violation of an order. Among the major problems of implementation are disparities in the extent of imposition of orders, in the length of orders, and in the use of sanctions against offenders who do not comply with orders. There have been few efforts to assess the impact of the use of orders on recidivism, and the results are inconclusive.

The definition of a community service program to be used is taken from Harris (1980): "A community service program is a program through which convicted offenders are placed in unpaid positions with nonprofit or tax-supported agencies to serve a specified number of hours

Ken Pease is Lecturer in Social Administration, University of Manchester.

performing work or service within a given time limit as a sentencing option or condition" (p. 6). Community service orders are thus distinct from restitution programs, which involve direct compensation to victims. Community service programs are more generally applicable than restitution programs, since they may be employed even when the victim is indemnified against loss, where no victim can be identified, and where an identified victim will not cooperate. Programs such as Earn-It (Klein 1981) that direct offenders to perform work whose proceeds are then used to compensate the victim are outside the scope of this review, since work in such schemes is simply a means to compensate victims rather than the (unpaid) substance of the sentence. The restriction of the scope of the review to convicted offenders excludes pretrial diversion, which may involve the performance of work.

In this essay, because of my own location and experience, British studies will be cited most often. Studies from other parts of the world, notably from North America and Australia, will be included where known and as appropriate. The essay is divided into five sections, beginning with a brief description of the schemes as they operate in the United Kingdom, largely to provide a framework and vocabulary for what follows.

In Section II a brief history of community service and its precursors is provided. Community service echoes some features of impressment and transportation. More recently, work has formed the substance of penal sanctions in many parts of the world. Work is a major currency of social exchange in capitalist society. The notion of work as a negative wage on crime is thus an attractive one. The recent burgeoning of community service sentencing stems from dissatisfaction with the cost, conditions, and effects of prisons. It also derives, in the United Kingdom at least, from the finding that the introduction of state welfare did not reduce the crime rate. Despite elements in common, community service sentencing must not be confused with schemes of reparation, restitution, or victim compensation. Community service can be regarded as a purely retributive sentence, restoring the balance of advantage between offender and sociey.

Section III reviews the evidence that community service, while notionally an alternative to custody, is not reliably used in this way. This is so however strong the wording of the legislation to achieve custody replacement. The practical effect of this mismatch between purpose and reality is undesirable. Offenders consent to community service orders to avoid prison sentences of which they are not in danger. Mismatch between the views of probation officers (writing reports on suitability for community service) and those of courts making orders can lead to offenders' being imprisoned even where the court did not originally intend this. If an offender fails to keep to the conditions of an order, his order will be revoked and another sentence will be substituted. Mismatch between the views of a court making an order and a court revoking an order can lead to a sentence that is at odds with the gravity of the original offense. The lesson of community service is consistent with that from other noncustodial sentences introduced to replace prison: it is that any achievement of the purpose has a high cost in confusion, inconsistency, and therefore unfairness. I will argue that community service owes its popularity to the inefficiencies of fining. A more precise relationship between means and fines would restrict or remove the appropriate use of the community service order. Evidence is reviewed suggesting that employment status rather than offense characteristics is critical in determining length of an order.

Section IV reviews issues of implementation. These have been markedly underresearched, which has meant that issues such as choice of order length have not been closely studied, although there is a suggestion that employment status, rather than offense characteristics and offender age and criminal history, influences order length. Community service (the fine on time) has never been properly considered alongside the fine. There is a case for saying that a system of fines that efficiently links penalty to wealth would reduce the proper scope of community service orders, and that research on wealth as a determinant of sentence choice should have high priority.

Such research as has been done suggests extensive disparities in all aspects of community service implementation. This has many implications. It means, for example, that revocation rates cannot be validly used as indices of success. It also means that the most successful work placements cannot be identified.

Section IV also addresses the social policy implications of work choice. Despite bland pronouncements that community service orders should not reduce normal avenues of employment, the availability of a pool of unpaid labor will inevitably change the budgeting of work-providing agencies, and in consequence the availability of paid work for those agencies.

Section V reviews studies of the success of community service orders. Attitudes to the sentence held by those given it are generally favorable, but this does not generalize to other aspects of the criminal justice system. British studies show no apparent effect of the sentence on levels of recidivism. A key Tasmanian study appears to show a lower rate of reconviction among those given community service who escaped a custodial sentence, and a higher rate among those who did not. Given the diverse and often unfocused operation of community service sentencing, the lack of dramatic evidence of the sentence's effect on recidivism should not be a cause for despair. Rather it should encourage the clear articulation of selection, work allocation, and revocation procedures so that indicators of the best practice emerge. This is necessary for the evaluation of the scheme's success or failure in terms of reconviction statistics.

I. The British Experience

Because the British experience of community service orders is referred to frequently, a brief account of its development will provide a background and vocabulary for what follows.

The community service order in England and Wales began life as a recommendation in the 1970 report "Non-custodial and Semi-custodial Penalties." This was the work of a subcommittee of the Advisory Council on the Penal System, chaired by Baroness Wootton of Abinger. The report is generally known as the Wootton Report. The recommendation of the community service order was followed by a feasibility study, and a modified form of the recommendation was enacted in the Criminal Justice Act 1972.[1] Some of its central features now are:

1. An offender given a community service order must be age sixteen or over.
2. He or she must have been convicted of an offense punishable by imprisonment.
3. Before imposing a community service order, the court must have considered a social inquiry report prepared by a probation officer or social worker, and be satisfied that the offender is suitable and that suitable work is available.
4. The extent of work obligation must be between forty and 240 hours, to be fulfilled within one year, during leisure time. There are no obligations other than work. The offender is not on probation.
5. If an offender does not attend for work, or does not work as in-

[1] The relevant statute in England and Wales is now the Powers of Criminal Courts Act 1973. In Northern Ireland it is the Treatment of Offenders (Northern Ireland) Order 1976. In Scotland it is the Community Service by Offenders (Scotland) Act 1978. The Scottish statute, unlike the others named, allows community service as a condition of a probation order.

structed, he is in breach of his order and can be returned to court, where he can be fined up to fifty pounds with the order to continue, or can have the order revoked. An order may also be revoked "in the interests of justice." This occurs when an offender becomes chronically ill or receives a prison sentence for another offense that makes him unavailable for community service work. Revocation revives the court's powers to deal with the original offense.

Six probation areas were chosen to pioneer community service orders. These "experimental" areas began operation during the early months of 1973. They were the subject of research by the Home Office, published in two reports (Pease et al. 1975, 1977) dealing with aspects of the process of the order (e.g., factors influencing recommendation for an order, choice of work, and attitudes to community service orders) and with the outcome of orders (revocation and reconviction rates). Techniques used included interviews with the participants in the process, analysis of social inquiry reports, press reports and criminal record information, decision-making exercises with probation officers, and participant observation on work sites. I even correlated rainfall with attendance at work.

From April 1975 the order was made available to courts in more and more areas until complete coverage of the United Kingdom was achieved less than six years later.

The number of community service orders imposed in England and Wales in 1982 was 30,830, which constitutes 8 percent of offenders sentenced for more serious crimes. The proportions given community service by courts in Scotland and Northern Ireland, where the scheme started later than in England and Wales, are tending toward the English level of usage. Within England and Wales, there are huge local variations. For example, judges in southeastern England used community service orders about one-third as often as judges in the northeast (Shaw 1983).

In the making and conduct of an order, the typical sequence of events is as follows: A probation officer writes a social inquiry report, a court (judge or magistrate) makes an order on the offender, who then has to report to a community service organizer (who is in almost all cases a trained probation officer). The organizer finds a suitable placement in an agency (typically a voluntary organization or local tax-supported enterprise), where the offender will have his work overseen by a supervisor, who may be a volunteer, an employee of the agency, or a probation service employee. The terms used here will be used in the same sense throughout the paper.

II. Background

The notion that effort expiates evil permeates education, religious practice, and penal history. Assuming the status of slave on falling foul of the law provides an early example. In 1547 the slavery statute (1 Edw. 6, ch. 3) provided that able-bodied vagrants who would not work could be enslaved to their former masters for a period of two years. If no master could be found, they could be enslaved by the borough and employed on road building and other public works. The statute's rationale was, in effect, that the Devil made work for idle hands to do. Draconian legislation of the sixteenth century against the vagabond and criminal did not end there, nor was it restricted to Great Britain. Bridewell Palace in London became a receptacle for the vagrant and petty criminal, and served as a prototype for the "houses of correction" that were set up throughout the country. The aims of the Bridewell and its successors were "to reform the inmates by means of compulsory labour and discipline; to discourage vagrancy and idleness outside its walls; and last but not least to ensure its own self-sufficiency by means of labour" (Melossi and Pavarini 1981, p. 14). The first Dutch workhouse was converted to its use (from its previous function as a convent) in 1596.

One penal strategy with particularly close links with community service orders as now conceived was impressment. As Radzinowicz (1956, p. 99) noted, "The primary object of impressment was to supply the forces necessary to safeguard British interests abroad and to defeat her foreign enemies. It had an important secondary function, however, as a weapon against those thought to threaten security at home. The internal enemy could thus be diverted to the defeat of the external, a striking example of penal economy." A Commission of 1602 was appointed by Queen Elizabeth to arrange that "except when convicted of wilful murder, rape and burglary" an offender might be reprieved from execution and impressed to the navy "wherein, as in all things, our desire is that justice may be tempered with clemency and mercy . . . our good and quiet subjects protected and preserved, the wicked and evil-disposed restrained and terrified and the offenders to be in such sort corrected and punished that even in their punishment they may yield some profitable service to the Commonwealth" (quoted in Ives 1914, p. 9). These sentiments anticipate the rationale put forward by the British Advisory Council on the Penal System nearly four centuries later, and aptly described by Thorvaldson (1982) as a smorgasbord of penal purpose. Community service, the council opined, "should appeal to adherents of different varieties of penal philosophy. To some it would simply be a more constructive and cheaper alternative to short sentences of imprisonment; by others it would be seen as introducing into the penal system a new dimension with an emphasis on reparation to the community; others again would regard it as a means of giving effect to the old adage that the punishment should fit the crime" (Advisory Council on the Penal System 1970, p. 13).

Many of the controversies that surround community service also surrounded impressment. For example, the reality of an offender's "consent" to community service when prison is the alternative has links with the fate of English debtors after 1696, whose discharge from prison was forbidden unless they enlisted in the army or navy (Insolvent Debtors Relief Act 1696, 7 and 8 Will. 3, ch. 12). Likewise, the question whether work groups composed solely of offenders on community service are a good idea echoes Radzinowicz's account of doubts expressed in 1812 about the wisdom of having whole regiments composed of convicts, and the indignation of a general who "did not want jail birds to lower the tone of the regular regiments" (1956, p. 99).

Transportation is another ancestor of community service. As Chappell (1982, p. 132) notes, "Community service by offenders in Australia began in 1788 when a British fleet arrived at Botany Bay in New South Wales and deported . . . 548 male convicts and 188 females. . . . Not only were the British able to clear their jails of troublesome, depraved and corrupt persons, including quite a number of political radicals, but the colonies 15,000 miles away were provided with a large pool of free labour."

As impressment and transportation fell into desuetude, public works came to be considered substitutes for short terms of imprisonment (see, e.g., Ruggles-Brise 1901). In fact there has been no modern period during which some form of work was not used as the substance of penal sanction. Partial reviews of the literature on this topic are available in Pease (1980a), Harland (1981), and Thorvaldson (1983).

The particular emphasis the twentieth century has brought to community service as a penal sanction has been its imposition as a noncustodial sentence rather than as a circumstance of custody or exile. The use of community service as a complete sentence is now widespread, and is to be found in such diverse places as Australia (Rook 1978a,

1978*b*; Leivesley 1983); Sri Lanka (Delgoda 1980); the United States (Harris 1980); Canada (Thorvaldson 1977; Polonoski 1981); Greece, Yugoslavia, and the Federal Republic of Germany (Lopez-Rey 1973); Poland (Drzewicki 1969); and the United Kingdom (Pease et al. 1975; Young 1978, 1979; Thomas 1979).

Melossi and Pavarini (1981), writing from a Marxist perspective, argue that in capitalist society human labor measured in units of time provides the conventional coin of exchange for goods. The wage worker exchanges quanta of his time for quanta of purchasing power. Thus the worker-employer contract in capitalism is a model for social relationships that can be applied to the punished/punisher relationship. Melossi and Pavarini quote Pashakunis's (1978) view that retribution is underpinned by an understanding of social wealth in terms of human labor measured in time. Punishment as a negative wage measured in hours worked, whose payment settles the wrongdoer's account (Kneale 1967), is the community service order.

Work as a currency of exchange is well understood. Performing work to obtain a wage or to eliminate an obligation relates ordinary social life with penal experience in a way that deprivation of liberty or conditional release does not. Studies of offender attitudes toward community service have consistently found an acceptance of the appropriateness of work as a punishment (Pease et al. 1975; Flegg 1976; Whittington 1977; Parker 1980; Polonoski 1980; Varah 1981; Novack, Galaway, and Hudson 1980).

The intuitive appeal of community service to those who engage in it is not evidence that the sentence rests on a firm theoretical footing. The "smorgasbord of penal purpose" is most likely when a sentence has intuitive appeal. Community service may be legislated on a frailer theoretical basis than, for example, branding, simply because its intuitive appeal floats it effortlessly onto the statute book.

There is rough consensus on the factors underlying the rapid adoption of community service schemes. Young (1979) argues that in the United Kingdom prison is perceived to be intrinsically harmful to the individual and of dubious deterrent value. There is concern about prison overcrowding and the cost of building new prisons. Increases of recorded crime and of prison receptions have cast doubt on the efficacy of existing noncustodial sentences and fostered interest in new, relatively severe, noncustodial options. Concerns to reconcile victims and offenders have also developed. Community service orders, as enacted, were the result of a confluence of these factors. Rook (1978*a*) identifies the roots of the Tasmanian work order scheme in a shortage of funds and overcrowding of prisons, allied to a recognition of the merits of the concept of community work developed in New Zealand for the adult periodic detention scheme. Harris (1980) writing from the United States, includes the ineffectiveness of prisons, institutional overcrowding, and a lack of imagination in noncustodial alternatives as the background to the introduction of community service schemes.

It thus appears that both the intuitive appeal of unpaid work by offenders and the urgent need for alternatives to custody hastened the development of community service by offenders. Baroness Wootton, who chaired the committee recommending the introduction of community service orders in England and Wales, seems aware of the confused penal thinking underlying community service. Of the smorgasbord of penal purpose mentioned earlier, she writes: "We did include a paragraph in the report of which I have always been slightly ashamed, as an undisguised attempt to curry favour with everybody" (1978, p. 128).

The consequences of confused thinking become evident when community service ceases to be words on paper and starts being work in a community. The choice of type of work, level of supervision, and contact with beneficiaries of service may be determined by the justifying aim of the sentence. If rehabilitative, organizers will seek to maximize contact between offender and nonoffender volunteers; if reparative, they may well seek to find work for crime victims. If rehabilitative, an organizer may be guided in the decision to revoke an order by the circumstances of the individual offender. Because the probation officer, the sentencer, the revoking court, and community service organizers may hold different views about the justifying aim, there are many possible confusions. Thorvaldson (1978) argues for the primacy of a reparative purpose, paying particular attention to the links between aspects of reparation and retributive and denunciatory sentencing purposes. My view is that reparation should strictly be confined to dealing with victims, and that community service should not be regarded as reparative in purpose. Community service orders benefit the victims no more than any penal alternative and less than some (notably compensation orders). It is misleading to smuggle the notion of reparation into community service by conflating the real victim of crime with the symbolic victim of crime in the abstraction of society as a whole. Yet this confusion is common, as is illustrated by the definition of restitution at the Second U.S. National Symposium on Restitution 1977 (see Galaway and Hudson 1978, p. 1) as "a sanction imposed by an official of the criminal justice system requiring the offender to make a payment of money or service to either the direct or substitute crime victim." Community service orders are neither restitution nor victim compensation. It can be argued that they are retributive. Short (1983, p. 562) defines retribution thus: "A retributive position holds that justice requires that criminals receive the punishment they deserve and that punishment is deserved because the person who violates rules has gained unfair advantage over those who abide by them. The function of punishment therefore is to restore the balance of effort and advantage that is entailed in citizenship." Such a definition allows the community service order to be regarded, together with the fine, as the most perfectly retributive sentence imaginable. Unlike other penalties, the community service order and the fine speak to the notion of contract between individual and society that requires redress for harm. Whereas sentences such as imprisonment exact spectacularly more in social costs than they yield in benefits, the "balance of effort and advantage" in community service seems at least to move in the direction of restoration. Conceived thus, the touchstone of success of the community service order would be the recognition by all concerned of the usefulness of the work being done and feelings of reconciliation resulting from the work.

III. Community Service as an Alternative to Custody

In this section, it is argued that community service orders have shared the fate of other sentences introduced explicitly as alternatives to custody. They have been used in many, perhaps most cases, to replace other noncustodial sentences. This is so even where a statute makes the intended use in principle obligatory. In consequence of this mismatch between rhetoric and reality, offenders may consent to an order fearing that they will otherwise receive a custodial sentence of which they do not stand in danger. Confusions between a probation officer recommending an order, a court making an order, and a court revoking an order are inevitable. Procedures are recommended to ensure that all participants in the process know to what each order is an alternative. Experience suggests that the consistent use of any noncustodial sentence as an alternative to custody is not an achievable aim, whereas clarity of its use may be.

In England and Wales and in Tasmania extensive community service schemes were introduced in the early 1970s; in both places the impetus was concern about the size of the prison population. In the Tasmanian

Probation of Offenders Act of 1971 the intended substitution of "work orders" for imprisonment was clear. Section 7 reads, "Instead of sentencing a person to undergo a term of imprisonment, the Supreme Court and courts of summary jurisdiction may, with the person's consent, adjudge that he for his offence attend at such places and times as shall be notified to him in writing by a probation officer or a supervisor, on so many Saturdays, not exceeding 25, as the court may order." In England and Wales, the Powers of Criminal Courts Act of 1973 specified only that the offense for which an order (of between forty and 240 hours) should be imposed, must be imprisonable.[2] However politicians in the debate leading to the Act delivered themselves of remarks such as, "I was attracted from the start by the idea that people who had committed a minor offence would be better occupied doing a service to their fellow citizens than sitting alongside others in a crowded gaol," and "the alternative would be to go to gaol" (see Pease 1980b, p. 29). The Home Office (1974) circular of guidance to the courts suggested that the use of the order instead of another noncustodial sentence would be only occasional. In the early days of the scheme almost all press coverage stressed that community service was an alternative to imprisonment (see Pease et al. 1975). Even the maximum number of hours to be worked was doubled from the 120 hours originally proposed to 240 hours to allow its more plausible use in place of custody. Even the number may be significant in being divisible by twelve. Noncustodial sentencing, notably to fines, tends to be decimal, and custodial sentencing duodecimal. To offer a noncustodial sentence in numbers that invite comparison with numbers used in custodial sentencing may itself be a subtle message that community service is meant to be an alternative to custody.

The major thrust of the introduction of community service in England encouraged its use as an alternative to custody. The Home Office has been consistent in its advocacy of this position. Most recently, a Home Office study of recidivism on community service (Home Office 1983c) describes community service as "intended to be an alternative disposal for offenders who might otherwise have received a custodial sentence" (p. 4).

There were, even in 1972, clear signs that the hope of its use in this

---

[2] Among the many ways of classifying offenses by gravity (indictable vs. nonindictable, felony vs. misdemeanor) the distinction used here is the simple one of whether an offense could be punished by imprisonment. Many imprisonable offenses are seldom punished by imprisonment.

way in a clear majority of cases was likely to be vain. Suspended sentences of imprisonment had been introduced in England and Wales in 1967. These, in law, were sentences of imprisonment. In principle, a suspended sentence should only be imposed when, by having eliminated all other alternatives, the court decides that the case is one for imprisonment, the final question being, given that imprisonment is unavoidable, Is immediate imprisonment necessary or can the sentence be suspended? The sense is clear, although the psychology implied is tortured.

Since the suspended sentence, like the community service order, was intended to replace active custody, the experience with suspended sentences should be instructive to those concerned with the extent to which community service orders would be used as intended. Researchers (see Bottoms 1981) have consistently found that suspended sentences were imposed mainly where a custodial sentence was unlikely. The implication must be that if the suspended sentence has been used instead of noncustodial sentences in many cases, then a fortiori so would the community service order. Sparks (1971) estimated from distributions of sentences passed that 40–55 percent of those given suspended sentences in 1968–69 had escaped custody. Oatham and Simon (1972) showed that "courts have used the suspended sentence both to replace immediate imprisonment and as a sentence in its own right. . . . It has been estimated that of all persons awarded a suspended sentence, only somewhere between 40% and 50% would, but for the new provision, have been sentenced to imprisonment" (p. 233). In Israel, Sebba (1969) found that in district courts suspended sentences were used in lieu of fines in about half of all cases. There is much force in Sparks's warning that "there is a danger that the experience of the suspended sentence will merely be repeated with these measures" (p. 400). The warning was not heeded, and the experience was repeated. It was clear that it would be even before the first order was made. A presentence report from a probation officer was mandatory; it was from these reports that courts were to assess offender suitability and work availability. Probation officers were therefore bound to be critical participants in the process. There were six areas of the country in which community service was introduced in 1973. In three of these areas the official policy of the probation service was that community service should primarily be an alternative to custody. In the remaining three areas this was not the policy. However, only 61 percent of probation officers held opinions on this matter that were consistent with policy handed down from their own chief probation officers (Pease et al. 1975). In areas where community service should have been an alternative to custody, 44 percent of probation officers asserted that community service was indeed primarily an alternative to custody. In the three areas taking a view of community service as a sentence in its own right, 30 percent of probation officers asserted that community service was primarily an alternative to custody. Further, officers in all areas were divided about whether a suspended sentence was to be regarded as custody for diversion purposes, thus introducing yet another opportunity for misunderstanding. The case in which the first community service order was made confirmed all suspicions. The offender was a first-time possessor of cannabis. Cannabis possession by a first offender rarely attracts a custodial sentence, still more so for someone who is described by the press as gentle and inoffensive and whose ambition was expressed as being to die on the banks of the Ganges (Pease 1980*b*).

The Home Office Research Unit set out to gather four types of information relevant to the diversion question (Pease, Billingham, and Earnshaw 1977). The first was the use of probation officers' prediction of sentence. This was a very small-scale exercise including only thirty-nine cases, yielding an estimate of 49 percent diversion from custody.

Second was an analysis of sentences passed on those who had been recommended for community service by probation officers, but who did not receive such an order. These offenders were at least arguable cases for community service. For a probation officer to recommend a community service order outside the plausible range would be to invite the court's ridicule. From among the population of possibles, a number (1,194) did not get orders. Fifty-three percent got noncustodial sentences and 47 percent custodial sentences. These proportions were assumed to correspond with what would have been the fate of those actually given orders in the absence of the order. On this reasoning, 47 percent of those given orders escaped custody. Local reports since that time have produced, with similar data, similar figures with remarkable regularity.

A third estimate of diversion is obtainable from examination of sentences substituted when orders are revoked, with fewer than one-fifth of the ordered hours having been worked, and where no further offense is involved. Of the forty-four cases of this kind, twenty-six had active custody substituted. Since these sentences were unlikely to be less severe than the ones they replaced, an estimate of at most 58 percent diversion is reached.

TABLE 1

Magistrate and Probation Officer Responses to the Question "Do You Think a Community Service Order Should Be Used Solely as an Alternative to Custody?"

	Magistrates (%)	Probation Officers (%)
Yes	27	22
No	45	50
Probably yes	28	28
Total	100	100
N	164	54

SOURCE.—Whittington (1977).

A fourth estimate yielded a much lower figure, based on the sentence passed on those for whom the sentencer requested a social inquiry report considering community service. As Pease et al. (1977) stressed, each of the estimates taken alone is open to criticism. But the errors to which they are prone are different, and the close correspondence of three of them is impressive. These estimates have been criticized by Young (1978). For example, the estimate based on those breached may be in error because "custodial sentences may well be passed upon those who are in breach of a community service order not because such a sentence would originally have been imposed, but because the offender's failure to take advantage of the order is in itself seen as warranting a custodial sentence" (p. 31). The effect of this criticism, as of Young's other criticisms, would be to reduce the levels of estimated diversion from custody. No criticisms of the Home Office work have been advanced that would serve to increase levels of estimated diversion from custody to community service.

Other British research (e.g., Whittington 1977; Duguid 1982; Smith et al. 1984) suggests the Pease et al. (1977) estimates may be reasonable. Tables 1 and 2 show relevant data from Duguid (1982) and Whittington (1977). The late Norman Whittington in a survey in Northumbria showed that around half of groups of both magistrates and probation officers stated their view that community service should not be used solely as an alternative to custodial sentences. Application of the second method of estimating diversion to local data almost invariably yields similar estimates. This gives greater credibility to the method itself,

TABLE 2
Community Service Orders in Scotland:
Probable Alternative Disposal by Assessor

Probable Alternative	Sheriff (Year 1) (%)	Social Worker (Year 1) (%)	Social Worker (Year 2) (%)
Custody	71	78	58
Fine	20	11	25
Probation	5	10	14
Deferred sentence	5	1	3
Total	100	100	100
N	147	99	105

SOURCE.—Duguid (1982).

since it will work across areas with differing degrees of trust between courts and probation officers. The major criticism of the method could be that it reflects the recommendation policy of probation services.

When community service was introduced into Scotland, both sentencer (sheriff) and social worker (in Scotland probation functions are discharged by social workers) estimated, in cases given community service sentences, the likely alternative disposal. In the first year table 2 shows that estimates of diversion are in excess of 70 percent; in the second year, less than 60 percent (Duguid 1982). Godson (1981) reports that nationally in England and Wales fewer than half of those whose orders are revoked for noncompliance were given custodial sentences, but he notes that in his local area (Hampshire) 83 percent of offenders received custodial sentences when community service orders were revoked for noncompliance with fewer than 20 percent of hours worked. It is unclear whether Godson included suspended sentences in his definition of custody.

In Britain, the approach to sentencing that emphasizes the gravity of the offense is termed the tariff approach. The term neatly incorporates the notion that the sentence is a payment for the crime. The tariff approach is contrasted with the individualized approach, which bases sentence on offender "needs." Custody is not a response to offenders' needs. It follows that alternatives to custody should likewise not be individualized sentences but tariff sentences. The seriousness of offenses committed should be similar for short custody and alternatives to custody. In his major study of the tariff position of community service orders, Young (1979, p. 135) concluded from an analysis of age, current offense, criminal record, and opinions expressed in courts in six English probation areas: "In each court the sentence was imposed upon offenders who had committed crimes of widely differing degrees of seriousness. While some were similar to those sentenced to imprisonment, others were at a stage where such a sentence would have been highly unlikely. . . . its initial purpose of effecting a substantial reduction in the prison population was blurred."[3] Willis (1977) reached a similar conclusion on the basis of a more limited but nationwide examination of statistics of the use of community service orders. More indirect, but highly relevant, are the observations of Roberts and Roberts (1982) on the relationship between probation service activity and the use of custody. In Great Britain, many offenders are given prison sentences without having been the subject of a social inquiry report written by a probation officer. The writing of such reports has widely been seen to be a way of reducing the use of custody. The probation officer, so the reasoning goes, makes recommendations of noncustodial sentences. These are accepted and custody is avoided. Writing more reports should therefore be linked with a reduced use of custody, particularly so because priority is supposed to be given in report writing to offenders at risk of custody. Roberts and Roberts tested the view that the more reports written by a probation service, the fewer the people imprisoned by the courts served. They found that the more reports, the more probation and community service. They found no relationship between the number of reports and the use of custody. This makes it difficult to believe that community service orders (made almost exclusively after a recommendation in a probation officer's report) substantially change the level of use of custody.

One final U.K. study demonstrates the confusion dramatically. Taking a sample of 153 reports in which community service was recommended, Andrews (1982) found that the probation officers writing them judged that in eighty-one cases (53 percent) custody was deemed "very unlikely" or "possible," rather than "probable." Despite this, the reasons they gave for 95 percent of all these recommendations was that the sentence was an alternative to custody. Thus, in around 40 percent

---

[3] Any hope that community service orders would substantially reduce the prison population was always arithmetically naive, given the brevity of the prison sentences that would be replaced and the high rate of reconviction among those it was intended to divert.

of all the cases in which community service was recommended, it was recommended as an alternative to custody even though it was not actually seen as such.

The limited extent to which community service replaces custody in England and Wales is not likely to be increased by the Court of Appeal judgment in the case of *R. v. Gillam* (1980), 2 Crim. App. Repts. (S) 267. This held that when in a case otherwise pointing to the imposition of an immediate prison sentence a judge decides against that course and requests the production of a report with a view to community service, the defendant should have a community service order imposed if the Probation Service agrees on the grounds that a feeling of injustice is otherwise aroused. Thus, in effect, a judge must decide against custody before putting in train the consideration of community service. This is bound to reduce those cases where consideration for community service really is a long-shot attempt to divert from custody.

Estimates of diversion from custody are also available from the Tasmanian scheme, and educated guesses from the United States and Canada. In Tasmania (Mackay and Rook 1976; Rook 1978*a*, 1978*b*), Rook's method of estimating diversion from custody was to extrapolate prison receptions before work orders were introduced and to compare the projection with the actual number of receptions to prison after work orders were introduced, and with the number of receptions to prison added to the number of work orders. If work orders are used only instead of prison the number of prison receptions plus the number of work orders should equal the projected prison receptions. If work orders are used only instead of nonprison sentences the projection of prison receptions should equal the actual number of prison receptions. The Tasmanian statute is a strong one in the sense that it sets out to restrict work orders to cases where imprisonment would otherwise have been imposed. As will be seen in figure 1 the real position is intermediate between the two described. Because regression lines based on so few points are liable to substantial error it is prudent to limit interpretation to the first years of the work order scheme. In 1971-72 the diversion estimate was 47 percent. In 1972-73 it was 53 percent. The Victoria Department of Correctional Welfare Services (1983) reviewing the first year of community service orders in that state reports (p. 11): "Estimates by programme staff suggest that approximately half of offenders placed on CSOs would otherwise have been imprisoned. This estimate is based on comments made by the Magistrates in Court, comparison of offenders' prior convictions and the perceptions of of-

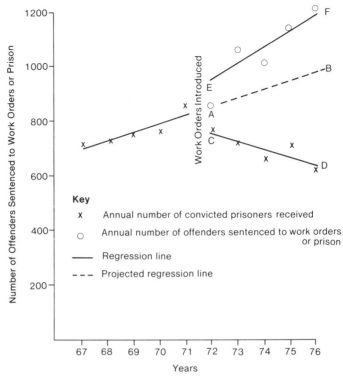

FIG. 1.—Regression lines for the number of convicted prisoners received before and after the introduction of the Tasmanian Work Order Scheme (from Rook 1978*a*). Also shown is the regression line for the number of offenders sentenced to work orders or prison. Offenders between lines *AB* and *CD* would be expected to receive a prison sentence had work orders not been available. Offenders between lines *AB* and *FE* would not be expected to receive a prison sentence had the work order scheme not been available.

fenders placed on CSOs." The Victoria Department of Correctional Services (1982) *Community Service Order Scheme Manual* estimates diversion from custody at 50 percent in New South Wales, but does not provide a reference.

The single Canadian observation on diversion from custody (Polonoski 1981) of which I am aware comes from Ontario's scheme. The basis for the observations seems to be the reasonably anticipated sentence for people of particular levels of criminality. We read: "Initially, CSOs were intended to provide an alternative sentence to the incarceration of offenders. Because of the low-risk nature of this CSO client population, however, it is unlikely that the CSO option is con-stituting an alternative to incarceration too extensively. These proba-tioners probably would not have otherwise been sentenced to a term of incarceration" (p. i).

Harris's (1980) review of community service programs in the United States yields no information about the extent to which programs de-signed to operate as alternatives to custody achieve this purpose. How-ever, as Harland (1981) points out, referring to the Harris review, "The tendency of community service programs to deal predominantly or exclusively with offenders who are extremely unlikely to be incar-cerated is reinforced by examination of a large majority of the programs that have been evaluated. Where formal eligibility criteria exist for admission to the program, they most commonly relate to those con-victed of minor property offenses or others for whom some form of community-based disposition might be expected" (p. 444). Despite this, the chairman of the Bar Association Support to Improve Correc-tional Services (Basics) program, writing the preface for Harris (1980), states: "My own positive attitude about community service sentencing may have best been summarized by the British observer who . . . said '. . . community service has yet to prove that . . . it is more effective . . . but as an alternative to custody it is at least more humane as well as cheaper'" (p. vi). Such a presumption surely requires the reporting of more empirical evidence on this point than has so far been presented. We must rest content with Harland's (1982) informed guess that "com-munity service . . . fits in the tariff, in the minds of American criminal justice practitioners . . . right smack dab in the middle between incar-ceration and probation" (p. 157).

There is thus remarkable consensus, wherever the proposition has been put to the test, that community service orders do not replace custody in a clear majority of cases in which they are imposed, even where it is clearly stated that the order was introduced for such a purpose. The precise estimates of diversion vary, both locally and nationally, but the figure 45–55 percent recurs with some regularity in England and Australia, with a variety of measurements being used. Does it matter that community service straddles the custody-noncustody divide? There are those (Winfield 1977; Godson 1981; Shaw 1983) who feel no unease. Certainly the precision of the diversion estimate is irrelevant, except insofar as it gives the lie to the rhetoric. The practical issues would be the same were 90 percent or 10 percent of those given orders diverted from custody. The real issue is nicely captured in an exchange between Donald Sinclair and Alan Harland in the British Columbia symposium on redress:

Sinclair: Just a point of clarification, Professor Harland, you made it clear to us that you object to the way that CSOs are used in the U.S., as an add-on to probation.

Harland: I'm sorry you misunderstood me, I don't object to it being used in that way, what I object to is intellectual dishonesty which is pervasive in the system in which judges and program administrators say they are not using it in this way, they are only using it as an alternative to incarceration when all the reports suggest otherwise. [P. 161]

I would prefer to think of the problem as self-deception rather than dishonesty. Whatever it is called, it has substantial practical implications. I have seen probation officers suggest strongly to offenders when soliciting their agreement to an order that custody was the likely alternative. Such suggestions are understandable, because the two types of error an officer can make differ in their consequences. Failing to obtain consent to community service when custody eventuates is a worse outcome than obtaining agreement when custody would not eventuate. It is significant that wherever offenders on community service are asked what sentence they would have received if community service had not been available, they estimate custody more often than is realistic (Flegg 1976; Whittington 1977; Parker 1980; Polonoski 1980). The reason for this is plausibly stated by the National Association of Probation Officers (1977), in the report of a working group on community service: "This disparity may have its roots in the drama of the court proceedings for the accused who may not be in the best position to appreciate the real probabilities of the different sentencing options, particularly when even mild sentences can often be combined with stern remarks and threats from the bench" (p. 17).

Now, there can be any combination of views among the various people involved about the position of community service relative to custody. A probation officer can, for example, recommend a community service order believing it to be an alternative to custody. The court can accept or reject that recommendation believing it not to be an alternative to custody, and the offender's perception could be either. If the offender has his order revoked, the revoking court can have a view of community service relative to custody different from that of the sentencing court or the probation officer who first recommended it. Particularly poignant misunderstandings can arise when the probation officer, believing the sentence not to be primarily an alternative to custody, does not recommend community service and the court thereupon locks up the offender, believing that the probation officer would have recommended community service if he had thought that it was an appropriate alternative to custody in the case. In other cases, the revoking court locks up someone who has failed on his community service order, although the court making the order did not think the original offense merited prison. There is some judicial pressure to keep the situation confused. For example, the Appeal Court criticized a probation officer for what it saw as an unrealistic recommendation in a case where the seriousness of the offense made custody inevitable (R. v. Blowers [1977] Crim. L. Repts. 51). If probation officers have to restrict their community service recommendations to cases where custody is otherwise uncertain, the kinds of confusion described are inevitable.

I believe that the person sentenced to community service should know to what his order is an alternative, and that this should be a matter of public record. Some unpublished local initiatives have been undertaken in this direction, for example the recording of sentencers' comments. Such initiatives prevent only some of the possible confusions.

In England a possible general solution would be agreement on a two-tier system, in which it is understood that orders in excess of 100 hours are alternatives to custody and shorter ones are not (see Pease 1978*a*; Pease 1978*b*; Trewartha 1978; Willis 1978). In this way, when invited to consent to an order of a particular length, the offender would grant or withhold his consent knowing what the alternative was. If he withheld his consent to a short order and the court then locked him up, this would be dealt with on appeal. He could also appeal against order length that seemed excessive. One of the more encouraging features of current practice is the increasing number of appeals now being entered against community service sentences. In 1982 there were sixty-eight (Home Office 1983*a*). These could apply some pressure for clarification of the tariff position of community service orders.

The two-tier proposal has been the subject of criticism, but Lord Justice Lane sitting in the Court of Appeal (R. v. Lawrence [1982] Crim. L. Repts. 377) held a community service order of 190 hours to be equivalent to a prison sentence of twelve months. This does not of course address the general point of being able to infer sentencing purpose from order length, but at least it maps one equivalence point and does suggest that it may be realistic to think of long community service orders as being equivalent to prison sentences of some length. Lord Justice Lane's decision may owe something to a recognition that it requires no effort of will to serve a prison sentence, but an effort of will to attend community service work. Lord Justice Lane sees community service as a much more severe sentence than do those (e.g., Thorvaldson 1978) who criticize the scaling of the community service order suggested in the two-tier proposal.

The lack of clarity concerning the place of community service in the tariff is regrettable. Apart from its direct consequences, it may indirectly lead to a process of penal inflation. Two instances will be selected to show that this is not fanciful. The first is a decision of the Appeal Court (R. v. Howard and Wade [1977] Crim. L. Repts. 683) stating, "When a community service order is made, it saves the person in respect of whom it is made from an immediate custodial sentence. It is to that extent an indulgence to him, although it is hoped it is also an advantage to the community if the order is complied with. If the order is not complied with, those who break the terms of the order cannot complain if a custodial sentence is imposed, when they have thrown away the advantage which was offered to them" (p. 683). Insofar as the Court of Appeal acts on such reasoning, it removes any protection from those sentenced on revocation of a community service order. They may well receive a sentence more severe than is merited by the offense. The second instance is taken from the deliberations of the Advisory Council on the Penal System (1977). The council argued for the extension of community service orders to those convicted of an offense not punishable by imprisonment. The council was exercised by the question how to discipline such people if they showed themselves disinclined to attend for work. The sanction of prison would not be available. One option considered, though rejected, was the creation of a new imprisonable offense, willful failure to attend for community service work! These instances have in common the willingness of those with influence to allow the gravity of an offense to be overridden by considerations of noncompliance with the penal process.

As an illustration of the tangled web of purpose attending the more severe noncustodial penalties, one can do no better than to quote without comment the remarks of the Lord Chief Justice Lane, in his attempt to clarify the issues in the case of *R. v. Clarke* [1982] 4 Crim. App. Repts. (S) 197.

> Before imposing a partly suspended sentence, the court should ask itself the following question: first of all, is this a case where a custodial sentence is really necessary? If it is not, it should pass a non-custodial sentence. But if it is necessary, then the court should ask itself secondly this: Can we make a community service order as an equivalent to imprisonment, or can we suspend the whole sentence? If not, then the point arises: What is the shortest sentence the court can properly impose? In many cases, of which an obvious example is the case of the first offender for whom a short term of imprisonment is a sufficient shock, without any suspension, that would be enough. If imprisonment is necessary, and if a very short sentence is not enough, and if it is not appropriate to suspend the sentence altogether, then partial suspension should be considered. [P. 200]

The best estimate of the extent to which partly suspended sentences replace fully custodial sentences is around one half of cases (Home Office 1983*a*). This is perhaps the most dramatic illustration yet of an increase in the net of social control. In half of those on whom partly suspended sentences are passed, people are now locked up who previously were not. This is direct diversion into custody, in contrast with the indirect diversion to custody that can happen with community service and the fully suspended sentence.

IV. Issues of Implementation

Consideration of community service orders in relation to imprisonment has tended to obscure equally important issues. Some of these issues will be discussed in this section. The general conclusion is that many points of principle have been little considered—among them the determinants of order length and revocation process—and that there is wide variation in all examined aspects of practice.

A. *The Length of Community Service Orders*

Little work has been done on this topic. Harris (1980) and Harland (1982) give instances in the United States of orders of thousands of hours, many times longer than the British maximum. Pease (1982) calculated the median length of order imposed in England and Wales by two tariff-relevant variables, prior record and age (current offense was not available in the statistics obtained) and concluded: "Neither youth nor lack of a criminal record buys a short order. A youth of 17 with no previous convictions has an order (on average) five hours shorter than a 30-year-old with previous custody" (p. 740). Northern Ireland data (Jardine, Moore, and Pease 1983) demonstrated that "type of present offence, number of previous convictions and number of previous custodial sentences were all unrelated to order length imposed, whether considered singly or in combination" (p. 19). The variable included that did predict order length was employment status, with the unemployed being given longer orders than the employed. The conclusions reached by Jardine et al. were that "employment status is a factor in determining the length of community service. . . . more generally, tariff considerations do not seem to govern length of order" (p. 20). King (1982), interviewing magistrates, also perceived a link between order length and unemployment. Jardine et al. (1983) regret the association; Ashworth (1983) argues its fairness on the basis of equality of impact.

To my knowledge, no study has been undertaken of the employment status of an offender and his chances of being given an order. Brown (1977) argues for community service as a fitting penalty for the unemployed. Goldstone (1982) argues against this position.

B. Community Service and Fines

Considerations of employment status lead naturally to thoughts of the relationship between community service and fines. Community service considered as retribution is a fine on time. Given the popularity of community service for fine defaulters (see, e.g., Powers of Criminal Courts Act 1973; Heath 1979), the relationship between fines and fines on time must be seen to be crucial. There is a case for saying that in the ideal world fining would be so precise in relation to income and wealth that default rates would be uniform across social class. That is not the case now, where both the rich and the poor present problems; the rich because of the dismissive ease with which they may pay fines, and the poor because they cannot pay fines. Numerically, the problem is with the poor. It is naturally attractive to the sentencer to use community service for the poor fine defaulter. However, as Harris (1980) perceptively remarks, this would be a reiteration of the Roman system where the citizen was punished in his property and the slave in his body.

An approach to the issue of community service and fines might be through the introduction of a day-fine system, where the court must obtain information about an offender's liabilities and capital. In general, the day-fine is assessed at one-thousandth of annual income. Once this calculation has been completed, the court can order a number of day-fines appropriate to the seriousness of the offense. Thus the two factors, the seriousness of the case and the offender's means, are determined independently. If day-fines were applied, would the community service order be necessary? It may be of significance that Sweden, which has day-fines, rejected community service in the following terms: "The group does not think that there is any need for alternative sanctions over and above those that already exist in the sanction system (fines, conditional sentences, probation and intensive supervision). The purpose of other new forms of imprisonment is unclear" (National Swedish Council for Crime Prevention 1978, p. 64). The only jurisdiction of which I am aware that operates both community service orders and a day-fine system is the Australian state of Victoria, and the community service scheme there is very new. Data emerging from Victoria are likely to be of especial interest.

There is at least a case for saying that community service orders only exist alongside an inefficient fining system. This is not to say that fine systems have nothing to learn from community service. It was earlier argued that community service could properly be regarded as a retributive sentence, because it restores the balance of effort and advantage between offender and society. So do fines. Yet community service work can be seen. Fine income cannot. Who knows what courts do with the income from fines? Thus, even in efficient fining systems, attention should perhaps be given to the perception of appropriateness of penalty to offense that is one of the strengths of community service orders.

C. Personal Suitability for Community Service Orders

In the United Kingdom, at least, empirical evidence about personal characteristics that make for particular suitability for community service is absent. There tend to be, rather, unsuitability lists, suggesting the kinds of offenders on whom an order should not be made. These lists generally refer to serious mental disturbance, strong addiction to alcohol or drugs, lack of settled address, and debilitating personal problems (W. McWilliams 1980). It is interesting to see how the early British exclusionary lists (see Pease et al. 1974; Pease and Earnshaw 1977) have reproduced themselves in lists elsewhere. For an American example, see Smith (1980). For an Australian example, see Victoria

Department of Correctional Welfare Services (1982). This being so, it is important to remind oneself that the lists are based on precautionary prudence, not evidence (except for opiate use, see Donnelly [1980]). Essentially, the lists amount to descriptions of groups on whom it would be difficult to impose the regular discipline of work appointments. Pease et al. (1974) pointed out that although certain factors were associated with likelihood of order completion (e.g., criminal record), no group could be identified that had breached in a majority of cases. More recently, length of order and age have been found to be associated with revocation rates (the young and those with long orders being less likely to complete the assigned work) but in no age or order length category are rates of revocation higher than 15 percent (Home Office 1983*b*). In any event, no conclusions about the failure of community service should be reached because of the wide discretion used in the administration of community service, which will determine rates and patterns of revocation. Neither should particular offenses be seen to confer suitability or unsuitability for community service on the basis of extant levels of use. This is because attitudes about the relative punitiveness of the community service order largely determine the offenses for which it is imposed. The picture it currently seems reasonable to depict is of organizers of community service who will, by and large, take anyone for whom work can be arranged and who is likely to attend. The extent to which pragmatism rules is limited by judicial and probation service idiosyncrasies in referring cases for consideration for community service. As to the probation service, an analysis of community service consideration (Hoggarth 1983) concluded: "In the survey that determined the categories of information thought important by probation personnel in relation to the task of preparing a social enquiry report, the community service organizers placed more emphasis on the practical issues of suitability, rather than on such matters as family history or childhood experience. These issues were more important to the probation officers" (p. 85). Hoggarth's extensive study goes on to suggest the openness of community service consideration by its organizers and the progressive easing of selection criteria as the scheme progressed.

However, the probation officer is the gatekeeper to community service consideration in the British system, and his or her mobilization is necessary. Given the relationship between views of the punitiveness of community service and the likelihood of custody, there is even less cause for complacency after considering Hoggarth's finding that probation officers varied widely in their prediction of sentence in the same case.

D. *The Operation of Community Service*

A review such as this is not the place to consider detailed operational aspects of community service schemes. Documents that can serve as manuals of this kind already exist (see, e.g., Harding 1974; Sussex 1974; Morgan 1977; Beha, Carlson, and Rosenblum 1977; Harland, Warren, and Brown 1979; Cooper et al. 1981; Victoria Department of Correctional Welfare Services 1982; Georgia Department of Offender Rehabilitation 1983). Rather it seems proper to consider aspects of the operation of the scheme central to judgments of its fairness, both internally and in relation to people generally. Two such aspects will be considered: disparity in operation and the relationship of community service work to paid work.

Disparity in Operation.   There is wide disparity in all aspects of community service operation that have been studied, from work selection and allocation of offenders to tasks, to criteria for discipline, including revocation. Variation in the decision to revoke an order is of particular interest. Current arrangements allow oversight of the decision to revoke, but not of the decision not to revoke. This leads to the development of a "hidden caseload" of offenders safe from revocation because of system failures that would be embarrassing if they came to the attention of the court.

Young's (1979) work and statistics from the Hertfordshire Probation and After-Care Service (1979) demonstrate the wide variation between courts and court areas in use of the community service order, showing that areas with the highest usage make around four times as many orders per hundred cases as those with least use. Young was unable to account for even half of this variation in terms of characteristics of offenders sentenced. The variation can be attributed in part to the number of offenders on whom probation officers prepared reports for the court (Roberts and Roberts 1982), area differences in perceived tariff position of the community service order (Ashworth 1983), and, speculatively, the unemployment level in an area. Once on an order, the type of work performed will vary widely, as do the circumstances in which it is performed. Pease et al. (1975) showed the wide variation in percentage of work appointments involving contact with beneficiaries and percentage of offender-only work groups in the experimental areas. During the period January–February 1974 the percentage of work appointments involving contact with beneficiaries varied between 16 percent and 92 percent. The percentage of offenders working in offender-only groups varied between 2 percent and 48 percent. Fletcher (1983) showed continuing variation in this and many other aspects of practice. Mackay and Rook (1976) demonstrated that projects involving individual assistance are characterized by lower levels of absenteeism and that the grant of informal "good time" by administrators also helped in this respect. Read (1980) showed continuing variation in placement type and particularly in area differences in the use of a common initial assignment and in the use of a fallback assignment from which breach proceedings may be initiated without involving a voluntary agency in giving evidence in court.

It appears to be a general finding that offenders fail on community service far more often by not turning up than by turning up and working badly (see, e.g., Pease et al. 1975; Mackay and Rook 1976). In general, probation officers, in the United Kingdom at least, have been reluctant to take offenders back to court when they are in breach of the requirements of a probation order (see Bridges 1976; Lawson 1978). Should there be similar reluctance concerning community service orders? While some organizers take the view that there should, others do not, resulting in the various inequities that are apparent between probation areas. Young (1979) highlights the conflict between the offender's needs and penal requirements when he notes that individualized considerations can lead to lenient treatment, which militates against the exaction of a proper penalty. In the areas he studied this often resulted from a recognition by the community service organizer of an offender's problems—domestic conflict, irregular work habits, depression, and so forth. Vass (1980) also shows a high rate of violations (unacceptable absences) on community service, but only a low rate of consideration for breach. He concludes that prosecutions are taken only as a last resort. This is also suggested by the fact that nearly half of all revocations coincide with convictions for further offenses, indicating perhaps that evidence for revocation was only used when a further conviction made clearing the books worthwhile.

Enforcement begins not with the community service organizers but with the work supervisor. Sympathy and understanding from a supervisor can express themselves in ways that can subvert the intentions of the sentencing court. Research by Shaw (1980) suggests how. Community service organizers and task supervisors were given four possible justifications for the introduction of community service orders. They were

1. the reduction of the prison population,
2. the imposition of a penalty on the offender,
3. increasing reparation to the community, and
4. the provision of help for the client (offender).

Community service organizers and supervisors were asked to rank these four reasons in order of importance. The order of the reasons in the two groups are mirror images. For task supervisors the most important justification of the scheme is the provision of help to the offender. To community service organizers, it is the least important. This being so, it is little wonder that there is a danger of task supervisors' placing the conduct of the work second to the welfare of the offender. There will always and inevitably be a degree of flexibility in the counting of hours, but a rough correspondence between the number of hours ordered and the number of hours worked seems a necessary condition of the proper application of the sanction.

Once a community service organizer becomes aware of problems on site, what happens next? A community service order can end, in England and Wales, in one of three ways: normally, with all the hours having been completed; "in the interests of justice," typically used when an offender is given a long custodial sentence for a further offense that makes it impossible for him to complete the order, or in case of prolonged illness; for failure to attend or to work once in attendance. It is also open to the courts, when someone fails to attend for work or to work adequately, to impose a fine and allow the order to continue. Organizers and courts vary substantially in the use which they make of the disciplinary procedures. Perhaps the most important feature of the process is what one may term the excuse classification process. The process whereby someone is classified as having failed to attend satisfactorily for work depends upon the circumstances of his nonattendance. For example, it would clearly be unreasonable for an offender with a written medical excuse who failed to attend on one occasion to have his order revoked.

Table 3 shows the number of orders made in England and Wales during 1979–82. It also shows the manner of termination of orders during the same period. This was a period of mushroom growth for community service. The proportion being completed successfully re-

TABLE 3

Numbers of Orders Made in England and Wales 1979–82, and
Manner of Termination of Orders

Manner of Termination	1979: 19,900	1980: 25,360	1981: 36,440	1982: 43,300
Hours completed (%)	74	75	74	74
Failure to comply with requirements (%)	14	13	13	12
Conviction of another offense (%)	10	9	10	10
Other (%)	3	3	3	5

SOURCE.—Home Office (1983*b*).
NOTE.—The number of orders is greater than the number of people on whom orders were made. More than one order may be made per person. The manner of termination data are based on terminations during the year, not orders made during the year.

mained remarkably constant. One would have supposed that changes in the kinds of offenders selected and administrative pressures in a period when work growth outstripped staff and resource increases would have affected revocation rates. Their constancy suggests the compensatory use of discretion by community service organizers.

Read (1980) noted that some organizers withdrew the offender to a probation-supervised work group as a prelude to possible breach action, others did not. B. McWilliams (1980) asked community service organizers about their breaching policy. Their answers varied: "Three unacceptable absences within a reasonable period of time will lead to a consideration of breach"; "We work on the principle of picking the worst four every week"; "Aim is to assist a community service worker towards a satisfactory completion of his order. However, when all attempts have failed, after due warning . . . breach action is initiated" (p. 67).

B. McWilliams (1980) asked a number of community service staff about the factors they would take into account in a "revocation imminent" situation. She found that a number of factors were generally associated with greater leniency (such as medical problems, domestic problems, and "system failures" like nonarrangements of placements). Factors predictably associated with less leniency included previous warnings of revocation and "poor attitudes." Most worthy of interest are a group of factors whose importance was acknowledged but whose implications for action are unclear. These factors are that:

1. offender has good employment record,
2. offender is currently employed,
3. some past placements have not been suitable,
4. there is less than one-quarter of the order to complete,
5. offender has poor relationships with co-workers,
6. offender has poor relationship with supervisor,
7. offender has financial problems, and
8. previous orders have been completed satisfactorily.

It is clear from these findings that social factors are taken into account in the decision to return an offender to court and, most interestingly, that these factors sometimes operate in different directions for different organizers. These findings perhaps suggest the need for greater contact and collaboration between community service organizers in different parts of a country and also between community service organizers and the courts. This is also suggested by differences among community service staff in their response to excuses for absence from work.

One of the most telling points (which I owe to conversation with Brenda McWilliams) is a difference in procedure and publicity attendant upon a decision whether or not to revoke an order. It is always the decision to revoke that has to be justified, and never the decision not to revoke. Thus, a community service organizer will only start to discuss revocation when he feels that there is a justifiable case to be proceeded with. It may well be that, much earlier in the process, the point is passed at which other community service organizers would have revoked an order. The process only becomes public when revocation proceedings start. Contrast this with an arrangement under which there had to be periodic inspection of community service records. In those circumstances the decision not to revoke would have to be justified. Whether this scrutiny should be by courts or more rigorously by an inspectorate such as exists for prisons, the police, and probation services, is open to question. The issue is particularly relevant given McWilliams's (1980) finding that what one might call system failures were associated with greater leniency toward the offender. If, for example, the first work appointment had been delayed, the organizer would be less likely to breach the offender. Courts may or may not regard that as appropriate. There is certainly an incentive for community service organizers not to breach those offenders who might report in court on the scheme's inefficiencies.

The foregoing urges the development of clear guidelines for community service revocation which would apply across areas, and McWilliams's research is directed toward at least partial achievement of this. Second, it should open the minds of community service organizers and probation management to the possibility of making more public the decision not to breach.

Community Service Work. From the very beginning of community service, the Wootton Report stressed that community service work should not replace paid work. It is of no little interest then to find that in the very earliest days of the scheme, a Nottingham project was being publicized in the following way: "The council were getting very concerned about the state of a certain building in the park which had fallen into a bad state of repair and had received the full treatment from vandals. It had previously been the tea and refreshment rooms. When the issue came up in council I was there again. The committee decided to spend some money on the place, . . . and it was at this point that I suggested to them—why not spend the money on materials and give the labour side of the job to community service?" (Harding 1974, p. 41). The only possible interpretation is that here, in a highly publicized booklet at the sensitive beginnings of community service, it replaced paid work. The Nottingham scheme is far from being the only published account of the replacement of paid work. For example the 1978 Kent Probation Department's booklet "North Kent Community Service Projects 1978" is one rich source of data among many.

There appears to be a considerable spread of opinion about what work is appropriate for community service. At one extreme lies the sophisticated formulation of the scheme in Victoria (Victoria Department of Correctional Welfare Services 1982), which refers to the need to ensure that community service work does not reduce normal avenues of employment and thus covers the possibilities of expenditure diversion evident in the Nottinghamshire example. In the North American context, despite the frequent mention of state, county, and municipal government agencies as recipients of work, there seems to be a complete absence of safeguards against substituting community service for paid work. Simply assigning offenders to agencies that put them to work (see Roe 1980) is the most extreme example of the surrender of responsibility to private agencies.

The issues in practice are difficult ones. Should community service organizers take on projects for old people in private housing as well as in the public sector? If so, should there be a means test? The experience of one English scheme is significant. A local authority's housing department found itself short of the resources necessary to carry out its normal program of gardening and decorating for old people, seized the opportunity of using offenders on community service, printed internal community service referral forms, and quickly became a major user of community service labor. The impact of community service was no doubt quickly reflected in the budgeting of the local authority concerned. Is it proper to allow such situations to develop, where agencies define their budgets in ways which take into account an expected contribution from community service labor? Should areas with low local taxation and in consequence low levels of service provision be subsidized by free labor?

Any pattern of work accepted by community service organizers is a covert statement of political position, a statement of what is acceptable for this kind of indirect public funding. Offenders share views of vulnerable and deserving groups with other people. To work where they feel service should be paid for creates sharp resentment (Pease and West 1977; Polonoski 1980). This in itself would be an obstacle to the recognition of fairness that is part of the achievement of retributive purpose. However the most telling reason for concern comes from Fred Phipps, the first community service organizer in County Durham. Ten years later Phipps, quoted in Medina Reygadas (1982) says: "I have seen perhaps the saddest side of the community service order scheme. . . . the sort of work available . . . should be done by paid labour. . . . we are now filling the gap created by . . . unemployment [and] the irony is that you can now have a situation . . . where a young man can become unemployed and because of his unemployment starts committing offences and is sent to court and given a community service order to do unpaid work of the type that made him unemployed in the first place" (p. 42).

V. Assessing the Success of Community Service Orders

Because of extensive discretion of supervisors and others, reported rates of successful completion of community service orders cannot be used as evidence of real success. A frequently reported index is continued work after the end of an order (see, e.g., Harding 1974; Hertfordshire Probation and After-Care Service 1979).

Such reports seldom distinguish between offenders who complete an afternoon's work rather than leave precisely when an order expires, and those who take on longer-term commitments to the work. What are more important are feelings of satisfaction and reconciliation that the community service order may bring about, in those on whom it is imposed and in the community on whose behalf it is imposed. Reconviction studies are also reviewed in this section. They are not retributively relevant, but will be regarded as relevant by those taking other views of the sentence.

A. *Public Opinion and Attitudes to Community Service Orders*

To my knowledge, no study has been undertaken among representative samples of the population of attitudes toward community service orders per se in any of the countries in which the sentence is available. Community agencies generally (press, trades unions, work-providing agencies, sentencers, probation officers, and their professional organizations) gave support early in the scheme's development in England and Wales (Pease et al. 1975). A representative sample of the adult population drawn in 1982 showed that 85 percent of respondents wished to see community service used more often for offenders who now end up in prison (Shaw 1982). The consensus among offenders given community service in support of the sentence was referred to earlier (Pease et al. 1975; Flegg 1976; Thorvaldson 1978; Novack et al. 1980; Parker 1980; Polonoski 1980; Varah 1981; Galaway et al. 1983).

The difficulty lies in deciding whether this goodwill is contingent on the use of community service as an alternative to custody. For example, the British Association of Social Workers (see Pease et al. 1975) took the view that they would "support an extension of the scheme to all probation areas if the findings of research support our impression that community service has made a contribution in reducing the numbers of offenders in custody, and is offering a constructive alternative to sentencers" (p. 64). Press reports have predominantly stressed community service orders as an alternative to custody and have approved of it on that basis. For example, under the heading "Useful Jobs Instead of Jail Sentences," the *Daily Telegraph* of December 30, 1972, argued: "Experiments in community service must not be allowed to fail through lack of government money to support them. The cost of keeping a man in prison was 25 pounds per week" (p. 2). On page one of the *Guardian* of December 29, 1972, a story appeared headlined "Community Work in Place of Prison." Whether goodwill would remain if people became aware of the actual levels of diversion from custody achieved by community service is open to question. Varah (1981), commenting on the 86 percent of offenders in his study who felt that they had gained from community service,[4] asserts that "if the 100 clients who took part in this exercise had all just been released from prison I doubt if 86 would have said that they had positively gained from the experience" (p. 123). That is true but disingenuous. It may be equally true to argue that half of them could be excused for attributing hypocrisy to a court that engineered their consent to an order by the threat of a custodial sentence of which they were not in danger.

Two studies have set out more rigorously to assess the effect of community service on offender attitudes. A small study by Wax (1977) observed changes in the asocial and immaturity indices of offenders who had served twenty hours of work, in comparison with a group not given a disposition involving work. As the author notes, the study is too small for confident interpretation. In a more substantial study Thorvaldson (1978, 1980) interviewed forty-two fined subjects, forty-two probationers, and forty-eight offenders given community service. Differences between the groups in criminal history and current offense were satisfactorily controlled. Groups were interviewed on average four to five months after sentence. Four types of measurement were undertaken:

1. attitude toward sentence,
2. attitude toward the criminal justice system,
3. general social attitude scales, and
4. short attitude scales taken from the literature.

It is clear from Thorvaldson's work that attitudes toward the community service sentence itself are very favorable in comparison with attitudes toward the other sentences concerned. Attitudes toward magistrates and court procedure are more favorable among those given community service than among those given fines, but not than among those given probation. Wider social attitudes, Thorvaldson found, were not related to receiving community service. Thus, it appears that reconciliation between offenders and society, at least in the perception of offenders, is achieved only insofar as the receipt of the sentence itself is concerned, with little generalization to the perception of the criminal justice system more generally. However, Thorvaldson (1980) observes, "In summary . . . I think we have some encouraging evidence about the

---

[4] Varah's study, in common with the others cited, is flawed in that it includes only those who complete orders.

effect of CS on offenders' attitudes. Certainly the CS group felt much more positively toward their sentences than did the fined offenders or the probationers. Further . . . it seemed that the CS group responded more positively for the right reasons. They tended to appreciate the principle of fair reciprocity that community service expresses" (p. 85).

As Thorvaldson notes, there are other possible reasons besides the sentence for the differences he found, such as greater enthusiasm for the new sentence by its practitioners communicating itself to offenders. One of the possible reservations about Thorvaldson's study is uncertainty about attrition in the subject groups. Results could obviously be greatly changed by differing rates of attenuation in the groups. Another point is that a higher proportion of community service offenders believed they had escaped a custodial sentence, thus arguably leading the study to confound relief at sentence with attitude toward sentence.

B. Reconviction Studies

Two studies of reconviction have been undertaken which attempt, however roughly, to assess whether community service affects levels of reconviction.[5] One is British (Pease et al. 1977), the other Tasmanian (Rook 1978a). A third large-scale descriptive study has recently been published (Home Office 1983a).[6] Pease et al.'s study confined itself to the 617 offenders given orders during the first year of operation in the six "experimental" areas, and used as a comparison group the 111 offenders considered for, but not given, community service orders in the same areas at the same time. The comparison group was subdivided into those given custodial sentences and those given noncustodial sentences. Reconvictions were recorded that occurred within one year of imposition of a community service order. In the comparison group, the period under study was one year from sentence in the case of noncustodial sentences, and one year from release in the case of custodial sentences. Forty-four and two-tenths percent of those given orders were reconvicted during the year. The reconviction rate of the comparison group was 33.3 percent (the reconviction rates of the custodial and noncustodial segments of the comparison group differed only

---

[5] Although written from a restitution standpoint, the review by Hudson and Galaway (1980) contains a wealth of relevant American material.

[6] This purely descriptive study is included primarily for purposes of comparison with the Pease et al. (1977) study. Descriptive studies in general give no indication of the effects of the community service sanction.

trivially). The community service group differed from the comparison group in terms of age, and post hoc elimination of cases to remove this difference narrows the gap in recidivism, which is not statistically reliable after adjustment.

Pease et al. also examined whether offenses of which the community service group were reconvicted were less serious than those for which the order had been imposed. They were not.

The recent British descriptive study looked at the reconvictions of the 2,486 people given community service orders in January and February 1979 within three years. Thirty-six percent of those given orders were reconvicted within one year, 51 percent within two years, and 59 percent within three years. The slightly lower reconviction rate of the later study could be the result of many factors. The most parsimonious explanation is in terms of the slightly broader definition of reconviction in the earlier study. The pattern of reconvictions by age, sex, and prior record mirrors that found with other sentences: young males with bad records are reconvicted most frequently. The 1983 study shows a lack of relationship between length of order and offense seriousness. In both Pease et al. (1977) and Home Office (1983c) studies, about one-third of first reconvictions led to an active custodial sentence.

The Tasmanian study (Rook 1978a) concluded that community service orders when imposed instead of prison yield lower rates of reconviction than one would expect. Rook showed that around half of those sentenced to community service (work orders) had avoided custody and half had not. He reasoned that recidivism should be examined in a way that allowed comparison of the community service order with each of the types of sentence they replaced separately. To do this he had to identify the group given noncustodial sentences in 1971 who would have attracted orders in 1974. Similarly, he had to identify those given custody in 1971 who would later have received orders. He had then to match the subgroups thus identified with a comparable subgroup of those actually given orders in 1974. The variables used in this matching process were age, marital status, offense type, prior convictions, and prior imprisonments. The number of those given orders included in Rook's study was 340. The period during which recidivism was measured was on average one year. An interesting feature of Rook's study is that he seems to measure time from sentence, even for sentences of custody. This has the effect of reducing the amount of recidivism after custody, because the prisoner is incapacitated from further crime dur-

88   Ken Pease

ing the term of his custody. Nonetheless Rook (1978a, pp. 220–21) concludes: "On all measures, the offenders sentenced to work orders in 1974 who would have received a prison sentence had work orders not been available . . . had lower rates of recidivism than those offenders sentenced to prison in 1971 who would have received a work order sentence had work orders been available at that time. In contrast, those given orders instead of a different non-custodial sentence were reconvicted more often than the comparable group of those given other noncustodial sentences in 1971." The overall one-year reconviction rate of those given orders was 47.1 percent. The overall reconviction rate of the combined 1971 comparison group was 50.2 percent.

The criticism to which the Rook study is vulnerable is that his crucial comparisons depend for their validity upon the adequacy of his matching process. His interesting pattern of results is thus perhaps not interpretable. Further, the size of the subgroups into which division took place is based on a projection that becomes increasingly suspect over time. Nonetheless, the type of interaction Rook's analysis suggests is a fascinating one and well worth futher thought and research. It would be remarkable if, on the lines of Rook's data, work orders increased recidivism for those who did not thereby escape custody, while decreasing it for those who did. There are no doubt more parsimonious explanations of the data than those offered by labeling theory. The data are consistent with labeling theory, however. It would be strange if the debate about the position of community service as an alternative to custody permeated even its capacity to change rates of recidivism.

VI. Concluding Remarks

The development of community service may take it in the direction of incorporation in local government. In this future, it becomes more obviously involved in the provision of local services at the expense of paid labor. To reduce overheads, large offender-only groups perform manual work with no identifiable beneficiary, often work in preparation to construction projects. The nature of the work would be such as to embitter those performing it.

A second direction of development would conflate community service with probation. The ethic of the probation service, with its purpose of advising, assisting, and befriending the offender would be brought to bear on community service. Community service would come to include tasks like looking for a job, discussing problems with probation staff, and so forth. Probation staff would be reluctant to revoke orders, either because revocation would be damaging to the offender or because the real nature of community service would become evident to the court. Despite this, courts would become aware of the development and community service would come to be made in fewer cases, and those on whom they were made would be less serious offenders.

A third direction of change would be in the clarification of the tariff position of community service orders, the development of guidelines of operation enforced by an inspectorate, a continuing research program to refine criteria of operation, and sanctions for nonperformance realistically imposed (see Pease and McWilliams 1980).

Community service is potentially a good retributive sanction. It has so far proved robust to confusion about its place in the range of sentencing alternatives and its conduct. It is not infinitely robust and eventual recognition of its difficulties may lead to its decline as a penal sanction, no doubt to be revived later in a different form. I see no prospect in Great Britain at least that the necessary standardization and refinement of community service will take place. As with so many penal matters, change of practice owes more to change of fashion than to the effects of consolidation. There is a better future for community service orders, but the last ten years give us no cause for optimism that we will live it.

REFERENCES

Advisory Council on the Penal System. 1970. *Non-Custodial and Semi-Custodial Penalties*. London: HMSO.
———. 1977. *Powers of the Courts Dependent on Imprisonment*. London: HMSO.
Andrews, J. E. 1982. *Alternatives to Custody: A Study of Social Inquiry Reports.* Mimeographed. Manchester: Greater Manchester Probation Service.
Ashworth, A. J. 1983. *Sentencing and Penal Policy*. London: Weidenfeld & Nicolson.
Beha, J., K. Carlson, and P. H. Rosenblum. 1977. *Sentencing to Community Service*. Cambridge, Mass.: Abt.
Bottoms, A. E. 1981. "The Suspended Sentence in England 1967–78." *British Journal of Criminology* 21:1–35.
Bridges, C. 1976. *Section Six*. Wakefield: West Yorkshire Probation Service.
Brown, B. 1977. "Community Service as a Condition of Probation." *Federal Probation* 41:7–9.
Chappell, D. 1982. "Community Service by Offenders: Some Australian Perspectives." In *Crime and Redress*, edited by S. A. Thorvaldson. Proceedings of

the National Symposium on Reparative Sanctions. Vancouver: Ministry of Attorney General, British Columbia.

Cooper, G., J. B. Blum, K. L. Sackett, and A. S. West. 1981. Handbook on Community Service Restitution. Denver: Denver Research Institute.

Delgoda, J. P. 1980. "Alternatives to Imprisonment." In *Corrections in Asia and the Pacific*, edited by W. Clifford. Canberra: Australian Institute of Criminology.

Donnelly, S. M. 1980. *Community Service Orders in Federal Probation*. Paper presented to the Fourth Symposium on Restitution and Community Service Sentencing. Minneapolis, September 24–26.

Drzewicki, J. 1969. "Some Problems of Criminal Justice in Voluntary Labour Brigades." *Przeglad Penitenajarny Warsaw* 4:62–73.

Duguid, G. 1982. *Community Service in Scotland: The First Two Years*. Edinburgh: Central Research Unit, Scottish Office.

Flegg, D. 1976. *Community Service: Consumer Survey 1973–6*. Nottingham: Nottinghamshire Probation Service.

Fletcher, A. E. 1983. *Organisational Diversity in Community Service*. M.A. economics thesis. Manchester University.

Galaway, B., and J. Hudson. 1978. *Offender Restitution in Theory and Action*. Lexington: Heath.

Galaway, B., J. Hudson, and S. Novack. 1983. *Restitution and Community Service: An Annotated Bibliography*. Waltham, Mass.: National Institute for Sentencing Alternatives.

Georgia Department of Offender Rehabilitation. 1983. *Community Service: General Guidelines*. Atlanta: Department of Offender Rehabilitation.

Godson, D. 1981. "Community Service as a Tariff Measure." *Probation Journal* 28:124–29.

Goldstone, Judge. 1982. "From the Crown Court: A Fresh Look at Community Service Orders." *Magistrate* 38 (May):71–73.

Harding, J. 1974. *Community Service by Offenders: The Nottinghamshire Experiment*. London: National Association for the Care and Resettlement of Offenders.

Harland, A. T. 1981. "Court-ordered Community Service in Criminal Law: The Continuing Tyranny of Benevolence." *Buffalo Law Review* 29:425–86.

———. 1982. "Discussion from the Floor." In *Crime and Redress*, edited by S. A. Thorvaldson. Proceedings of the National Symposium on Reparative Sanctions. Vancouver: Ministry of Attorney General, British Columbia.

Harland, A. T., M. Q. Warren, and B. J. Brown. 1979. *Guide to Restitution Programming*. National Evaluation of Adult Restitution Programmes, Research Report no. 5. Albany, N.Y.: Criminal Justice Research Center.

Harris, M. K. 1980. *Community Service by Offenders*. Washington, D.C.: American Bar Association, Basics Program.

Heath, M. 1979. "Fine Option Program: An Alternative to Prison for Fine Defaulters." *Federal Probation* 43:22–27.

Hertfordshire Probation and After-Care Service. 1979. *Annual Report*. Bedford: Hertfordshire Community Service.

Hoggarth, E. 1983. *Strategies and Pressures in the Selection Process for Community Service Orders*. Mimeographed. Birmingham: Birmingham Polytechnic School of Social Work.

Home Office. 1974. *Community Service Orders: Memorandum of Guidance*. London: Home Office.

Home Office. 1983a. *Criminal Statistics England and Wales*. Cmnd 9048. London: HMSO.

Home Office. 1983b. *Probation Statistics: England and Wales 1982*. London: Home Office.

Home Office. 1983c. "Reconvictions of Those Given Community Service Orders." *Home Office Statistical Bulletin 18/83*. Surbiton, Surrey: Home Office Statistical Department.

Hudson, J., and B. Galaway. 1980. "A Review of the Restitution and Community Service Sanctioning Research." In *Victims, Offenders and Alternative Sanctions*, edited by J. Hudson and B. Galaway. Lexington, Mass.: Heath.

Ives, G. 1914. *A History of Penal Methods*. London: Stanley Paul.

Jardine, E., G. Moore, and K. Pease. 1983. "Community Service Orders, Employment and the Tariff." *Criminal Law Review*, pp. 17–20.

Kent Probation and After-Care Service. 1978. *North Kent Community Service Projects—1978*. Maidstone, Kent: Probation Service.

King, J. A. 1982. *Community Service—Perceptions Held by Magistrates, Community Service Organisers, Probation Officers and Offenders and Implications for Philosophy and Practice*. M. A. dissertation, Birmingham University.

Klein, A. W. 1981. *Earn-It: The Story So Far*. Quincy, Mass.: Quincy Court.

Kneale, W. 1967. "The Responsibility of Criminals." In *The Philosophy of Punishment*, edited by H. B. Acton. London: MacMillan.

Lawson, C. 1978. *The Probation Officer as Prosecutor: A Study of Proceedings for Breach of Requirement in Probation*. Cambridge: Institute of Criminology.

Leivesley, S. 1983. *Community Service: An Evaluation of the Impact of the Community Service Order Scheme in Queensland*. Brisbane: Queensland Probation and Parole Service.

Lopez-Rey, M. 1973. "The Present and Future of Non-institutional Treatment." *International Journal of Criminology and Penology* 1:301–17.

MacKay, J. G., and M. K. Rook. 1976. *An Evaluation of Tasmania's Work Order Scheme*. Launceston: Tasmania Probation and Parole Department.

McWilliams, B. 1980. *Community Service Orders: Discretion and the Prosecution of Breach Proceedings*. Mimeographed. Manchester: Manchester University, Department of Social Administration.

McWilliams, W. 1980. "Selection Policies for Community Service: Practice and Theory." In *Community Service by Order*, edited by K. Pease and W. McWilliams. Edinburgh: Scottish Academic Press.

Medina Reygadas, M. A. 1982. *A Decade of Community Service Orders: A Study of Experience in Six Probation Areas*. M.A. economics dissertation, University of Manchester.

92   Ken Pease

Melossi, D., and M. Pavarini. 1981. *The Prison and the Factory.* London: Mac-Millan.

Morgan, C. 1977. *Community Service Orders in Gwent.* Cwmbran, Wales: Gwent Probation Service.

National Association of Probation Officers. 1977. *Community Service Orders: Practice and Philosophy.* Thornton Heath: Ambassador House.

National Swedish Council for Crime Prevention. 1978. *A New Penal System: Ideas and Proposals.* Stockholm: National Swedish Council for Crime Prevention.

Novack, S., B. Galaway, and J. Hudson. 1980. "Victim and Offender Perceptions of the Fairness of Restitution and Community Service Sanctions." In *Victims, Offenders and Alternative Sanctions,* edited by J. Hudson and B. Galaway. Lexington, Mass.: Heath.

Oatham, E., and F. Simon. 1972. "Are Suspended Sentences Working?" *New Society* (August 3), pp. 233–35.

Parker, M. A. 1980. *Community Service Orders: Interviews with Offenders in Inverclyde and Dumbarton 1978–9.* Dumbarton: Statistics and Information Office, Social Work Department, Argylle/Dumbarton Division.

Pashakunis, E. B. 1978. *Law and Marxism: A General Theory,* edited by C. Arthur. London: Lawrence & Wishart.

Pease, K. 1978a. "Community Service and the Tariff." *Criminal Law Review,* pp. 269–75.

———. 1978b. "Community Service and the Tariff: A Reply to the Critics." *Criminal Law Review,* pp. 546–48.

———. 1980a. "A Brief History of Community Service." In *Community Service by Order,* edited by K. Pease and W. McWilliams. Edinburgh: Scottish Academic Press.

———. 1980b. "Community Service and Prison: Are They Alternatives?" In *Community Service by Order,* edited by K. Pease and W. McWilliams. Edinburgh: Scottish Academic Press.

———. 1982. "Community Service." *Justice of the Peace* (November 27), p. 740.

Pease, K., S. Billingham, and I. Earnshaw. 1977. *Community Service Assessed in 1976.* Home Office Research Study, no. 39. London: HMSO.

Pease, K., P. Durkin, I. Earnshaw, D. Payne, and J. Thorpe. 1974. *Community Service Orders: The Suitability of Offenders and Local Administration.* Mimeographed. Manchester: Home Office Research Unit.

———. 1975. *Community Service Orders.* Home Office Research Study, no. 29. London: HMSO.

Pease, K., and I. Earnshaw. 1977. "Community Service Orders: A Suitability Check-List." *Probation Journal* 28:15–22.

Pease, K., and W. McWilliams. 1980. "The Future of Community Service." In *Community Service by Order,* edited by K. Pease and W. McWilliams. Edinburgh: Scottish Academic Press.

Pease, K., and J. S. M. West. 1977. *Community Service Orders: The Way Ahead.* Home Office Research Bulletin, no. 4. London: Home Office Research Unit.

Polonoski, M. 1980. *The Community Service Order Programme in Ontario: Partici-*

pants and Their Perceptions. Islington: Ontario Ministry of Correctional Services, Planning and Research Branch.

————. 1981. *The Community Service Order Programme in Ontario: Summary.* Islington: Ontario Ministry of Correctional Services.

Radzinowicz, L. 1956. *A History of English Crim·nal Law.* London: Stevens.

Read, G. 1980. "Area Differences in Community Service Operation." In *Community Service by Order,* edited by K. Pease and W. McWilliams. Edinburgh: Scottish Academic Press.

Roberts, J., and C. Roberts. 1982. "Social Enquiry Reports and Sentencing." *Howard Journal* 21:76–93.

Roe, J. 1980. "Involving the Private Sector in Administering the Ontario (Canada) Community Service Order Programme." Paper presented at the Fourth Symposium on Restitution and Community Service Sentencing. Minneapolis, September 24–26.

Rook, M. K. 1978*a. Practical Evaluation of the Tasmanian Work Order Scheme.* M.A. thesis, University of Tasmania.

————. 1978*b.* "Tasmania's Work Order Scheme: A Reply to Varne." *Australia and New Zealand Journal of Criminology* 11:81–88.

Ruggles-Brise, E. 1901. *Two Prison Congresses—Paris 1895, 1900: Report to the Secretary of State for the Home Department on the Proceedings of the 5th and 6th International Penitentiary Congress.* London: HMSO.

Sebba, L. 1969. "Penal Reform and Court Practice: The Case of the Suspended Sentence." *Scripta Hierosolymitana* 21:133–48.

Shaw, I. 1980. *Community Service Attitudes and Practice.* Cardiff: South Clamorgan Probation and After-Care Service.

Shaw, S. 1983. *Community Service: A Guide for Sentencers.* London: Prison Reform Trust.

Short, J. F. 1983. "Criminology. Modern Controversies." In *Encyclopedia of Crime and Justice,* edited by S. H. Kadish. New York: Free Press.

Smith, M. 1980. "Community Service Sentencing Project: Experiences of a Pilot Project." Paper presented at the Fourth Symposium on Restitution and Community Service Sentencing. Minneapolis, September 24–26.

Smith, D. E., D. Sheppard, G. Mair, and K. Williams. 1984. *Reducing the Prison Population.* Research Paper, no. 23. London: Home Office Research and Planning Unit.

Sparks, R. F. 1971. "The Use of Suspended Sentences." *Criminal Law Review,* pp. 384–401.

Sussex, J. 1974. *Community Service by Offenders: Year One in Kent.* Chichester: Rose.

Thomas, D. A. 1979. *Principles of Sentencing.* 2d edition. London: Heinemann.

Thorvaldson, S. A. 1977. *Development of the Community Service Order in British Columbia.* Vancouver: Ministry of Attorney General.

————. 1978. *The Effects of Community Service on the Attitudes of Offenders.* Ph.D. thesis, Cambridge University.

————. 1982. *Crime and Redress: An Introduction.* Proceedings of the National Symposium on Reparative Sanctions. Vancouver: Ministry of Attorney General.

————. 1983. *Public Service by Offenders: A Brief International Review*. Mimeographed. Vancouver: Ministry of Attorney General, Research and Evaluation Division, Policy Planning Branch.

Trewartha, R. 1978. "Community Service and the Tariff (2). A Further Comment." *Criminal Law Review*, pp. 544–46.

Varah, M. 1981. "What about the Workers? Offenders on Community Service Orders Express Their Opinions." *Probation Journal* 28:121–24.

Vass, A. A. 1980. "Law Enforcement in Community Service: Probation, Defence and Prosecution." *Probation Journal* 27:114–17.

Victoria Department of Correctional Welfare Services. 1982. *Community Service Order Scheme Manual*. Melbourne: Victoria Department of Community Welfare Services.

Victoria Department of Correctional Welfare Services. 1983. *Community Service Order Scheme for Adult Offenders*. Report on the first twelve months of the Pilot Scheme. Melbourne: Victoria Department of Community Welfare Services.

Wax, M. L. 1977. *Effects of Symbolic Restitution and Presence of Victim on Delinquent Shoplifters*. Ph.D. dissertation, Washington State University.

Whittington, N. 1977. *Community Service by Offenders Survey*. Newcastle: Newcastle Polytechnic.

Willis, A. 1977. "Community Service as an Alternative to Imprisonment: A Cautionary View." *Probation Journal* 24:120–25.

————. 1978. "Community Service and the Tariff (1). A Critical Comment." *Criminal Law Review*, pp. 540–44.

Winfield, S. 1977. "What Have the Probation Service Done to Community Service?" *Probation Journal* 24:126–30.

Wootton, B. 1978. *Crime and Penal Policy*. London: Allen & Unwin.

Young, W. A. 1978. *Community Service Orders: The Development of a New Penal Measure*. Ph.D. thesis, Cambridge University.

————. 1979. *Community Service Orders*. London: Heinemann.

Gerald G. Gaes

The Effects of Overcrowding in Prison

ABSTRACT

Prison crowding is often identified as the cause of inmate ill health and misconduct and of postrelease recidivism. Crowding can be measured objectively in several ways: in terms of floor space per prisoner, prisoners per living unit, and institutional population relative to stated capacity. Whether an inmate perceives conditions as crowded depends on objective crowding conditions and on the relative differences in crowding within a prison's housing accommodations. Research on prison crowding has not, however, convincingly demonstrated many adverse effects of crowding. The major findings on which most researchers agree are (1) that prisoners housed in large, open bay dormitories are more likely to visit clinics and to have high blood pressure than are prisoners in other housing arrangements (single-bunked cells, double-bunked cells, small dormitories, large partitioned dormitories); (2) that prisons that contain dormitories have somewhat higher assault rates than do other prisons; and (3) that prisons housing significantly more inmates than a design capacity based on sixty square feet per inmate are likely to have high assault rates. The relationship of crowding to the distribution and availability of prison resources has not been investigated. Crowding may act as an intensifier of stressful conditions that have been precipitated by other causes. Under extreme conditions, crowding can itself induce stress reactions. The limited number of research findings that can be asserted with confidence is the product of inherent difficulties confronting efforts to conduct well-controlled research studies in prison.

Gerald G. Gaes is Senior Research Analyst with the Federal Bureau of Prisons. Opinions expressed are the author's and do not necessarily reflect the policies or procedures of the Federal Bureau of Prisons. The author wishes to thank Michael Tonry, Alfred Blumstein, Norval Morris, Lloyd Ohlin, David Farrington, Paul B. Paulus, Peter Nacci, Tom Kane, Mike Janus, Susan Czajwokski, and J. Michael Quinlan for their critical comments, suggestions and advice in revisions of this manuscript. Thanks also to R. M. for his help in preparation of this paper's tables and figures.

Prison crowding has become a critical criminal justice issue in recent years. The number of sentenced state and federal prisoners rose from 229,721 in 1974 to 438,830 in 1983. Prison population increased especially rapidly in the early 1980s—by 12.2 percent in 1981, by 12.0 percent in 1982, and by 5.9 percent in 1983. These rapid increases have created managerial, financial, and other strains on prison systems. They have also been a subject of litigation in many jurisdictions. The Bureau of Justice Statistics reported in April 1984 that twenty-three jurisdictions were then under court orders or consent decrees due to prison crowding.

The crowding problem has been approached in different ways. Several states—Michigan was the first—enacted emergency crowding laws that authorize early release of prisoners when population exceeds some specified level. Other states have used parole release to achieve that end. In yet other states—Illinois is an example—the provisions of "good time" laws have been made more generous and have thereby shortened prison terms. However, the increases in prison population have occurred notwithstanding emergency crowding laws and parole and good time adjustments, and many jurisdictions have had no choice but to undertake major renovation and construction programs. Nearly forty-two thousand prison beds were added to correctional institutions as a result of renovations and new construction during 1981 and 1982. At the end of 1982, thirty-nine jurisdictions reported that new beds had been added, fifty-one reported that new beds were then under construction, and forty-nine reported that new beds were being planned.

Inextricably connected with the developments surveyed above have been concerns about the effects of crowding on prison management, on prison programming, on the prospects for prisoner rehabilitation, and on the physical and psychological well-being of prisoners and staff. Unfortunately, while deeply held views about the effects of crowding are common, the core of scientific knowledge on which informed opinion must be based is small and is constrained by methodological limitations that caution against generalizing from it. This essay reviews that scant body of research, focusing almost exclusively on the impact of crowding, in various forms, on the physical and mental well-being and behavior, in prison and after, of confined persons.

The overcrowding problem is complex and implicates the ability of prison administrators to manage their institutions, the evolution of prison standards, the public attitude toward confinement, the courts' intervention into prison conditions, and the role of legislators who must anticipate and weigh all of these concerns. Overcrowding has been proposed as the underlying cause of rapes, riots, hostage taking, and assaults. Newspaper accounts of prison life commonly link inmate tension to the degree of crowding.

One reason crowding may be the foremost explanation of prison disturbances is that it is easily identified. It is much simpler to count the number of inmates above some design capacity than to scrutinize procedures, reexamine management and fiscal policies, or change habitual responses to existing conditions. The role of the crowding researcher is to define when and if crowding manifestations occur and the degree of crowding that is detrimental. Only with a clear understanding of these phenomena can prison officials monitor problems related to crowding, judges make rational determinations of cruel and unusual confinement, the public understand the limitations of the correctional system, and legislators consider the cost-benefit relationships involved in increasing or limiting future prison capacities.

When crowding and its manifestations are treated synonymously, other underlying problems may be concealed. Consider two institutions, each with a five-hundred-bed capacity. Institution A has seven hundred men and institution B has five hundred. If institution A has twice as many assaults as B, overcrowding may be blamed. Yet the difference may result from management policies, a difference in the propensity to violence of each institution's inmates, or a failure of institution A's custodial staff to control violence.

This essay reviews the findings of research on the effects of prison crowding on inmate health, inmate violence within the prison, and postrelease recidivism. Section I discusses theoretical frameworks within which laboratory and applied crowding research has been conducted and identifies causal hypotheses by which crowding is linked to human well-being and behavior. Crowding research too often suffers from terminological imprecisions and confusion. Section II therefore reviews the different conceptions of crowding and identifies the various measures—individual, aggregate, contextual—that have been employed. Sections III, IV, and V comprise a substantive review of prison crowding research. Section III reviews the evidence on the relationships between prison crowding and measures of inmate health. Section IV reviews the evidence concerning crowding and inmate violence, and Section V reviews findings on crowding and postrelease recidivism. Section VI isolates the relatively few generalizations about which most crowding researchers agree concerning the effects of prison crowding on human well-being and behavior, identifies plausible but more tentative hypotheses, suggests the most promising directions for prison crowding research, and discusses some theoretical approaches that may clarify some of the current ambiguity in the data. The final section considers the implications for policy and analysis of the research that has thus far been done.

I. Theories of Crowding and Crowding Models

Theories of crowding have focused on the psychological mechanisms that produce immediate and latent effects from both temporary and prolonged exposure to a crowded environment. The psychological theories have emphasized the distinction between objectively defined crowded settings and a personal, subjective state. Objective indicia of crowded settings are discussed in Section II. The conceptual basis for subjective crowding is considered in this section.

The major psychological theories of crowding include behavioral interference (Schopler and Stockdale 1977), crowding helplessness (Rodin and Baum 1978), attentional or informational overload (Cohen 1978; Saegert 1978), and social interaction demands (Cox, Paulus, and McCain 1984).

Behavioral interference concerns the extent to which an individual's goal-directed behavior is interrupted or discontinued by other people in the setting. The individual weighs the costs of reaching a goal against the benefits derived. Costs refer to the stress-related consequences of operating in a crowded environment. To the extent additional effort must be expended to reach a goal, or to the extent an individual will experience anxiety or irritability due to actual or potential failure, that individual will have greater feelings of crowding and exhibit behavioral changes.

Crowding helplessness is a generalized expectation, based on crowding experiences, that one's behavior has little or no effect on situational outcomes. The theory derives from Seligman's (1975) theory of learned helplessness, which postulates that people can learn that outcomes are not contingent on their responses, which results in a degree of apathy even when control is restored. Rodin and Baum (1978) argue that continued exposure to crowded situations reinforces the individual's feeling of helplessness because in a crowded setting there are so many outcomes that the individual is helpless to control. Unwanted interactions, noise, and unexpected requests are examples of social and physical stimuli that impinge on the individual in a crowded setting. Helplessness may occur only in similarly crowded situations or possibly generalize to other settings.

Attentional overload theories posit that, to the extent a crowded situation overloads or taxes an individual's attentional capacity, the individual's attention to other tasks will be diminished (Cohen 1978). Saegert (1978) has amplified this theory to include the effects of limited space and other social dimensions. The diminution of attention to selected stimuli results in strategies that limit the amount of information the individual must coordinate. Thus, the individual might rely on stereotypes or other preconceptions in a high-density environment. Attentional overload has implications for the development of simple cognitive strategies that may generalize to other situations.

A theory of *social interactional demands* has been developed by Cox et al. (1984) from a combination of the helplessness, overload, and behavioral interference theories. They argue that crowded conditions can affect all three types of hypothetical constructs previously mentioned. The major difference between this model and the others it incorporates is the relative unimportance it assigns to people's perception of crowding in mediating the effects of objective indicia of crowding. This issue is addressed in greater detail below after a discussion of Stokols's (1972) emphasis on the role of perceived crowding.

In contrast to the variety of psychological models of crowding effects, sociologists have focused more on an explication of the measurement process. Booth (1976), Gove, Hughes, and Galle (1979), and Baldassare (1981) are the most systematic studies of household density. Much of the research effort in these studies was directed at better subscales of objective and subjective measures of crowding rather than providing a theoretical framework, though Baldassare's (1979) work examines crowding in a broader sociological framework.

Although there are various levels of support for the psychological theories of crowding in nonprison research settings, prison crowding studies generally have failed to address or contrast these theories. Schopler (1980) tested the behavioral interference model by assessing whether inmates who had a high perception of control of their environment experienced dissatisfaction in a crowded setting. Schopler argued that inmates who believe they have control of their environment are less susceptible to interference from other inmates. The data do not support this hypothesis. Had Schopler's hypothesis been confirmed, it would not have supported the interference theory to the exclusion of others. One could postulate from a helplessness perspective, for example, that the degree of perceived control is a direct consequence of helplessness learning. Since interference and helplessness are components of the social demands model, the same conclusions would result from three different theories.

The crowding theories lack a construct that relates system resource allocation to its effects on individuals. When correctional administrators or practitioners refer to crowded environments, they usually are talking about a strain on the system's ability to provide clothing, food, medical care, and basic safety needs. Crowding theories and studies of crowding are more oriented toward the effect of the social environment, including the effect of human density on the physical and psychological well-being of the individual, than toward the indirect results of few resources for too many people.

Stokols (1972) was one of the first to distinguish between environmental density and the subjective experience of crowding. Individuals in a crowded environment do not always feel crowded. As a common example, consider spectators at a baseball game: density is very high, yet the individuals do not feel crowded. Stokols argued that objective density is a necessary but not sufficient condition of subjective crowding. Stokols (1978) later argued that subjective or perceived crowding, as it is usually called, is a necessary and sufficient condition of crowding effects. That is, although objective crowding will not always result in the subjective experience of crowding, when the latter occurs, whatever its objective basis, effects such as withdrawal, aggression, and stress-related pathology will always result. Perceived crowding is determined by crowding density and other social and personal variables that define the person's response to a high-density setting. Perceived crowding has both a stress and a motivational component. According to Stokols, when the individual's demand for space exceeds the amount available, a stress reaction occurs and the individual is motivated to reduce his stress.

Figure 1 is a simplification of the crowding model underlying Stokols's conceptualization and the helplessness, behavioral interference, and attentional overload theories previously described. The top diagram is the theoretical model, the lower half sets out various indicators of each of the constructs. The *objective antecedents* are different measures of crowding density, explicated in Section II. *Moderators* are personal and situational dimensions that determine variations in the perception of crowding and whether the individual will experience stress. The *intervening processes* are proposed psychological and phys-

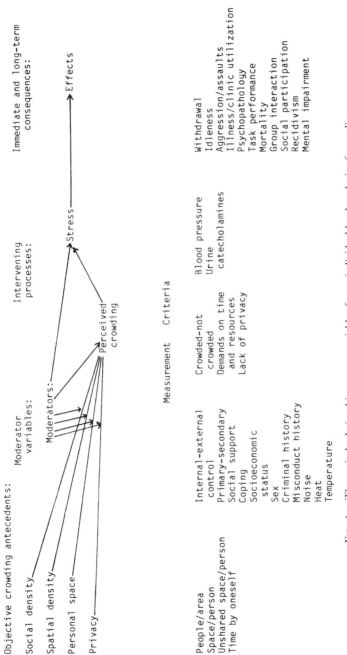

m o d e l

Objective crowding antecedents: Moderator variables: Intervening processes: Immediate and long-term consequences:

Social density

Spatial density

Personal space

Privacy

Moderators:-

Perceived crowding

Stress

Effects

Measurement   Criteria

People/area
Space/person
Unshared space/person
Time by oneself

Internal-external control
Primary-secondary
Social support
Coping
Socioeconomic status
Sex
Criminal history
Misconduct history
Noise
Heat
Temperature

Crowded-not crowded
Demands on time and resources
Lack of privacy

Blood pressure
Urine catecholamines

Withdrawal
Idleness
Aggression/assaults
Illness/clinic utilization
Psychopathology
Task performance
Mortality
Group interaction
Social participation
Recidivism
Mental impairment

FIG. 1.—Theoretical relationships among variables for an individual-level analysis of crowding

iological constructs that are intermediate to the objective antecedents and the objective consequences. These include perceived crowding and stress. It is not clear from the exposition of the other psychological theories of crowding whether a subjective experience of crowding is a necessary and sufficient condition of crowding consequences such as psychopathology. Nonetheless, these other theories generally postulate some form of cognitive mediation of the crowding consequences. One could postulate that cognitions of helplessness, goal interference, and informational or attentional overload are either concomitant or causal perceptions of subjective crowding. Items that assess all of these dimensions may prove to be a more fruitful measure of the subjective experience of crowding than simple questions about crowding, space, or privacy.

Freedman (1975) and Cox et al. (1984) have proposed crowding theories unlike the causal sequence in figure 1. Freedman (1975) has argued that density intensifies both negative and positive effects that are caused by some set of factors other than crowding. This intensification hypothesis is partially based on Freedman's findings that task performance in a laboratory setting is unaffected by density manipulations. Cox et al. argued that the subjective crowding response may be a manifestation of the other crowding constructs, social overload, helplessness, and interference; however, the perceived crowding reaction does not mediate other crowding consequences such as illness, psychopathology, or aggression.

There are many studies in both prison and nonprison settings that demonstrate crowding effects unrelated to the degree of subjective experience of crowding. This is quite apparent in the prison crowding and health literature reviewed in Section III. It is the basis for the assumption of Cox et al. that cognition has no role in the mediation of crowding effects. As Stokols (1978) points out, the failure to find perceived crowding–crowding effect relationships may be attributable to a lack of refinement in the way perceived crowding is measured. In Section VI, I outline a social comparison process explanation of perceived crowding that is intended to refine the construct and its measurement. Stokols (1978) has also refined the concept by distinguishing among moderator variables that determine whether a high-density environment will result in the subjective experience of crowding.

Moderator variables may interact—that is, combine with the crowding antecedents in figure 1—or directly affect perceived crowding. If a moderator variable interacts with a crowding antecedent such as social density, the moderator can be interpreted as some stable characteristic of the person or the social situation that determines whether a crowding antecedent precipitates the subjective experience of crowding. The moderator can affect either the level of subjective experience or the occurrence of such an experience. The interaction of a moderator with objective crowding is indicated by the arrows in figure 1 that originate at the moderator and terminate on the arrows drawn from the crowding antecedents to perceived crowding. If a moderator variable directly affects the subjective experience of crowding without interacting with objective crowding antecedents, then the variable buffers or compensates the subjective crowding experience or exacerbates or intensifies the experience independently of crowding antecedents. This is indicated in figure 1 by the lines drawn directly from the moderator to perceived crowding. Variables that directly affect the subjective experience of crowding are indicative of another cause of perceived crowding absent any objective crowding density manipulations.

Moderators may be grouped into personal and situational variables. Personal variables include both personality measures and demographic characteristics. Among these are (1) internal versus external control—a scale measuring the extent to which an individual believes he has control over his environment (it is presumed that internals are better able to manage a crowded setting because they are not fatalistic about their circumstances); (2) crowding history—the extent to which individuals have been previously exposed to overcrowding (the presumptions for this variable are less clear, in that previous crowding experience may sensitize and thus exacerbate current crowding experience, or the individual may adapt to crowding over time); (3) sex—laboratory studies have found that under some limited conditions females react positively to crowding and males negatively; (4) socioeconomic status—the household density studies that controlled for SES have found that the variable is generally a more potent predictor of effects than crowding.

In prison crowding studies the following moderator variables have been examined: (1) ethnicity—Mexican aliens and Mexican nationals demonstrate fewer health-related crowding effects than other ethnic groups; (2) race—blacks tend to use prison clinics more often than whites regardless of crowding levels; (3) criminal history—few or no effects of sentence length, custody level, and offense type; however, there are better measures of criminal history that may be more fruitful; (4) age—there is limited support for a crowding-age interaction on inmate assault levels.

Situational variables include (1) primary versus secondary environments (Stokols 1978)—primary environments are those in which individuals relate to each other on a personal basis (home, school); secondary environments are those in which encounters are relatively anonymous, transitory, and unimportant (subways, baseball parks)—subjective crowding is more likely to occur in primary environments; (2) task structure—the degree to which a task is focused, requiring concentrated attention—under crowded conditions, subjective crowding is more likely to occur with low structured tasks. Other situational variables include environmental variations of noise, temperature, and architecture. It has been postulated that noisy, hot, architecturally unpleasant environments intensify crowded conditions.

This essay does not review the effects of moderator variables and crowding antecedents in laboratory and applied research settings other than in prisons. Reviews by Freedman (1975), Booth (1976), Schopler and Stockdale (1977), Stockdale (1978), Sundstrom (1978), and Paulus (1980) have attempted to integrate the findings although conclusions have differed.

The stress construct postulated in the model of figure 1 is sometimes explicit and often implicit in crowding theories. It is an intervening variable used to explain immediate and latent crowding effects. As a motivational construct, it is used to explain why and how the individual attempts to alleviate his momentary stress in a crowded situation by such behavior as aggression or withdrawal. More important, prolonged exposure to crowding is assumed to produce chronic responses attributable to stress-related sources. These include suppression of the immune system (Rogers, Dubey, and Reich 1979) and a decline in mental health. Stress is an intervening construct that is also used to explain why some subgroups exposed to chronic crowding do not exhibit problems and others do. Thus, even though some individuals are exposed to chronic crowding and do experience subjective crowding, the stress reaction is mitigated or buffered by other personal or situational effects. Two examples of these moderators are coping strategies (Lazarus 1966) and social support (Finney et al. [1984] have a methodological discussion).

Coping and social support have been invoked in the life events–stress literature. Some people exhibit a higher prevalence or incidence of pathology soon after a stressful life event. Others who have developed coping strategies or who are supported by close friends or relatives are less likely to exhibit these stress-related manifestations. Crowding too may be a stressor that can be ameliorated by coping strategies or support from peers and relatives.

The final element in the crowding model is the measurement of crowding evoked effects. These include measures of withdrawal, aggression, illness, psychopathology, task performance, mortality, group interaction, social participation, discomfort, and mental impairment. The prison crowding literature has been primarily concerned with health, aggression, and recidivism.

Figure 2 amplifies the theoretical distinction about the allocation of system resources. Crowding density as measured by larger units of analysis may affect the quantity and quality of resources. This may be especially true where resource allocation is only partially based on the client or population size. These system-level effects may affect per capita expenses and service quality. If the decline is severe, the quality of life is affected. These quality-of-life effects may not be mediated by subjective crowding. As an example, it may be difficult for the individual to attribute his failure to receive adequate medical care to an overtaxed staff. There are two levels of effects described in figure 2. Macro-level consequences are those that affect the institution while affecting the individual not at all or only indirectly. Individual effects are the impact of the macro-level variables on the individual.

Most research by psychologists and sociologists concerning crowding and its effects has not concerned prisons. Probably no more than 5 percent of the data collected have come from prisons. Unfortunately, it is not clear that the nonprison research is a valid basis for inferences about prison research or policy. There are several reasons for this. First, the generalizability of laboratory and "free world" research to prison settings as well as the converse must be based on a theoretical and empirical foundation. However, no integrated theory explains the differences among the research findings in both prisons and these other areas of study. Second, laboratory research conducted with college students typically involves unfamiliar participants for extremely short time periods (fifteen minutes to three hours). A prison environment houses familiar cohabitants over intervals of weeks, months, or years. Third, the prison environment is relatively harsh compared to a benign lab setting or the relative comfort of one's home, dormitory, or ship, the settings of other applied crowding research (Dean, Pugh, and Gunderson 1975, 1978; Baum and Valins 1977). When this is considered in conjunction with the differences in the research populations, it is clear that generalizations from nonprison to prison settings must be made

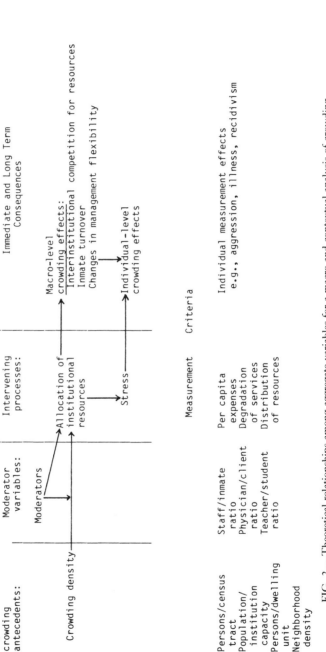

FIG. 2.—Theoretical relationships among aggregate variables for a macro and contextual analysis of crowding

cautiously. For these reasons I focus on the prison crowding research almost exclusively. Others have attempted to integrate some of the diverse applied literature (see Cox et al. 1982).[1]

In summary, most crowding theories postulate that objectively defined crowding antecedents evoke a cognition directly or indirectly related to the perception of crowding, which depends on the presence of some factors and the absence of others. Crowding is presumed to affect some biologically based mechanism associated with stress. The result of all of these prior events is a wide variety of crowding responses and effects, some of which are short term (e.g., aggression), some of which are long term (e.g., health impairment). Before reviewing the prison crowding literature, it is important to distinguish among the various conceptualizations of crowding antecedents and their measurement.

II. Crowding Measurement and Unit of Analysis

There are at least two measurement levels of crowding, an individual and an aggregate level. There is also an interrelationship between these levels referred to as contextual effects. In this section I treat crowding antecedents with reference to these analytical distinctions.

A. Individual-Level Data

Individual-level data consist of responses or characteristics of each subject or participant. Inferences from such data refer to individuals. At an individual level, objective crowding is measured as spatial density, social density, personal space, and privacy, and subjective crowding is measured as perceived crowding.

1. *Spatial density.* In a defined area such as a room, spatial density refers to the amount of space per occupant. It is usually measured as the number of square or cubic feet per person. In a prison cell, the amount of spatial density per person is the area in square feet divided by the number of occupants.

2. *Social density.* Social density refers to the number of people in a given area. It is usually measured as the total number of occupants. Hence, the social density of a two-man cell is two. In defining social

---

[1] Cox et al. (1982) have noted parallel results to the prison crowding research from other applied research. The best studies among the applied research are the major household density studies. Although Cox et al. conclude this research supports a general crowding framework, a close examination of the data shows very little consistency. This research is considered in Sec. VI of this paper.

density, the area of occupancy must be explicit—it might refer to the number of people per census tract, per prison, or per household. Often social and spatial density are dependent on each other; for example, an increase in the occupancy level in a cell or prison causes an increase in social density and a decrease in spatial density. However, if increases in population were accompanied by increases in available housing, the effects on spatial and social density would depend on the extent of the respective increases.

3. *Personal space.* Personal space refers to the amount of space that does not have to be shared. If we consider inmates in an open bay dormitory with sixty square feet per person versus individual rooms having sixty square feet per person, the distinction is obvious. In the former the amount of personal space is virtually nonexistent.

4. *Privacy.* Privacy, though related to personal space, is the proportion of time the individual can be alone. An inmate may have a single cell yet only be allowed to be there during the night, while spending most of the day with many other inmates.

5. *Perceived crowding.* Perceived crowding is a subjective experience. Very often it is measured with a single scale asking a respondent to rate the degree of crowdedness by choosing from alternatives such as very crowded, crowded, moderately crowded, somewhat crowded, not at all crowded. Part of the failure to find crowding effects mediated by perceived crowding is the lack of refinement in this measure. At a minimum, a crowding scale should address other crowding antecedents. There is also some evidence from McCain and his colleages (personal communication) that there are individual differences in the relative importance of spatial and social density. There are probably different individual needs for personal space and privacy as well.

Table 1 contrasts typical prison housing configurations in relation to the four objective crowding antecedents and the presumed resultant perception of crowding. There is limited support for some of the relationships in table 1 concerning social and spatial density. The table represents the inmate's subjective experience of crowding under different housing conditions on a range of one (the least unpleasant experience) to seven (the worst experience of crowding). The question marks in the columns under partitioned dormitories result from studies (McCain et al. 1980; Gaes 1982) that have shown that partitioned dormitories in which inmates have their own cubicles are more like single cells than dormitories. An implication of table 1 is that comparisons among institutions as well as within institutions may often contrast

TABLE 1

The Relative Comfort of Spatial Density, Social Density, Personal
Space, and Privacy for Different Kinds of Inmate Housing

Bunking Arrangement	Spatial Density	Social Density	Personal Space	Privacy
Cell (room):				
Single bunked	1	1	1	1
Double bunked	2	2	2	2
Small dormitory (3–10 men):				
Single bunked	1	3	3	3
Double bunked	2	4	4	4
Large partitioned dormitory (cubicles):				
Single bunked	1	?2–3	?1	?2–3
Double bunked	2	?3–5	?2	?3–4
Large open bay dormitory:				
Single bunked	1	6	5	5
Double bunked	2	7	6	6

housing units that differ on all four crowding antecedents simultaneously. The relative impact of all of these variables is unknown; however, there is some evidence that social density has more impact than
spatial density (McCain et al. 1980; Gaes 1982).

B. Aggregate Crowding Measures

Aggregate data are collections of individual data. At an aggregate
level, the measures of crowding depend on the unit of analysis or point
of reference that determines the number of individual data that enter
into a particular statistic. If one has averages based on an entire prison's
population, then the prison is the particular unit of analysis and inferences drawn from the data should reflect differences among prisons,
not individuals. There are exceptions to this rule that are beyond the
scope of this paper (Firebaugh 1978). One could conceive of larger,
more encompassing units such as state prison systems or even international comparisons. The most typical aggregate-level unit of analysis
used among prison crowding researchers is the prison. The most common measure is a density ratio based on the number of inmates housed
in a prison relative to its capacity.

1. *Crowding density ratio.* In order to measure this ratio, it is important to define capacity. Capacity typically depends on some standard of
space allotted to each inmate. A commonly used standard is sixty

square feet per inmate. This is not a magical number below which there is base and indecent living and above which there is luxurious comfort. In the Northeast very few prisons have single-cell spatial capacities of sixty square feet (Mullen and Smith 1980). In such instances capacities are sometimes defined as the number of single-inmate cells and the number of beds that can be put in a dormitory meeting a fifty- or sixty-square-foot capacity. Some standard must be made explicit when determining an institution's capacity, and exceptions to the standard must be known.

2. *Aggregate measures of prison housing.* Although crowding density is the most frequently used measure of aggregate prison crowding, it is not as closely linked to the quality of life in inmate housing as individual crowding measures. The emphasis of individual-level measurement has been on bunking arrangements in relation to space and occupancy levels. Corresponding to these individual variables, one could compute the percentages of a prison's population housed in different bunking arrangements—single cell, double cell, small dormitories, large partitioned dormitories, and large open bay dormitories. Gaes and McGuire (1984) used such measures and found that both the typical crowding density ratio and the percentage of occupancy in dormitories contributed to the explanation of assault levels.

At an aggregate level of explanation, crowding density may affect resource allocation, while the more specific housing variables are linked to interference, helplessness, and overload relationships. To test these assumptions, intervening variables that distinguish among the aggregate antecedents should be measured simultaneously. Crowding density may be expected to affect aggregate crowding effects through such variables as per capita operating expenses or measures of service degradation. Variables such as the percentage of inmates housed in double cells might be mediated by inmate ratings of perceived control of their environment, or other measures implied by the psychological crowding theories.

3. *Crowding in common areas.* Considering Stokol's distinction between primary and secondary environments, prisons may be divided into inmate housing and common areas. Crowding in dayrooms, recreation yards, libraries, and dining halls may be more appropriately measured as the average occupancy per unit of time. Hence, a library may have a usage rate of thirty men per hour, a dayroom ten men per hour. No study to date has employed these measures. They may also provide an insight into the effect of overall crowding density on the usage and demands placed on the prison's staff and operations.

C. Contextual Effects

Although frequently measured with aggregate data, contextual effects refer to the impact of system-level variables (often referred to as macro level) on the individual (Hauser 1970). A system's effect on a prison might be the impact of the institution's density ratio on the individual, whether housed in a single-bunked unit or otherwise. Other contextual effects of crowding should be recognized. Similar to neighborhood density considered in household density studies, a housing unit's density is intermediate to the overall prison's density and the particular bunking arrangement of the inmate. For example, a housing unit consisting of single-person cells may have an overall capacity of one hundred, while another similar unit may be self-contained and house only forty. When open bay dormitories are considered, this contextual level is synonymous with the dorm's social density.

With these definitions of crowding, researchers can specify crowding manifestations and compare different institutions, inmates, or both under different crowding conditions. Although there are potentially many measurable crowding differences among inmates and prisons, a small subset of these variables may be the crucial antecedents. Complicating the problem of assessing crowding effects is that there are many differences among institutions and inmates other than their crowding levels. These other differences may be the primary cause of changes in aggression, debilitation, or psychopathology.

Sections III, IV, and V, which follow, review the prison crowding literature. Most of the research has been atheoretical. Researchers have characterized crowding by one of the many measures reviewed in this section and then examined concomitant changes in criteria assumed to be affected by crowding.

III. Inmate Health, Morbidity, and Mortality

This section separately considers aggregate and individual-level data. Although most of the data come from individual-level analyses, a recent paper by Cox et al. (1984) includes a section on aggregate data in which the authors claim there is a consistent set of findings implicating crowding as the source of increased morbidity and mortality. I examine these data before turning to the larger set of studies examining individual measures of health.

A. Population Crowding and Morbidity/Mortality Rates

Cox et al. (1984) review data they have collected from prison systems in Texas, Illinois, and Oklahoma, and from a prison in Mississippi. The data were collected from prison archives including death certificates and reports published by each state. The authors report changes in prison populations (not density measured as a ratio of capacity) and concomitant changes in crude death rates, psychiatric commitments, suicides, disciplinary infraction rates, and homicides. Although the latter two measures are not morbidity measures, the present discussion emphasizes the nature of archival aggregate data and hence is included. With few exceptions, Cox and his colleagues report the bivariate relationship between the total yearly population of a prison system (e.g., Texas) or a prison (e.g., Menard Unit in Illinois) and the yearly rate of a particular morbidity, mortality, or misconduct index. In each of the bivariate relationships, there was a concomitant change in mortality or morbidity with changes in population increases or decreases.

Although these data seem compelling, there are several reasons, both theoretical and methodological, why further scrutiny of these relationships is required.

First, except for data pertaining to the Texas Department of Corrections, crowding is represented as population and not density changes. Even with the Texas data, the authors state that there was a 200 percent increase in population with only a 30 percent increase in capacity; however, their data do not account for capacity changes by mapping density (population/capacity) against the criteria.

Second, the data represented as yearly aggregates of entire prison systems may reflect longitudinal processes that affect both morbidity or misconduct and population increases. A "law and order" policy may increase prison population and make the prison more punitive. This could affect both crowding and the health and morbidity criteria. As an alternative to the Cox et al. crowding hypothesis, this model views the covariation of population changes with mortality, misconduct, and morbidity as caused by a more primary process.

A third problem is a result of aggregation itself. The data reported by Cox et al. concerning disciplinary reports for the Texas Department of Corrections from 1976 to 1977 show that although the inmate population increased 200 percent in that time period, misconduct rates increased 600 percent. When these same data are disaggregated to the prison level, the relationship between population and the misconduct rate becomes convoluted (Ekland-Olsen, Barrick, and Cohen 1983). Using the same data, Ekland-Olsen et al. demonstrated that when each Texas prison was graphed separately, there was an inconsistent pattern in the population misconduct relationship. For most of the prisons there was no relationship. For a youth prison, population increases were associated with misconduct rate increases; however, for an adult institution, population increases were inversely related to misconduct rates. Whether this discrepancy among levels of aggregation holds for the other prison systems and other indicators, this inconsistency does raise a serious question about the appropriateness of some yearly aggregates collapsed across entire prison systems.

A fourth problem is that other sources of aggregate statistics are inconsistent with data reported by Cox et al. These include data gathered in the Georgia State Prison System (Carr 1980), the Federal Prison System (Lebowitz and Pospichal 1979), and an aggregation of data from over five hundred state prisons throughout the United States gathered in 1978 (Greenfeld 1982). The data from the Georgia State Prison System showed no relationship between quarterly population changes and cardiovascular death rates. Within the Federal Prison System, there was no relationship between population changes and either suicide rates or homicides. Greenfeld (1982) examined death and suicide rates using data collected by Abt Associates from 571 state prisons. Greenfeld reported there was an inverse relationship between state prison populations and their reported death rates. Furthermore, prisoner death rates controlling for age, race, and sex were lower than analogous parolee and general population rates.

The data reported by Greenfeld (1982) were collapsed across distinctions among state prison systems and time-related changes. It may be that the level and point of aggregation partly determines the results of these studies. Nonetheless, without some theoretical basis for determining which level of aggregation is the most appropriate, the data must be considered inconclusive.

A fifth problem is that, whether aggregate or individual-level data are being analyzed, the simple analysis of a bivariate relationship may be misleading if there is some underlying variable or subset of variables responsible for the relationship. As an example of a well-controlled study of morbidity and mortality in a nonprison setting, Manton and Myers (1977) and Myers and Manton (1977) analyzed crowding and death rates. They demonstrated certain crowding density effects while using ten measures of density, and fourteen measures of crude and age-specific death rates for certain disease categories, while controlling for fourteen indicators of socioeconomic and demographic differences in the census tracts being studied. Similar prison crowding studies would not only bolster one's confidence in the bivariate relationships, they would also provide information on population and prison differences that could be used in policy decisions and changes.

A final problem with the aggregate analysis of population changes and their effects on morbidity and mortality over time is that the yearly point of analysis equates the level of risk as if it were the same throughout the unit of time. It has been observed in several studies (Twaddle 1976; Gaes 1982) that morbidity decreases with the amount of time an inmate has served. There are at least two theoretical reasons for this. The first is that many new commitments are suffering from impaired health, drug related or otherwise. The second is that prisoners are adapting to the "shock" of prison. Thus, newly committed inmates are at a higher level of health risk than inmates who have spent some time in prison. The implication of this result for an aggregate analysis is that increases in population levels may represent increases in the percentage of inmates who are new commitments. Thus, what appears to be a relationship between population and mortality or morbidity is a relationship between increased risk attributable to new commitments and morbidity or mortality. If this analysis is correct, there are at least two basic implications: if a prison system's population levels off, morbidity and mortality would decrease as the system's population reached higher levels of average time served; second, an analysis controlling for average time served or percentage of new commitments may eliminate a population-level and morbidity or mortality relationship.

B. Individual Crowding Measurement and Inmate Health

The most extensive research program on effects of prison crowding on individual inmates has been conducted by Paul B. Paulus, Garvin McCain, and Verne Cox of the University of Texas at Arlington. Their data on aggregate measures of morbidity and misconduct have already been reported. The majority of their data collection has come from research sponsored by the National Institute of Justice. In that study, information was gathered on approximately 1,400 inmates housed in six federal prisons. The particular prisons were selected based on their variety of housing. For each inmate, housing information, demographic information, criminal history, and clinic visits were recorded. Each inmate also responded to a questionnaire which measured his subjective experience of crowding and numerous other scales of satisfaction with his housing unit. In some prisons, an inmate's blood pressure was recorded. I will focus on the relationship between an inmate's particular housing unit, his subjective experience of crowding, and indicators of his health, either blood pressure or clinic utilization. Although other subjective reactions are interesting, it is clearly the behavior of inmates that must form the objective basis for decisions, policy or otherwise, about inmate housing.

Clinic utilization refers to any voluntary visit an inmate makes to the prison infirmary. Prescription refills, blood pressure clinics, or mandatory physicals are excluded from the data reported by McCain et al. (1980) and Gaes (1982). For each clinic visit, an inmate's complaints, symptoms, or a physician assistant's diagnosis was recorded along with the date of the visit; however, the data that will be reported are not distinguishable by type of symptom or complaint.

Although McCain et al. have examined categories of illness responses, such as contagious or noncontagious, no consistent pattern has emerged. Paulus and Gaes have had a sample of physicians and physician's assistants rate over 50 of the typical symptoms or complaints inmates report. The sample of medical professionals categorized the complaints by judging whether the symptoms were verifiable, stress related, psychosomatic in origin, or contagious. Based on these categories, as well as the statistical co-occurrence of symptom complaints, Paulus and Gaes are attempting to refine the analyses of clinic utilization. This could result in more theoretically meaningful complaint categories. The results of this analysis are pending. A rough categorization of the complaints is reported in Gaes (1982) and appears in table 2.

The results of the NIJ-supported research in six federal prisons are

TABLE 2

Examples of the Most Frequent Contagious and Noncontagious Illness Symptom Classifications and Their Percentage of Occurrence among Inmates

Contagious	%	Noncontagious	%
Venereal disease	1.8	Neuroses, psychoses	7.0
Eye, ear, nose, throat		Headache	5.2
infections, problems	11.9	Circulatory heart problems	2.1
Cough, cold, flu	18.2	Joints, bursitis, arthritis	4.6
Gastrointestinal, stomach	8.3	Neck, shoulder, hip pain	5.9
Skin, subcutaneous	11.3	Chest pain	2.8
Virus, chills, fever	5.2	Back pain	6.9

NOTE.—The values indicate the percentages of these inmates who reported a particular complaint. Of the entire sample, 35 percent of the inmates had no clinical visits.

reported in McCain et al. (1980). The other studies of prison housing and health are D'Atri (1975), McCain, Cox, and Paulus (1976), Twaddle (1976), Paulus et al. (1978), and Gaes (1982). Where appropriate, different prisons are recorded as sites. In some cases, contrasts involving different housing units within a prison are reported. These are recorded as a site and a particular comparison,·or visit.

The data reported in tables 3–7 contrast different types of bunking arrangements within the prison housing. For example, table 3 contrasts large open bay dormitories to single-bunked cells or cubicles. For each contrast the average number of clinic visits per week per inmate is recorded in the column headed "Clinic Utilization." "Utilization/ Perceived Crowding" is a column heading that measures the relationship between the inmates' subjective experience of crowding and their clinic utilization. "Blood Pressure" designates the average blood pressure per group. Either systolic or diastolic pressures are recorded depending on a particular study and the particular results. Finally, the "Sample Size" per group is listed. In several cases, utilization or blood pressure results are reported in a study without specifying group means. These appear as NR entries in the tables. If row entries are blank, the data were not collected for a particular study. For the utilization/perceived crowding relationship, different studies adopted different covariation procedures. For this reason a coding scheme was used to report a negative relationship ($-$), a positive relationship ($+$), or no relationship (0). Significant results in tables 3–7 are noted by an asterisk.

The results are set out below according to the major types of housing contrasts.

1. *Single cells or rooms versus large open bay dormitories (table 3).* The data in table 3 indicate that higher clinic utilization rates and higher average blood pressure levels are associated with living in dormitories in contrast to single cells or rooms. One exception to this pattern is Twaddle (1976), who reported that there was a greater percentage of inmates housed in single cells who reported to sick call than the inmates housed in dormitories. When the data are reported, there is rarely a relationship between perceived crowding and either of the health criteria.

2. *Single- versus double-bunked rooms or cells (table 4).* Table 4 indicates very little consistency in the double versus single contrast. McCain et al. (1980) have found opposite and null results in the three sites they assessed. Neither blood pressure nor clinic utilization indicated differences among these types of housing.

TABLE 3
Comparisons of Open Bay Dormitories and Single Cells

Studies	Clinic Utilization Single Cells	Dorms	Significance	Blood Pressure Single Cells	Dorms	Significance	Utilization/ Perceived Crowding Single Cells	Dorms	Sample Size Single Cells	Dorms
McCain et al. 1980:										
Site 3-comp 1	.081	.165	*					—	60/75	47/63
Site 4-comp 1	.140	.280	*	63.0	63.5	N.S.		0	73/82	55/77
Site 4-comp 2	NR	NR	N.S.						NR	NR
Site 6-comp 1	NR	NR	N.S.						82	39
McCain et al. 1976:										
Site 1	NR	NR	*						20	20
Gaes 1982:										
Site 1	.119	.208	*				0	+	21	85
Twaddle 1976[a]	54%	21%	*						79	43
D'Atri 1975:[b]										
Site 1				109.63 / 67.78	133.57 / 79.29	*	0	0	27	7
Site 2				112.11 / 68.65	127.31 / 76.79	*	0	0	52	39
Site 3				114.90 / 69.54	131.03 / 76.55	*	0	0	97	29

[a] Twaddle reported results as the percentage of inmates who reported to sick call in one month.
[b] Both systolic and diastolic blood pressure were significantly different for each site.

TABLE 4
Comparisons of Single and Double Cells

Studies	Clinic Utilization			Blood Pressure			Utilization/ Perceived Crowding		Sample Size	
	Singles	Doubles	Significance	Singles	Doubles	Significance	Singles	Doubles	Singles	Doubles
McCain et al. 1980:										
Site 1	.07	.14	*	55.6	51.2	*		+	52	40
Site 4-comp 1	.14	.08	*	63.0	65.4	N.S.		0	73/82	35/40
Site 4-comp 2	NR	NR	N.S.						NR	NR
Twaddle 1976	54%	45%	N.S.						79	100
Wener and Keys 1984[a]	1.51	1.51	N.S.						18	12

[a]Wener and Keys computed monthly sick call rates.

3. *Single-bunked cells versus single-bunked cubicles (table 5).* A quick modification to existing dormitory structures is to subdivide the space with partitions. These partitions may be simple room dividers, or they may be more elaborate modules containing desks and clothes lockers. The data in table 5 indicate that clinic utilization is typically the same for cubicles and single rooms, with one exception, McCain et al. (1980). The institution reported as site 3 in the McCain et al. data is the same institution recorded as site 1 in Gaes (1982). The discrepancy in the findings may indicate either instability in this data or longitudinal changes attributable to any number of factors.

4. *Double- versus single-bunked dormitories (table 6).* Table 6 indicates very little consistency among the three studies contrasting single- versus double-bunked dormitories.

5. *Multiple-bunked cells versus single- or double-bunked rooms or large dormitories (table 7).* The data reported in table 7 contrast intermediate size housing units with larger or smaller units. It is not important whether such intermediate units should be called small dormitories or large cells. In McCain et al. (1980), site 2, and Paulus, McCain, and Cox (1978), the size of the unit is the same for the double-bunked and higher social density units. The blood pressure and utilization data are inconsistent for McCain et al., site 2, although the utilization data suggest that there is a qualitative distinction between singles and triples versus higher social densities.

6. *Other studies assessing crowding and inmate health.* Several other notable studies do not easily fit into the format of tables 3–7. Rather than measure blood pressure differences by contrasting different inmates in different housing units (cross-sectional measurement), D'Atri et al. (1982) took blood pressure readings from the same inmates when they transferred to different housing units (longitudinal measurement). Although the longitudinal measures were reliably higher among inmates who transfer from single cell to dormitory accommodations than when those inmates were housed in single cells, their data indicate much smaller changes in blood pressure in the longitudinal results as opposed to the cross-sectional results.

In a study conducted by Gaes (1982), the major purpose was to ascertain whether the amount of space an inmate has (when he is confined to either a cell or cubicle and he does not have to share his area with another inmate) has any effect on his clinic utilization. In the same study, the contrast of dormitory and single cell or cubicle housing was assessed as an attempt to replicate the findings of McCain et al. (1980).

TABLE 5
Comparisons of Single Cells and Single-bunked Cubicles

Studies	Clinic Utilization			Blood Pressure			Utilization/ Perceived Crowding		Sample Size	
	Singles	Doubles	Significance	Singles	Doubles	Significance	Singles	Doubles	Singles	Doubles
McCain et al. 1980:										
Site 3-comp 1	.081	.183	*	55.6	55.6	N.S.		...	60/75	20/24
Site 1	.07	.07	N.S.						52	42
Site 6-comp 2	NR	NR	N.S.						88	44
Gaes 1982:										
Site 1	.119	.127	N.S.				0	0	21	113
Site 2	.123	.128	N.S.				0	0	42	79

TABLE 6
Comparisons of Single- and Double-bunked Dormitories

Studies	Clinic Utilization			Blood Pressure			Utilization/ Perceived Crowding		Sample Size	
	Singles	Doubles	Significance	Singles	Doubles	Significance	Singles	Doubles	Singles	Doubles
McCain et al. 1980:										
Site 1	.07	.14	*	55.6	51.2	*	...	...	42	49
Site 3–comp 1	.183	.165	N.S.						20/24	47/63
Site 3–comp 2	.105	.152	N.S.						NR	NR

TABLE 7

Comparisons among Large Dormitories, Intermediate Units, and Single- or Double-bunked Rooms

Studies	Significance	Rooms-Cells		Intermediate Units Number of Inmates				Large Dormitories
		Single	Double	3	4	5	6	
McCain et al. 1980:								
Site 2:								
Utilization	*	.09		.12	.22	.21	.25	
Blood pressure	*	60.9		52.7	65.7	64.8	52.4	
Sample size		54		59	44	35	29	
Site 5-time 1:								
Utilization	N.S.		.13		.16			
Blood pressure	N.S.		NR		NR			
Sample size			25		27			
Site 5-time 2:								
Utilization	N.S.				NR			NR
Blood pressure	*				126			117
Sample size					49			38
Paulus et al. 1978:								
Utilization	*							
Blood pressure			126.5	132.7			133.9	
Sample size			37	38			41	

The replications have already been discussed and reported in table 3. Cell sizes ranging from forty-three square feet to eighty-eight square feet were included. This range falls above and below the typically recommended standard of sixty to eighty square feet. Based on the clinic utilization criterion, there were no adverse effects of spatial density on reported inmate complaints. Although McCain et al. had found contradictory evidence in two sites when two levels of spatial density were contrasted to one another, there were several differences among the housing units in program participation and criminal history that may have produced these discrepancies, a fact noted by McCain et al. Gaes (1982) controlled for criminal history, ethnicity, race, program participation, age, and the particular week or season an inmate entered his housing unit and found no negative relationship between space and clinic utilization. In the same study Gaes was able to assess inmates living in combination housing units containing both single-bunked cubicles and open bay areas. Inmates in the single-bunked cubicles had lower clinic utilization rates.

Finally, Walker and Gordon (1980) reviewed epidemiological evidence demonstrating higher rates of contagious diseases among occupants having less space. These data were based mostly on research in Army and Navy barracks, a commercial airliner, and a large urban jail. In this last study (King and Geis 1978), 107 inmates were housed in 1,980 square feet, an average of 18.5 square feet per person.

In summary, the individual-level data (1) support a crowding hypothesis when open bay dormitories are contrasted to single rooms and cells, (2) marginally suggest high-density cells produce health effects contrasted to low-density cells, and (3) show that Walker and Gordon's (1980) review of epidemiological evidence demonstrates a density-contagion relationship. The null effects are (1) the amount of space among single-bunked cubicles or cells is not important between forty-three and eighty-eight square feet, (2) double-bunked versus single-bunked contrasts are ambiguous, (3) single cells and single-bunked cubicles are similar in their clinic utilization effects, and (4) the effect of double bunking in open bay dormitories is ambiguous.

There are several problems and many limitations among the results and studies reported. The epidemiological issue addressed by Walker and Gordon (1980), and this study is often cited, fails to consider the important dimension of ventilation. In testimony before the court in a crowding suit involving this issue (Miles v. Bell, Civil No. B-79-137, D. Conn., filed April 12, 1979), an epidemiologist cited ventilation and not space as the primary factor in the transmission of air-borne diseases. Since I am not an expert in epidemiology, I only raise this issue without attempting to resolve it. It is certainly the case that schoolchildren, armed services personnel, and office workers are also exposed to contagious disease transmission without being housed in the same quarters. If identified, inmates having a virulent contagious disease such as tuberculosis or syphilis can be isolated from the remainder of the population. This health standard is independent of crowding phenomena.

Two mechanisms have been proposed as mediating the contagion effect. The first, as previously discussed, is the exposure to or contact with the disease mechanism. Thus, a pathogen is transmitted to the crowded individual. The second mechanism is the suppression of the immune system (cf. Rogers et al. 1979), which ordinarily protects us from disease. No research to date has been designed to examine the extent to which crowding effects occur through one mechanism or the other.

The most consistent and demonstrative finding among the crowding-health data is that within the same institution, inmates living in open bay dormitories have higher clinic utilization rates and blood pressure averages than inmates living in single cells or rooms. Inspection of tables 3–7 indicates that other than the open dormitory rate of site 4, comparison 1, of McCain et al. (1980), other dormitory clinic utilization rates are not much different than the rates in some single cells, double cells, or other types of housing in different institutions. Clearly, there are interinstitutional differences that determine some base level of clinic utilization among prisons. These differences may include the overall crowding density of the institution; however, other variables that contribute to the level of health of the inmate population and the level of care provided by the particular clinic will also influence these averages.

For several reasons the dormitory versus single-cell comparison may not be as conclusive a crowding finding as some have suggested. Furthermore, there are theoretical limitations to the meaning and significance of this finding.

Theoretically, differences among dormitories and single cells represent changes in all of the crowding dimensions identified in table 1—social density, spatial density, personal space, and privacy. Because each of these variables can be measured in different ways, it is possible to examine not only the direct or main effects of these variables but the combination of effects as well. The differences in clinic utilization or blood pressure between two housing units may be a difference in some combination of all or several of the crowding measures. This is not just an esoteric methodological point. Depending on the particular combination of crowding factors associated with increased values of the health measures, the approach taken to ameliorate problems may be very different. As an example, if it is privacy per se that is the major problem, then dormitories may be tolerable under conditions where inmates are provided separate reading or study time areas.

There are also problems associated with interpreting the differences in clinic utilization rates. There is no necessary relationship between clinic utilization and actual illness. That more inmates from a dormitory use a clinic may not mean these inmates have more acute health problems. Inmates in dormitories may visit the health clinic more often yet have the same health problems as inmates in single cells. This is because the decision to visit a health clinic may involve factors other than one's actual level of health. There is evidence from the medical sociology literature which shows that the self-evaluation of one's health depends as much on one's subjective happiness as on one's actual health (Tessler and Mechanic 1978). One implication is that health care providers attend to psychological as well as medical problems. A second implication is that there may be similar symptoms or illness patterns in two housing units; however, illness complaint rates will be higher in a unit perceived as less satisfactory.

A second reason dormitory-housed inmates may have higher clinic utilization is that these inmates are more likely to complain because of characteristics other than their health. A paper by McGurk, Graham, and McEwan (1980) found that prisons housing greater numbers of inmates with disciplinary problems had higher illness complaint rates. Preferential housing assignments typically are given to inmates with longer tenure and better conduct records. Thus, inmates with good conduct are more likely to live in single cells than in dormitories. These data suggest that the least preferred units housing inmates with more disciplinary problems also contain inmates who complain about their symptoms. To date, no research has assessed complaints of illness while controlling for the disciplinary records of the inmates. Although Paulus et al. have controlled for length of housing in most of their analyses, a purer test would have controlled for the inmates' institutional adjustment.

The last caveat concerning illness complaint data concerns the meaning of clinic utilization. Prison clinics are used to meet virtually all health care needs of the population. For obvious reasons, inmates are dependent on the clinic for the most minor prophylactic medication, treatment of minor accidents, and preventive medicines. One study assessing clinic utilization in the Federal Prison System has shown that inmates average twelve ambulatory visits per year (LaJolla Management Corporation 1981). That is, prison clinics are used at four to five times the public rate of two-and-a-half clinic or doctor visits per year (U.S. Department of Health and Human Services 1981), even though the incidence or prevalence of diseases such as hepatitis or tuberculosis is the same for incarcerated and nonincarcerated subjects when they are matched on the basis of risk factors (LaJolla Management Corporation 1981). The relative differences among dormitory and single-cell-housed inmates reflect differences in nonvirulent symptoms.

Additional evidence suggests differences other than health may contribute to clinic utilization disparities in dormitories and singles. The magnitude of the differences between the longitudinal results and the cross-sectional results reported by D'Atri, Ostfeld, and their colleagues reinforces the inference that the higher magnitude of the cross-sectional results is attributable to differences in the populations of the particular housing units. The *same* inmates who changed from singles to dorms had much smaller blood pressure increases than would have been anticipated from the cross-sectional results.

When biological measures such as blood pressure have been measured they have not been related to clinical or diagnostic assessments. Thus, the presumed relationship between increased blood pressure and increased pathology has never been tested in a prison crowding study.

To pin down a relationship between crowding and health, there are two basic research strategies which could be taken. The first is to show that crowding is related to some biological indicator of stress and then show that the indicator is related to clinic utilization. Such a study would demonstrate that persistent crowding produces a reaction when the body exceeds a stress threshold. A second and complementary approach would be to assess independently the health status of individuals assigned to different housing types. The assessment would be done by health care providers who are "blind" to the housing conditions of the inmates they would examine. Such a study is costly because it entails expensive diagnostic tests. A modification would be to select inmates with chronic health problems such as diabetes or heart disease problems. This sample would be tested for acute episodes of the problems. Of course, the proper controls would have to be observed.

The first type of study has already been conducted by Shaffer,

Baum, Paulus, and Gaes, and the results are pending. The biological indicator used was catecholamine production (Baum, Grunberg, and Singer 1982). The results of the study may indicate whether we can identify the clinic utilization rates as genuine illness responses.

IV. Crowding and Violence

One of the effects suggested by Calhoun's (1962) classic study of crowded rats was the emergence of a dominant, aggressive type. Many characterizations of prison life portray the belligerent, predacious inmate taking advantage of the unknowing or unwilling inmate. It has been suggested that, as in Calhoun's rat colony, crowded prisons exacerbate the predatory nature of prison life. How and why crowding excites a violent response has rarely been detailed by researchers.

Unlike the health criteria, most of the violence research involves aggregate data analyses with the prison as the unit of analysis. Table 8 summarizes findings from eight studies of the relationship between crowding and inmate violence. The columns of table 8 describe for each study the following: *criteria*—the measure chosen to represent inmate violence; *results*—0 indicates no relationship, + a positive relationship, and − a negative relationship between crowding and a particular violence measure after controlling for all other variables in the study; *level of analysis*—the level of aggregation and the time period (day, month, or year) for each variable incorporated into the study; *number of cross-sectional data points*—the number of individuals or prisons for which the variables were measured; *number of longitudinal data points*—the number of days, months or years the variables were measured; *crowding level*—the average density (population as a ratio of capacity) level of an institution or prison system; *total incident/100 or assault/100 averages*—the overall level of violence in a prison or prison system as measured by the number of misconduct infraction or assault rates per 100 inmates; *other variables*—all other variables incorporated into the study.

Other than studies by Carr (1980), Ruback and Carr (1984),[2] Nacci et al. (1977), Ekland-Olsen et al. (1983), and Gaes and McGuire (1984), there were few data points over which the crowding, violence levels, and other variables were assessed (table 8). The reader should be cautioned about studies that claim results based on large numbers of

---

[2] Ruback and Carr (1984) contrasted symptom self-reports for inmates housed in small rooms (two men), large rooms (four men), and trailers (twenty men). There were no effects of housing type on the self-reports. These data were excluded from table 2 because there were no objective indicia to support the authors' findings.

TABLE 8

Comparison among Studies Evaluating the Effect of Crowding on Prison Assault Rates

	Criteria	Results	Level of Analysis	Number of Cross-sectional Data Points	Number of Longitudinal Data Points	Crowding Level	Total Incident/100 or Assault/100	Other Variables
Megargee 1974	Total incidents	+	Monthly aggregate	1	48	1.18*	13.23	None†
Nacci et al. 1977	Adjudicated incidents	+	Yearly aggregate	37	3	1.14		Institution type
	Assaults	+						
Ekland-Olsen et al. 1983:								
Study 1	Total incidents	0	Yearly aggregate	14	5	1.25–1.51	16.5–25.0	Age
	Assaults	0						Sentence length
Study 2	Solitary confinement	0	Aggregate	10	0		1.74–2.74	Time served
								Proportion of sentence served
Study 3	Total assaults	0	Individual (some aggregate predictors)					Yearly population

Study	Dependent variable	Effect	Level of analysis	N				Controls
Carr 1980: County and state prisons	Log of infractions per year	0	Individual and aggregate‡	5,645	…	1.00–1.25		Race County§ Arrests Age
Youth prison	Log of infractions per year	+	Individual and aggregates	1,112			9–10	Property offense Time served
Jan 1980	Assaults	+	Monthly aggregate	4	12	1.18	.3	Institution type
	Disciplinary confinement	+						
McCain et al. 1980	Total incidents	+	Yearly aggregate	2	5	…	8.3–31	None
Ruback and Carr 1984	Log of total incidents	+	Individual and aggregate‖	561	…	…	…	Race Density of home county Previous arrests History of violence Time served

TABLE 8 (*CONTINUED*)

Criteria	Results	Level of Analysis	Number of Cross-sectional Data Points	Number of Longitudinal Data Points	Crowding Level	Total Incident/100 or Assault/100	Other Variables
Gaes and McGuire 1984		Monthly aggregate	19	33	1.35 S.D. .31	2.2	Capacity Penitentiary Staff-inmate ratio Percentage of staff corrections officers Inmate turnover Inmate age Race White-collar occupation Drug abuse Time remaining on sentence
Assaults against inmates with weapon	+						
without weapon	+						
Assaults against staff with weapon	−						
without weapon	+						

Number of previous commitments
Crimes against person
Inmate program participation
Inmate work participation

*This density measure was derived from Megargee's reporting of the amount of average space and the proportion which was used for sleeping, excluding that proportion used for bathroom, TV room, game room, and vestibule area. This derived measure was divided by the ACA standard of sixty square feet to produce a capacity estimate of 474 men.

†Megargee (1974) reported a partial correlation in which the average monthly population and average amount of space were partialed from their respective relationships with incident measures. Concomitant with decreases in space, increases in population were also occurring in the sample ($r = -.33$).

‡Carr's study of the Georgia prison system assessed individual infraction rates in relation to individual measures of race, numbers of arrests, age, property offense, and time served. The crowding measures were contextual variables in that the institution crowding level was ascertained for each institution in which the inmate served a portion of his sentence. Furthermore, density was determined as the actual population level as a ratio of the average level.

§County of residence was also a contextual variable.

‖Ruback and Carr (1984) also employed a contextual measure of crowding and home county density.

131

inmate populations using aggregate data. For example, a study that considers yearly averages over several years for an entire prison system's population is based on a few data points (one for each year), not the twenty-five thousand or so inmates whose data might enter into those yearly averages.

Carr (1980) and Ruback and Carr (1984) examined crowding in the Georgia state prison system. In both studies the authors computed the density levels of institutions, in which a particular inmate was housed, as the inmate's crowding level. This represents a cross between individual-level data and aggregate data. The problem is that an inmate may have been housed in a single cell at a particular institution yet the institution may have been populated above its capacity. This would have caused an inmate who had rather comfortable housing to be assigned a high crowding index. For this reason, the results are ambiguous. After numerous analyses, Carr found the institution density measure was related to misconduct in the one major youth institution in Georgia and not in any of the regular adult institutions. Ruback and Carr found that both the institution crowding level and the inmate's age were associated with misconduct in a women's prison. Both studies suggest an interesting approach. The assignment of the institution's crowding index to the individual is tantamount to ascertaining a contextual effect. It would be interesting to ascertain both the contextual and individual housing effects in one study. Although several studies have aggregate and individual data, they do not have aggregate and individual crowding measures on the same inmate.

Both the Nacci et al. and Ekland-Olsen et al. studies focus on age as the major determinant of aggregate prison crowding effects. Nacci et al. found that the average prison density measure and the average level of serious misconduct rates were only related for youth institutions. Ekland-Olsen et al. went one step further in their analysis and conclusions and argued that the average age of the population, and not the crowding levels, was the cause of increased misconduct rates. The lower the average age of a prison population, the more likely misconduct will occur. Ekland-Olsen et al. argued that population increases which create crowded prisons result in more youths being incarcerated. Since younger inmates are more predisposed to violence, what appears to be a crowding phenomenon is actually attributable to an average decrease in inmate age. Ellis (1982), in a related argument, contends that the increases in prison populations are coincidental with inmate transiency. As new inmates enter the system, there is a tension created by new power relationships. Both Ellis's and Ekland-Olsen's arguments presume that crowding is only superficially related to increased violence levels and that the real underlying causes are attributable to pressures evoked by either the nature of the young inmate or the renegotiation of power within the inmate subculture.

Both of these assertions were tested and rejected by Gaes and McGuire (1984). The data were gathered from nineteen federal prisons for each of thirty-three months. This resulted in 619 data points for each variable in the analysis. During the time period of this study, there was a 40 percent increase in the population of these institutions. Thus, there was variability both in the cross-sectional measurement (prisons) and in the longitudinal measurement (changes over time for any given prison). Aside from the typical crowding density measure, Gaes and McGuire incorporated averages of inmate age, transiency, institution capacity, staff to inmate ratios, inmate program participation, inmate characteristics including race, preincarceration occupations, history of substance abuse, previous number of commitments, and the percentages of crimes that were against property or the person. The comprehensiveness of the data set allowed the isolation of crowding effects while equating the prisons sampled on these other characteristics.

To test the age-crowding-violence hypothesis of Ekland-Olsen et al., Gaes and McGuire ran analyses with variables equivalent to those used by those authors. Age preempted crowding as the most important variable. When the remaining variables were added, crowding was by far the most consistent and demonstrative variable. Gaes and McGuire interpreted these findings to mean that the average age of inmates at an institution represents many other institutional differences, which suppresses the crowding effect. Prisons housing younger inmates differ in their composition. When these differences are measured and accounted for, age is much less predictive of assaults. The age effect was also depressed, and the crowding effect enhanced by adding only an effects vector to the prediction equation. The effects vector represented the different institutions whose data were incorporated in the analyses. These effects vectors had nearly the same impact as adding the remaining variables discussed above.

Gaes and McGuire were similarly able to test Ellis's transiency hypothesis. Once again, crowding, not transiency, was the important factor. Prison administrators also view inmate turnover as an important determinant of violence. The common view is that inmate transfers are a way of handling management problems. Gaes and McGuire did not find any relationship between inmate transfer rates and prison violence.

The other important finding in the Gaes and McGuire study concerned the assessment of other aggregate crowding variables. These included the percentages of a prison's housing that were single cell, double cell, dormitory, or partitioned dormitory. In addition to the density ratio, the percentage of inmates housed in dormitories was also related to assault levels. These findings mean that a prison with an excessive number of inmates housed mostly in dormitories is particularly likely to have higher assault rates. In summary, crowding not age or transiency is the best predictor of assault rates.

V. Crowding and Recidivism

Whatever one's view of the purpose of incarceration, increased recidivism would be an undesired side effect of crowding. Ironically, a cycle of crowding and recidivism would be tantamount to releasing individuals from crowded prisons only to ensure their eventual return to the same or worse conditions.

The one study of crowding and recidivism was conducted by Farrington and Nuttal (1980). Their primary aim was to test the assumption that larger prisons are more susceptible to violence. As an ancillary issue, Farrington and Nuttal used a prison density ratio and correlated the measure with a derived effectiveness index. The effectiveness index was based on the difference between the predicted reconviction rate and the actual reconviction rate for each prison. The predicted reconviction rate was estimated in previous research based on the following set of predictors: offense type, number of previous commitments, interval of most recent arrest, age at first conviction, age, marital status, employment history, and living arrangements (note that crowding was not one of the variables). On the basis of these variables, each prison could be assessed a predicted recidivism rate.

Farrington and Nuttal found that the prisons in England and Wales with higher density ratios had lower effectiveness ratings. I have criticized this research on a number of bases (Gaes 1983): density may not be as important as other crowding measures; aggregate prediction of recidivism is unsatisfactory, because it overestimates individual relationships; the authors failed to control for variables other than crowding that might be the crucial determinants of reconviction. Farrington and Nuttal (1983) responded that most of the prisons they studied were constructed to house one inmate per cell, hence their density ratio was synonymous to other crowding measures. Since this was the case, their results may not be generalizable to the U.S. prison system in which 30–40 percent of prisoners are housed in multiple occupancy cells. Farrington and Nuttal also point out that they were not presenting their data as if individual reconviction rates could be ascertained.

Farrington and Nuttal reiterated that they controlled for other inmate and hence institutional characteristics by using their derived effectiveness measure. It is certainly reasonable to establish base rates for recidivism using criminal history and demographic variables and then to examine the contribution of crowding to the elevation or depression of these base rates.

This is not the same, however, as adjusting both the recidivism rates and the crowding levels by the criminal history and demographic variables. The advantage to this latter technique is that if crowding is representative of or related to these other controlling variables, then the effect of this relationship can go unnoticed in the analysis using the base-rate approach. To illustrate, suppose that the higher security prisons were the most crowded. Crowding would then be positively related to the criminal history variables. The relationship between recidivism and crowding might result from the higher recidivism rates of higher risk groups, and the crowding, recidivism relationship would be spurious.

The relationship between crowding and recidivism warrants further examination. The theoretical hypotheses should be spelled out. Does crowding interfere with otherwise salutary rehabilitative conditions? Does crowding intervene in the specific deterrent effects of prison, and in what manner? It would be curious if the otherwise harsh, punitive conditions of a prison, on which specific deterrence is based, would be ameliorated by crowding.

A second step would be to develop a methodology for assessing crowding and recidivism over time and among different prisons. The longitudinal data would allow inferences about crowding and recidivism both related and unrelated to differences among the institutions' inmate characteristics.

VI. Conclusions and an Agenda for Further Research
In this section, I review some of the major conclusions concerning the effects of prison crowding on which researchers are in substantial agreement, cite those findings which are tentative or over which there is disagreement, discuss the methodological and statistical limitations of

the extant research, briefly review the status of nonprison crowding literature, and propose an agenda for further systematic research including an alternative theoretical presumption for the role of the subjective experience of crowding.

A. The Effects of Prison Crowding

There are two basic conclusions warranted by the prison crowding research: dormitories are associated with higher illness complaint rates; and prisons that have higher density ratios are also more likely to have higher assault or misconduct rates.

Even if illness complaining is not indicative of differences in underlying sickness rates, the increased utilization rates present an administrative problem. This conclusion, however, is not strong enough to make prison crowding synonymous with cruel and unusual confinement conditions. The data cited by Cox et al. (1984), in which aggregate population measures were related to morbidity, mortality, and psychiatric commitment rates, are indicative of the presumed adverse effects of crowded confinement; however, other data do not support their conclusions.

Both the average age of the prison population and crowding density are related to inmate violence. Under certain measurement conditions (aggregate analysis, controlling for other population characteristics), crowding is much more influential than age composition, suggesting that age composition may be a proxy for other institutional characteristics.

B. Tentative Conclusions

It remains unclear whether the subjective perception of crowding is a necessary and sufficient condition of adverse crowding effects. This lack of clarity may be attributed to either the relative unimportance of the question or to the difficulty inherent in measuring a variable that is presumed to have an effect over time. There may be specific instances in which crowding effects are not mediated by subjective experience (for example, contagious disease transmission) and other instances where the effects depend on the subjective perception of crowding. Thus, it would appear that the significance of perceived crowding depends on the possible effect being investigated.

The limited data concerning spatial density in single-person cells or dormitories suggest that space is not as important as social density, with the constraint that this generalization applies to a range of between forty-three and eighty-eight square feet. Conclusions regarding the amount of space necessary under multiple occupancy conditions have not been addressed.

There is limited evidence that higher-density institutions may be associated with higher recidivism rates. Further analysis must be done to clarify the role of other influential variables.

C. Methodological and Statistical Limitations

The essential differences between prison crowding and other applied or experimental settings involve (1) the nature of the subject populations and (2) the relative differences in the harshness of the environments. One method of addressing the subject population differences is to assess crowdedness among probationers, parolees, and unconvicted people in a neighborhood density study while matching these subjects on socioeconomic status and race. It is much more difficult to isolate and assess the effect of environmental harshness on crowdedness. An indirect approach would be to compare the effect of crowding with that of other stressors in a prison, as is done in the medical sociology and medical psychology literatures on stressful life events. If the differences in applied settings can be overcome or adjusted for, then researchers can draw inferences from one setting to the other.

One way to bolster the perceived crowding analysis is to assess many different dimensions of subjective crowding simultaneously. The various inputs to perceived crowding in table 1 have never been scaled for their different weightings. Some of the imprecision in the perceived crowding-utilization relationship may result from measurement error in perceived crowding.

An additional difficulty for prison crowding research is that most research has involved smaller institutions and adverse crowding effects may be greatest in larger prisons. Most of the individual-level data on crowding have come from prisons with relatively smaller prison populations. The one major exception was Paulus et al. (1978). Crowding in small prisons may present fewer problems than crowding in large prisons; yet crowding in large prisons is rarely studied. Many large prisons are located in state systems that are reluctant to allow prison crowding research—in view of the abundance of suits against specific prisons or systems (Mullen and Smith 1980).

A methodological and analytical problem with most of the research has been the statistical approach adopted. Rather than consider many single indicators and different contrasts individually, a multiple indicator modeling approach (Joreskog and Sorbom 1983) may clear up some of the ambiguity.

D. Nonprison Crowding Research

There are three major bodies of human crowding research other than prison studies. The first is laboratory research among college students, the orientation mostly psychological. The second is crowding in applied settings among individuals. These studies are of relatively limited exposures (half an hour to several hours) or prolonged exposures such as in the household density literature. The research has been both psychological and sociological in orientation. The third body of research is the social areal analysis of crowding. These studies contrast aggregate relationships within social areas, such as census tracts, or neighborhoods, examining morbidity and age specific death rates in relation to crowding and sociodemographic factors.

The few credible generalizations that emerge from laboratory crowding research are not germane to prison crowding. A comprehensive theory of short- and long-term crowding might incorporate these laboratory results; however, such a theory is beyond the scope of this essay.

The most comprehensive and systematic crowding research has been the work on household density (Booth 1976; Baldassare 1979, 1981; Gove et al. 1979). Earlier versions were aggregate studies (Winsborough 1965; Schmitt 1966; Galle, Gove, and McPherson 1972; Levy and Herzog 1974; Freedman, Heshka, and Levy 1975a, 1975b; Manton and Myers 1977; Myers and Manton 1977), the results of which were inconsistent. The more recent household density studies employed a methodology in which individual household members were interviewed. In Booth's study (1976), subjects were also examined at a clinic where they were given diagnostic tests and a brief clinical evaluation. The crowding results of these studies are also inconsistent; however, as a group of studies they suggest two generalizations that are potentially applicable to prison crowding research: (1) crowding studies should assess the socioeconomic status and related variables of participants, and (2) crowding must be measured with multiple indicia for both objective and subjective scales.

Both Booth (1976) and Gove et al. (1979) have found that socioeconomic status contributes much more to the variation in crowding effects when crowding is also measured. Because crowding and socioeconomic status are often related, the researcher must adjust for this relationship. In prison studies, although socioeconomic status may not be as important a factor, certainly criminal history may be related to crowding, crowding history, and measures of debilitation.

"Crowding" may mean different things in different settings. Baldassare (1981) found that the demands on one's time and resources were key. Rather than restrict perceived crowding measurement to a simple Likert scale of "How crowded do you feel?" researchers must broaden their assessment by scaling other dimensions.

E. The Next Generation of Prison Crowding Research

Figures 1 and 2 list some of the variables necessary for a comprehensive analysis of prison crowding effects. There are two methodological prerequisites if some of the more important prison crowding questions are to be answered. The first is a study that assesses aggregate and individual crowding measures for the same subjects. This would allow inferences about the effects of both the inmate's immediate housing and the institution's composite crowding on the individual inmate. This will allow researchers to assess resource limitations as well as environmental effects on debilitation.

A second methodological issue is the assessment of effects longitudinally. A longitudinal design allows inferences about causal relationships that could not be made otherwise. If objective crowding, subjective crowding, and stress are assessed over time, researchers can isolate whether a causal stress relationship exists among these variables and criteria of debilitation.

A third issue, which is more conceptual than methodological, is the expansion of the currently limited number of crowding effect criteria to include other measures that prison administrators, judges, and crowding researchers would find meaningful. Figures 1 and 2 list some of these, including measures of inmate illness, psychological impairment, disease-specific suppression of the immune system, intellectual or motivational impairment, and the effects on staff's ability to meet inmate's needs. A related issue is the effect that institutional crowding has on staff's reactions reflected in their health, motivation, and safety.

A fourth issue has to do with another approach to the role of perceived crowding in the assumed causal relationship. If there were a functional relationship between social density and clinic utilization, contrasts that compare any higher-social-density housing unit with any lower-social-density housing unit should be uniformly significant with an occasional sampling error. This is not the case in tables 3–7. Sometimes double-occupant cells have higher utilization rates than singles;

very often they do not. Multiple-bunked rooms are sometimes higher than single- or multiple-bunked rooms with fewer occupants, but here again the data are inconsistent. In several cases in which there is a variety of housing available (singles, doubles, small dormitories, and large dormitories), dormitories have higher utilization rates than all other kinds of housing (McCain et al. 1980, site 4, site 5). One parsimonious explanation of these exceptions is that perceived crowding may be a social comparison process (Festinger 1954).

Social comparison theory describes the relative judgments an individual makes about his performance and abilities. Although the theory does not detail cognitive comparisons and appraisals, such as other social judgment theories (Hovland, Harvey, and Sherif 1957), it does incorporate the roles of other individuals in the judgments. Thus, an individual will make self-appraisals of his status, knowledge, or power by comparing his assets with those of others of similar potential. It follows from this reasoning that an inmate's subjective assessment and reaction to crowding is based on the relative housing conditions available. If only dormitories are available, some of which are double bunked, then the single bunked are perceived as less crowded. If double-bunked cells are added to this configuration, the dormitory comparisons are less important.

This suggests that below some level of severe overcrowding, there is no absolute level of social density associated with clinic utilization but that less favorable housing will have relatively higher clinic utilization rates. One possible test of this hypothesis can be conducted at an aggregate level of data. Prisons containing all dormitories or all rooms (singles or doubles) and a mixture of housing could be examined. If there is a systematic relationship between density and health, then prisons can be expected to be rank ordered on clinic utilization according to their social density arrangements. Prisons with all or mostly singles would be the lowest; those with mixtures of doubles, dormitories, and singles intermediate; and those with nearly all dormitories would be the highest on measures of health impairment. If a social comparison hypothesis is correct, institutions having all or mostly singles will have the same overall utilization rates as institutions with only dormitories or mixed varieties of housing. Among institutions with mixed varieties of housing, there will be higher clinic utilization in the less preferred units even though the absolute levels of clinic utilization will differ from institution to institution.

The implications of social comparison theory for individual measurement would require that the assessment of perceived crowding should focus on scales which contrast an inmate's housing relative to other housing available in his institution.

Finally, although the role of crowding in illness and violence etiology has been stressed in this essay and the prison crowding literature, crowding may be more important as a moderator or buffer variable rather than antecedent. In a prison setting this may be particularly true. There are many primary sources of stress in a prison. Among these are the separation from family, job, and friends; the loss of freedom; the dependence on prison staff for even the most mundane tasks; the cohabitation with inmates who for the most part are unfamiliar; and the potential danger (at least perceived if not actual) of assault or exploitation. Given these other sources of stress, crowding may act to exacerbate an already stressful environment; however, by itself crowding may not induce stress or stress-related pathology unless it occurs at extreme levels. This is very similar to Freedman's intensification theory of crowding with the restriction that crowding only exacerbates negative situations and the additional postulate that when crowding reaches some threshold it becomes a primary cause of pathology rather than merely an intensifier.

VII. Implications of Prison Crowding Research

There are issues that prison crowding research can and cannot address. Optimistically, prison crowding research can define the parameters of prison crowding (when and if crowding effects occur), the extent of debilitation, and the role of intervening variables that may allow intervention in the crowding, debilitation process. These data could be used to examine individual crowding suits and help administrators set standards. What prison crowding research cannot do is distinguish levels of risk associated with imprisonment from levels of risk that are considered cruel and unusual punishment. This latter determination falls under the auspices of the courts, the influence of legislators, and the conventional wisdom and morality of the community.

Paulus, McCain, and Cox (1981) have recommended that correctional institutions be limited to between five hundred and one thousand men, preferably the first. They have also recommended that the housing units consist solely of single rooms or cubicles. These recommendations are concordant with American Correctional Association Standards (1981). Under physical plant, the American Correctional Association lists the following standards: (1) five-hundred-man limitations on semiautonomous housing units (2-4127); (2) populations do not exceed rated bed capacity (2-4128); (3) one inmate per cell in cells designed for one inmate (2-4129); (4) the cell has a minimum of sixty square feet if confinement is less than ten hours and eighty square feet if more than ten hours (2-4129); (5) multiple occupancy cells are only allowed in minimum security institutions (2-4130); (6) multiple occupancy cells should house no fewer than three inmates and no more than fifty inmates (2-4131); (7) each inmate in multiple occupancy cells should have a minimum of fifty square feet (2-4132). These standards do not allow two inmates in single-person cells, nor do they call for partitions in open bay dormitories. It is strongly implied, though not specifically stated, that new institutions should not exceed a capacity of five hundred.

Given these criteria, in 1978 30–40 percent of all inmates housed in state and federal prisons were living in substandard housing. There were 411,800 inmates in housing designed for 256,500 (Mullen and Smith 1980). In that period, among federal and state prisons, there were from 2 percent (North Dakota) to 90 percent (Texas) of each system's inmates housed in dormitories. There are approximately 450,000 inmates in confinement in the United States, and increases in prison capacity have not matched population increases (Mullen and Smith 1980). If the standards concerning spatial and social density were completely and unequivocally enforced, drastic measures would have to be taken to reduce current prison populations.

It is a very different matter to show a statistical relationship between crowding and measures of debilitation, safety, and recidivism than to confront the moral question concerning the level of risk the courts or the community think is appropriate for a prison population. Most of the data gathered by Paulus, McCain, Cox, and Gaes on illness complaint rates are based on relatively nonvirulent symptoms such as colds, flu, lower back pain, and headaches. Some of these may be symptomatic of a more serious underlying problem or may lead to a serious disease. Similar risks are faced by men in the armed services (LaJolla Management Corporation 1981). The level of risk associated with higher levels of crowding is ambiguous based on the current research data.

Despite the highly publicized potential and actual effects of overcrowding, and the alarm signaled by the recent increases in the prison population, the prison crowding research itself is neither compelling nor specific. It is unfortunate that those conditions of crowding that are the most egregious have rarely been the focus of research endeavors.

REFERENCES

American Correctional Association. 1981. *Standards for Adult Correctional Institutions*. 2d ed. College Park, Md.: American Correctional Association.

Baldassare, M. 1979. *Residential Crowding in Urban America*. Los Angeles: University of California Press.

———. 1981. "The Effects of Household Density on Subgroups." *American Sociological Review* 46:110–18.

Baum, A., N. E. Grunberg, and J. E. Singer. 1982. "The Use of Psychological and Neuroendocrinological Measurements in the Study of Stress." *Health Psychology* 1(3):217–36.

Baum, A., and S. Valins. 1977. *Architecture and Social Behavior: Psychological Studies in Social Density*. Hillsdale, N.J.: Erlbaum.

Booth, A. 1976. *Urban Crowding and Its Consequences*. New York: Praeger.

Calhoun, J. B. 1962. "Population Density and Social Pathology." *Scientific American* 206(1):139–48.

Carr, T. S. 1980. "The Effects of Crowding on Recidivism, Cardiovascular Deaths, and Infraction Rates in a Large Prison System." Unpublished Ph.D. dissertation, Georgia State University.

Cohen, S. 1978. "Environmental Load and the Allocation of Attention." In *Advances in Environmental Psychology*, vol. 1, edited by A. Baum, J. Singer, and S. Valins. Hillsdale, N.J.: Erlbaum.

Cox, V. C., P. B. Paulus, G. McCain, and M. Karlovac. 1982. "The Relationship between Crowding and Health." In *Advances in Environmental Psychology*, vol. 4, edited by A. Baum and J. P. Singer. Hillsdale, N.J.: Erlbaum.

Cox, V. C., P. B. Paulus, and G. McCain. 1984. "Prison Crowding Research: The Relevance for Prison Housing Standards and a General Approach Regarding Crowding Phenomena." *American Psychologist*, in press.

D'Atri, D. A. 1975. "Psycho Physiological Responses to Crowding." *Environment and Behavior* 1:237–52.

D'Atri, D. A., E. F. Fitzgerald, S. V. Kasl, and A. M. Ostfeld. 1982. "Crowding in Prison: The Relationship between Changes in Housing Mode and Blood Pressure." *Journal of Psychosomatic Medicine* 43:95–105.

D'Atri, D. A., and A. Ostfeld. 1975. "Crowding: Its Effects on the Elevation of Blood Pressure in a Prison Setting." *Preventive Medicine* 4:550–66.

Dean, L. M., W. M. Pugh, and E. K. E. Gunderson. 1975. "Spatial and Perceptual Components of Crowding: Effects on Health and Satisfaction." *Environment and Behavior* 7(2):225–36.

———. 1978. "The Behavioral Effects of Crowding: Effects on Health and Satisfaction." *Environment and Behavior* 10(3):417–31.

Ekland-Olsen, S., D. Barrick, and L. E. Cohen. 1983. "Prison Overcrowding and Disciplinary Problems: An Analysis of the Texas Prison System." *Journal of Applied Behavioral Science* 19:163–76.

Ellis, D. 1982. "Crowding and Prison Violence: An Integration of Research and Theory." Unpublished manuscript. Toronto: York University.

Farrington, D. P., and C. P. Nuttal. 1980. "Prison Size, Overcrowding, Prison Violence, and Recidivism." *Journal of Criminal Justice* 8(4):221–31.

———. 1983. "Overcrowding and Recidivism: A Response to Gaes' Comment." *Journal of Criminal Justice* 11:268.

Festinger, L. 1954. "A Theory of Social Comparison Processes." *Human Relations* 7:117–40.

Finney, J. W., R. E. Mitchell, R. C. Cronkite, and R. H. Moos. 1984. "Methodological Issues in Estimating Main and Interactive Effects: Examples from Coping/Social Support and Stress Field." *Journal of Health and Social Behavior* 25(1):85–98.

Firebaugh, G. 1978. "A Rule for Inferring Individual-Level Relationships from Aggregate Data." *American Sociological Review* 43:557–72.

Freedman, J. L. 1975. *Crowding and Behavior.* San Francisco: W. H. Freeman.

Freedman, J. L., S. Heshka, and A. Levy. 1975a. "Crowding as an Intensifier of Pleasantness and Unpleasantness." (Abstract) In J. L. Freedman, *Crowding and Behavior.* San Francisco: W. H. Freeman.

———. 1975b. "Crowding as an Intensifier of the Effect of Success and Failure." Abstract. In J. L. Freedman, *Crowding and Behavior.* San Francisco: W. H. Freeman.

Gaes, G. G. 1982. "The Effect of Spatial and Architectural Housing Variations on Inmate Clinic Utilization Rates." Washington, D.C.: Office of Research, Federal Prison System.

———. "Farrington and Nuttal's 1983 'Overcrowding and Recidivism.' " *Journal of Criminal Justice* 11:265–67.

Gaes, G. G., and W. G. McGuire. 1984. "Prison Violence: Crowding versus Other Determinants of Prison Assault Rates." *Journal of Research in Crime and Delinquency*, in press.

Galle, O. R., W. R. Gove, and J. M. McPherson. 1972. "Population Density and Pathology: What Are the Relations for Man?" *Science* 176:23–30.

Gove, W. R., M. Hughes, and O. R. Galle. 1979. "Overcrowding in the Home: An Empirical Investigation of Its Possible Pathological Consequences." *American Sociological Review* 44:59–80.

Greenfeld, L. A. 1982. "Prison Population and Death Rates." Washington, D.C.: National Institute of Justice.

Hauser, R. M. 1970. "Context and Consex: A Cautionary Tale." *American Journal of Sociology* 75:645–64.

Hovland, C. J., O. J. Harvey, and M. Sherif. 1957. "Assimilation and Contrast Effects in Reaction to Communication and Attitude Change." *Journal of Abnormal Social Psychology* 55:244–52.

Jan, Lee-Jan. 1980. "Overcrowding and Inmate Behavior: Some Preliminary Findings." *Criminal Justice and Behavior* 7:293–301.

Joreskog, K. G., and D. Sorbom. 1983. *LISREL: Analysis of Linear Structural Relationships by the Method of Maximum Likelihood—Users Guide.* Chicago: National Education Resources.

King, L., and G. Geis. 1978. "Tuberculosis Transmission in a Large Urban Jail." *Journal of the American Medical Association* 237:790–93.

LaJolla Management Corporation. 1981. "Final Report: The Status of Health Care in the Federal Prison System." Washington, D.C.: Federal Prison Systems.

Lazarus, R. S. 1966. *Psychological Stress and the Coping Process.* New York: McGraw-Hill.

Lebowitz, H., and T. Pospichal. 1979. "Federal and State Inmate Deaths, 1972–1978." Unpublished manuscript. Washington, D.C.: Federal Bureau of Prisons.

Levy, L., and A. N. Herzog. 1974. "Effects of Population Density and Crowding on Health and Social Adaptation in the Netherlands." *Journal of Health and Social Behavior* 15:228–40.

Manton, K. G., and G. C. Myers. 1977. "The Structure of Urban Mortality: A Methodological Study of Hannover, Germany, Part II." *International Journal of Epidemiology* 6(3):213–23.

McCain, G., V. C. Cox, and P. B. Paulus. 1976. "The Relationship Between Illness Complaints and Degree of Crowding in a Prison Environment." *Environment and Behavior* 8(2):283–90.

———. 1980. "The Effect of Prison Crowding on Inmate Behavior." Washington, D.C.: Law Enforcement Assistance Agency.

McGurk, B. J., F. Graham, and A. W. McEwan. 1980. "An Abortive Attempt to Examine the Institutional Climates of Twenty-three British Prisons." London: Directorate of Psychological Services, Home Office.

Megargee, E. I. 1974. "Population Density and Disruptive Behavior in a Prison Setting." In *Experimental Behavior: A Basis for the Study of Mental Disturbance,* edited by J. H. Cullen. Dublin: Irish University Press.

Mullen, J., and B. Smith. 1980. *American Prisons and Jails.* Vol. 3: *Conditions and Costs of Confinement.* Cambridge, Mass.: Abt.

Myers, G. C., and K. G. Manton. 1977. "The Structure of Urban Mortality: A Methodological Study of Hannover, Germany, Part I." *International Journal of Epidemiology* 6(3):213–23.

Nacci, P. L., H. E. Teitelbaum, and J. Prather. 1977. "Population Density and Inmate Misconduct Rates." *Federal Probation* 41:26–31.

Paulus, P. B. "Crowding." 1980. In *Psychology of Group Influence.* Hillsdale, N.J.: Erlbaum.

Paulus, P. B., G. McCain, and V. C. Cox. 1978. "Death Rates, Psychiatric Commitments, Blood Pressure, and Perceived Crowding as a Function of Institutional Crowding." *Environmental Psychology and Nonverbal Behavior* 3(2):107–16.

———. 1981. "Prison Standards: Some Pertinent Data on Crowding." *Federal Probation* 45(4):48–54.

Rodin, J., and A. Baum. 1978. "Crowding and Helplessness: Potential Consequences of Density on Loss of Control." In *Human Responses to Crowding*, edited by A. Baum and J. M. Epstein. Hillsdale, N.J.: Erlbaum.

Rogers, M. P., D. Dubey, and P. Reich. 1979. "The Influence of the Psyche and the Brain on Immunity and Disease Susceptibility." *Psychosomatic Medicine* 41(21):147–63.

Ruback, R. B., and T. S. Carr. 1984. "Crowding in a Women's Prison: Attitudinal and behavioral effects." *Journal of Basic and Applied Psychology*, in press.

Saegert, S. 1978. "High Density Environments: Their Personal and Social Consequences." In *Human Responses to Crowding*, edited by A. Baum and J. M. Epstein. Hillsdale, N.J.: Erlbaum.

Seligman, M. 1975. *Helplessness*. San Francisco: W. H. Freeman.

Schopler, J. 1980. "A Study of Crowding Effects at Butner, FCI, Preliminary Report." Butner, N.C.: Federal Prison System.

Schopler, J. and J. E. Stockdale. 1977. "An Interference Analysis of Crowding." *Environmental Psychology and Non-verbal Behavior* 1:81–88.

Schmitt, R. C. 1966. "Density, Health and Social Disorganization." *American Institute of Planners Journal* 32(1):38–40.

Stockdale, J. E. 1978. "Crowding: Determinants and Effects." In *Advances in Experimental Social Psychology, Vol. II*, edited by L. Berkowitz. New York: Academic Press.

Stokols, D. 1972. "On the Distinction between Density and Crowding: Some Implications for Future Research." *Psychological Review* 79(3):275–77.

———. 1978. "A Typology of Crowding Experiences." In *Human Responses to Crowding*, edited by A. Baum and J. M. Epstein. Hillsdale, N.J.: Erlbaum.

Sundstorm, E. 1978. "Crowding as a Sequential Process: Review of Research on the Effects of Population Density on Humans." In *Human Responses to Crowding*, edited by A. Baum and J. M. Epstein. Hillsdale, N.J.: Erlbaum.

Tessler, R., and D. Mechanic. 1978. "Psychological Distress and Perceived Health Status." *Journal of Health and Social Behavior* 19:254–62.

Twaddle, A. C. 1976. "Utilization of Medical Services by a Captive Population: An Analysis of Sick Call in a State Prison." *Journal of Health and Social Behavior* 17:236–48.

U.S. Department of Health and Human Services. 1981. *Current Estimates from the National Health Interview Survey, United States, 1980*. Hyattsville, Md.: National Center for Health Statistics, Office of Health Research, Statistics, and Technology, Public Health Service.

Walker, B., and T. Gordon. 1980. "Health and High Density Confinement in Jails and Prisons." *Federal Probation* 44:53–58.

Wener, R., and C. Keys. 1984. "The Effect of Changes in Jail Densities on Perceived Crowding, Spatial Behavior and Sick Call: Absolute and Contrast Effects." New York: Polytechnic Institute of New York.

Winsborough, H. 1965. "The Social Consequences of High Population Density." *Law and Contemporary Problems* 30:120–26.

Ronald V. Clarke and Derek B. Cornish

Modeling Offenders' Decisions: A Framework for Research and Policy

ABSTRACT

Developments in a number of academic disciplines—the sociology of deviance, criminology, economics, psychology—suggest that it is useful to see criminal behavior not as the result of psychologically and socially determined dispositions to offend, but as the outcome of the offender's broadly rational choices and decisions. This perspective provides a basis for devising models of criminal behavior that (1) offer frameworks within which to locate existing research, (2) suggest directions for new research, (3) facilitate analysis of existing policy, and (4) help to identify potentially fruitful policy initiatives. Such models need not offer comprehensive explanations; they may be limited and incomplete, yet still be "good enough" to achieve these important policy and research purposes. To meet this criterion they need to be specific to particular forms of crime, and they need separately to describe both the processes of involvement in crime and the decisions surrounding the commission of the offense itself. Developing models that are crime specific and that take due account of rationality will also demand more knowledge about the ways in which offenders process and evaluate relevant information. Such a decision perspective appears to have most immediate payoff for crime control efforts aimed at reducing criminal opportunity.

Most theories about criminal behavior have tended to ignore the offender's decision making—the conscious thought processes that give purpose to and justify conduct, and the underlying cognitive mechanisms by which information about the world is selected, attended to, and processed. The source of this neglect is the apparent conflict between

Ronald Clarke was until recently Head of the Home Office Research and Planning Unit and is now Professor of Criminal Justice, Temple University. Derek Cornish is Lecturer in Psychology in the Department of Social Science and Administration, London School of Economics.

decision-making concepts and the prevailing determinism of most criminological theories. Whether framed in terms of social or psychological factors, these theories have traditionally been concerned to explain the criminal dispositions of particular individuals or groups. More recently, faced with the need to explain not just the genesis of people's involvement in crime but also the occurrence of particular criminal acts, greater attention has been paid by theory to the immediate environmental context of offending. But the resulting accounts of criminal behavior have still tended to suggest deterministic models in which the criminal appears as a relatively passive figure; thus he or she is seen either as prey to internal or external forces outside personal control, or as the battlefield upon which these forces resolve their struggle for the control of behavioral outcomes.

A number of developments, however, have combined to question the adequacy of explanations or models of offending that do not take account of the offender's perceptions and thought processes. Interest in the criminal's view of his world—characteristic of the "Chicago School" of sociology—revived during the early 1960s within the sociology of deviance that was beginning to stress the importance of developing an understanding of the offender's perspective. In mainstream criminology a similar revival of interest was also fueled by the apparent failure of the rehabilitative ideal—and hence, many argued, of deterministic approaches to criminological explanation. Disenchantment with treatment also shifted attention and resources to other means of crime control, such as incapacitation, deterrence, and environmental approaches to crime prevention; and it became apparent that offenders' perceptions might be salient to the success of these alternatives. As a result, interest grew in the 1970s in ecological studies of criminal activity, in criminal life histories, in cohort studies of criminal careers, and in offenders' accounts of how they went about their activities. At the same time, other academic disciplines such as economics and psychology were exploring, and in some cases applying to criminological problems, concepts and models of information processing and decision making.

Despite the vigor with which these diverse developments have been pursued, little serious attempt has been made to synthesize them; in particular, no concerted attempt has been made to draw out their implications for thinking about crime control policies. This may not be surprising given that most sociologists of deviance—whose theoretical concerns most directly corresponded to those of criminologists—had repudiated criminology's crime control goals (see Sparks 1980). And the antideterministic rhetoric that accompanied the explorations of deviancy sociologists, to say nothing of the ideological climate within which their studies tended to be conducted, further limited the impact both of methodologies and findings on mainstream criminology.

This essay reviews these developments primarily from the standpoint of their possible contribution to crime control policies. This might seem unnecessarily and even harmfully restrictive, but a narrowing of focus can sometimes be an advantage in policy-relevant research. When describing the long-term development of the Home Office Research Unit's program of crime control research, we have argued (Clarke and Cornish 1983) that simple and parsimonious accounts of criminal behavior—such as those provided by dispositional or situational theories—can have considerable heuristic value. They do not have to be "complete" explanations of criminal conduct, but only ones "good enough" to accommodate existing research and to suggest new directions for empirical enquiry or crime control policy. As soon as they no longer serve these ends they should be modified or discarded. We illustrated our argument by tracing the successive development of (i) dispositional theories "good enough" to guide research into treatment effectiveness; (ii) "environmental/learning" theories that accounted for the principal findings of the treatment research (that under the powerful influence of the contemporary environment the effects of intervention tend to dissipate rapidly); (iii) "situational" accounts that were developed from the environmental/learning perspective in order to guide the direction of research into crime prevention; and (iv) rudimentary "choice" theories that were developed to provide a means of understanding crime displacement (which is often the result of situational crime prevention measures).

It is with the enhancement and refinement of rational choice models of crime, made necessary by the recent growth of research interest documented below, that this essay is concerned. Section I documents the convergence of interest among a variety of academic disciplines—the sociology of deviance, criminology, economics, and cognitive psychology—upon a conception of crime as the outcome of rational choices and decisions. A brief and selective review is undertaken of each discipline's major contributions to the notion of crime as the outcome of rational choices—the intention being to provide a flavor of each approach and a summary of what seem to be its main limitations. Section II outlines the main requirements of decision models, temporarily "good enough" to explain the processes of criminal involvement (initial involvement, continuance, and desistance) and the occurrence of criminal events. In essence, these models are flowchart diagrams that identify the main decision points and set out the groups of factors bearing upon the decisions made. For reasons that we discuss, decision models need to be specific to particular kinds of crime, and we have chosen to illustrate the construction of such models with the example of residential burglary. In conclusion, Section III discusses the implications of the decision models for ways of thinking about crime control policies and associated research efforts.

I. Relevant Concepts

The following discussion of research relevant to the rationality of offending is couched in the form of brief reviews—and even briefer critiques—of the contributions made by each of the disciplines concerned. The reviews are intended to illustrate the confluence of interest in rationality and to provide the material for the synthesis of concepts and findings attempted in Section II.

A. Sociology of Deviance

In contrast to most earlier sociological formulations, the "deviancy theories" that were developed in the 1960s explicitly emphasized the cultural relativity of definitions of delinquency, the relationship between social control and the distribution of political and economic power in society, and the need to appreciate the meaning of deviance from the actor's perspective. Of greater relevance for our purposes, these theories also explicitly rejected deterministic and pathological explanations of crime in favor of those emphasizing its purposive, rational, and mundane aspects (see Taylor, Walton, and Young 1973; Box 1981)—concerns also shared by much previous oral history research (Bennett 1981). For example, Taylor et al. asserted that ". . . a social theory must have reference to men's teleology—their purposes, their beliefs and the context in which they act out these purposes and beliefs. . . . Thus men rob banks because they believe they may enrich themselves, not because something biologically propels them through the door . . ." (p. 61).

A substantial body of ethnographic work illustrates and supports many of the tenets of deviancy sociology. The following examples relate to the rational, largely nonpathological, and commonplace nature of much crime and illustrate how it is accommodated in the individual's day-to-day life:

i) Howard Becker's (1963) observation—based on his studies of marijuana use among jazz musicians in the 1950s—that deviants frequently see their conduct as a rational and obvious response to the pressures and opportunities of their particular circumstances. They may come to this position in a series of rationalizing "private conversations" in which they reconcile public and private morality. To justify their conduct, they may make use of "techniques of neutralization" (Matza 1964; Sheley 1980) such as: "everyone else does it"; "I am only borrowing it"; "he shouldn't have started it," and so on.

ii) Evidence from the life histories of individual offenders that criminal involvement is frequently initiated by relatives, friends, or acquaintances, and hence that the drift into crime is seen as unremarkable and almost natural (Samuel 1981); that legal and illegal ways of earning a living are not necessarily in conflict and may even be complementary (Klockars 1974; Prus and Irini 1980; Maguire 1982); that offenders frequently develop an increasingly more sophisticated and businesslike approach to crime (Shover 1972); and that certain forms of crime, such as bank robbery or truck hijacking, provide both the excitement and the large sums of money that are requirements of "life in the fast lane" (Gibbs and Shelly 1982).

iii) Documentation from participant-observation research that in many (if not most) occupational groups, such as waiters (Henry 1978), bread roundsmen (Ditton 1977), and dockworkers (Mars 1974), pilfering and cheating are commonplace and are largely accepted by managers and workers alike as legitimate perquisites. Indeed, as Denzin (1977) suggests in his case study of the American liquor industry, illegal activity may be routine, institutionalized, and essential to the satisfactory performance of the industry.

iv) Evidence that offenders may decide that the risks of continued criminal behavior are not justified by the rewards: among Parker's (1974) group of adolescents many gave up shoplifting and opportunistic theft of car radios when, as a consequence of increased police activity, some of their number were apprehended and placed in custody. West's (1978) study of the careers of young thieves provides similar evidence of the rational nature of decisions to desist.

v) Matza's (1964) observation that much delinquency is "episodic"— that individuals choose to engage in delinquency at certain times but not at others; that "manufacture of excitement" provides the reason for much adolescent delinquency; and that much offending is of a petty, everyday, even "mundane" character. Similarly, Humphreys's (1970) findings showed that even behavior commonly viewed as patho-logical—casual homosexual encounters in public lavatories—often rep-resents clearly encapsulated episodes within essentially normal hetero-sexual and "respectable" life-styles.

vi) The observation made by Cohen (1972) in his study of clashes between groups of "mods" and "rockers" and by Marsh, Rosser, and Harre (1978) in their studies of football hooliganism, that much of the "uncontrollable" violence between rival gangs of youths is highly ritualized; it rarely causes serious injury and is calculated to produce maximum effect upon onlookers.

vii) Evidence from interviews with offenders convicted of serious violence (Athens 1980; Felson and Steadman 1983) that many appar-ently unpremeditated or impulsive acts of violence are in fact the result of intentions formed during a sequence of confrontations between of-fender and victim immediately prior to the incident or sometimes even days or weeks beforehand.

While deviancy theory has generated a mass of suggestive data on the perspectives, attitudes, and life-styles of offenders, its limitations in terms of the crime control orientation of this discussion stem from three of its fundamental premises—the deliberate eschewal of the test of immediate practical or policy relevance, the belief that individuals are in a position to provide comprehensive and valid accounts of the rea-sons for their behavior, and the rejection of more quantitative and controlled methods of data collection. The end result is that although the ideas produced may provide valuable insights and hypotheses, their validity and generalizability are frequently suspect.

B. *Criminology*

The past two decades have seen a great expansion of criminological research—largely the result of direct funding by governments—and a marked change in the topics investigated. General disillusion with the rehabilitative ideal and criticisms of the determinism of mainstream criminology, especially in Britain, meant that credence was once more given to "classical" views about crime that emphasized the offender's own responsibility for his conduct. This has been reflected in the reaffirmation of the importance of such sentencing principles as just desert and due process for juvenile offenders, as well as an increased interest in deterrent sentencing and incapacitation. And in response to the same disappointment with rehabilitation, criminologists began to explore methods of prevention focused not upon the offender's inner personality but on the immediate circumstances surrounding the offense. Improved understanding was sought about the rewards of crime, the relationship between criminal opportunities and crime, and the ways in which crime becomes part of the offender's everyday life. Some of the themes of these new lines of research can be grouped together as follows:

i) The findings of *longitudinal cohort studies* (e.g., Wolfgang, Figlio, and Sellin 1972; Petersilia 1980; West 1982) that, while large proportions of boys in any age group may commit acts of delinquency, most even of the more persistent offenders appear to desist from crime as they reach their late teens or twenties. This may be because they decide that continued criminality is incompatible with the demands of holding a full-time job or settling down to marriage and a family (see Greenberg 1977; Trasler 1979)—or for some it may represent a shift from "street crime" to occupational deviance.

ii) Recent research in the *ecological* tradition that has inferred from the distribution of particular crimes that offenders make rational choices. For example, on the basis of findings that it is the homes on the borderlines of affluent districts that are at most risk of burglary, Brantingham and Brantingham (1975) suggested that burglars preying on such districts will select the nearest of the suitable targets because escape may be easier and because they prefer to operate where they feel least conspicuous. Similar considerations of reducing risk and effort, minimizing inconvenience, and trading on familiarity explain other findings about the ecology of crime, such as that juvenile offenders seldom stray far from their immediate neighborhoods (e.g., Downes 1966); that crimes tend to be committed en route between an offender's place of residence and his habitual place of work or leisure (Rengert and Wasilchick 1980); that offenses tend to cluster along main roads (Fink 1969; Luedtke and Associates 1970; Wilcox 1974); that neighborhoods with easily understandable "grid" layouts tend to have higher rates of victimization than those with more "organic" street layouts, that is, with winding avenues, culs-de-sac, or crescents (Bevis and Nutter 1977); and that offenders' "images of the city"—their familiarity with its different parts or their perception of the differential ease or rewards of offending—correspond with observed crime patterns (Carter and Hill 1979).

iii) *Crime-specific* studies of burglary (Scarr 1973; Reppetto 1974; Waller and Okihiro 1978; Walsh 1980; Maguire 1982; Winchester and Jackson 1982), vandalism (Ley and Cybrinwsky 1974; Clarke 1978), and shoplifting (Walsh 1978), which have shown that the vulnerability of particular targets can be explained largely on the basis of factors such as ease of opportunity, low risk, and high gain. For example, Winchester and Jackson (1982) found in their study of burglary in Southeast England that the most important factors determining victimization were the apparent rewards, the chances that the house was occupied, and the siting of the building, which either facilitated or restricted access. Thus they found that houses standing in their own grounds were much more likely to be burglarized than ones in the middle of a terrace. Waller and Okihiro (1978) and Reppetto (1974) found that apartment blocks given protection by a doorman had particularly low levels of burglary. Shoplifters are more likely to operate in large self-service stores where it is easy to steal, and which provide a more impersonal target (Walsh 1978). As for vandalism, the targets are more likely to be public property such as telephone kiosks or bus shelters (Sturman 1978) or private property that has been abandoned or left in a state of disrepair (Ley and Cybrinwsky 1974). In other words, vandals appear to choose targets that are afforded less protection or (perhaps) where repair will not cause individual owners too much hardship.

iv) These findings from crime-specific studies about target vulnerability are complemented by information obtained from offenders themselves. For example, *interviews* with convicted burglars by Reppetto (1974), Waller and Okihiro (1978), Walsh (1980), Maguire (1982), and Bennett and Wright (1983, 1984) confirm that, the decision having been made about the locality in which to commit burglary, the choice of the particular house is made on judgments of the likelihood of its being occupied and the difficulty of entering without being seen. And interviews with muggers (Lejeune 1977) have shown that victims are chosen as being unlikely to resist while yielding an acceptable payoff.

v) Studies of the *opportunity structure* for crime have shown that fluctuations in levels of offending reflect the supply of available opportunities. This has been demonstrated for auto crime by Wilkins (1964), Gould (1969), and Mansfield, Gould, and Namenwirth (1974) and for residential burglary by Cohen and Felson (1979). The latter mounted a persuasive case for regarding increases in burglary as the outcome of the increased portability of electronic goods and of an increase in numbers of unoccupied houses as more women go out to work.

vi) *Crime prevention experiments* have shown for a wide variety of offenses (including vandalism, car theft, football hooliganism, aircraft hijacking, and theft or robbery on public transport) that reducing opportunities or increasing risks through environmental management and design can achieve reductions in the incidence of crime (see Clarke 1983). In many cases offenders appear to decide that the risks and effort of offending are no longer worthwhile. For example, few of the motorists prevented from using illegal "slugs" in a particular district of New York by the installation of redesigned meters are likely to have parked their cars in some other more distant place so as to save a few pennies (Decker 1972). In other cases, reduction of opportunities has simply displaced the attention of offenders to some other time, place, or target of crime (see Reppetto 1976). For instance, the introduction of steering-column locks on all new cars from 1971 onward did not produce the expected immediate reduction of car thefts in England and Wales—because most car theft is for temporary use, offenders simply turned their attention to unprotected pre-1971 models (Mayhew et al. 1976).

These various strands of research provide much useful information about offenders' decision making, but they have been pursued too much in isolation from each other and without the benefit of a coherent theoretical perspective. The decision-making concepts employed have been derived from common sense or culled from the unsystematic accounts of offenders. In consequence the relevance of the research for policy is limited. For example, the concept of displacement—of central importance for policy-making—has not been disassociated from its theoretical origins as the outcome of powerful internal drives toward criminality. This has meant that much, perhaps undue, skepticism has been expressed about the value of situational crime prevention. But it is not difficult to see how displacement could be accommodated within a decision-making framework (i.e., as the outcome of choices and decisions made by the offender in the face of changed circumstances) and how this might give a better basis for advocating the reduction of criminal opportunities.

C. Economics

As with recent work in the sociology of deviance and criminology, developments in the economic analysis of criminal behavior have tended to revive some of the concerns of classical criminology. Located in the utilitarian tradition of Beccaria and Bentham, these approaches argue that individuals, whether criminal or not, share in common the properties of being active, rational decision makers who respond to incentives and deterrents. In Gary Becker's words, "a useful theory of criminal behavior can dispense with special theories of anomie, psychological inadequacies, or inheritance of special traits and simply extend the economist's usual analysis of choice" (1968, p. 170).

In contrast to classical economic and criminological theories, however, the new economic formulations take account of the existence and influence of a restricted number of potential individual differences (see Ehrlich's [1979] discussion of the role of "preferences" and Cook's [1980] discussion of subjective evaluation). The economists' emphasis on the importance of the concepts of rewards and costs and their associated probabilities has much in common with the accounts of behavioral psychology. Where economic models depart radically from behavioral ones is in their stress on the importance of the concept of choice.

To chart the various economic models of criminal behavior and the econometric studies to which these models have given rise is outside the purpose of this brief review (but see Palmer 1977; Orsagh and Witte 1981; Freeman 1983; Orsagh 1983; Pyle 1983), as is the extension of economists' interests into the fields of resource allocation by law enforcement agencies (Pyle 1983) or the development of complex mathematical models to study criminal justice decision making (Garber, Klepper, and Nagin 1983; Klepper, Nagin, and Tierney 1983). The relevance of economic models of rational choice to the present discussion may be summarized as follows:

i) Whatever their current limitations, economic models of criminal decision making effectively demystify and routinize criminal activity. Crime is assumed a priori to involve rational calculation and is viewed essentially as an economic transaction or a question of occupational choice—a view compatible with many of the recent sociological and criminological studies of crime as work (e.g., Letkemann 1973; Inciardi 1975; Akerstrom 1983; Waldo 1983). In the same way, phenomena such as displacement or recidivism can be provided with economic rationales as alternatives to explanations that emphasize offender pathology (see, e.g., Furlong and Mehay's [1981] econometric study of crime spillover).

ii) Such economic models are currently extending their analysis beyond crimes motivated predominantly by financial gain. Thus, attempts are being made to find room for nonpecuniary gains as a component of expected utilities (through their translation into monetary equivalents) and to suggest models for so-called expressive crimes—

such as those involving violence to the person (Ehrlich 1979)—which emphasize their responsiveness to incentives and deterrents.

iii) Economic models suggest that law enforcement agencies are justified in proceeding on the basis that criminals are deterrable; thus they both provide some grounds for optimism and suggest a range of factors (beyond traditional deterrence theory's preoccupation with certainty and severity of punishment) which might be manipulated in the interests of crime control. These include, for example, the potential rewards of crime and the degree of effort required. Similarly, exploration of the relationship between unemployment and crime (Orsagh and Witte 1981; Freeman 1983) also provides some economic rationale for rehabilitative programs designed to improve offenders' prospects of legitimate work.

Despite the welcome rigor these contributions have brought to criminological theorizing and to the evaluation of policy, there are a number of problems that for the purposes of the current discussion limit the usefulness of existing economic models of criminal decision making. A variety of economic models have recently been proposed (e.g., Heineke 1978; Orsagh and Witte 1981), which recognize the need to include individual differences, but they have generated little empirically based micro analysis of individual criminal behavior. Some attempts to study such models using individual-level data have recently been made (e.g., Witte 1980; Ghali 1982). But it remains the case that, as Manski (1978) pointed out, economic modelers seem largely unaware of the growing empirical data on criminal behavior from other disciplines; they continue to produce theoretical accounts of individual choice behavior which "are too idealized and abstract from too much of the criminal decision problem to serve as useful bases for empirical work" (p. 90). Where empirical investigations are undertaken they tend to be macro analyses using aggregated crime data; and the interaction between micro analysis (uninformed by empirical data) and macro analysis (using imperfect and inadequate data, and uninformed by relevant information about the bases of individual criminal decision making) may be impoverishing both efforts.

These criticisms suggest that current economic models have yet to achieve satisfactory accounts of the bases upon which individual criminals actually make choices, and that they may also underplay individual differences in information-processing capacities and strategies (Cook 1980). The question whether the increasingly sophisticated empirical research on deterrence using aggregated data provides a valid means of monitoring the effectiveness of criminal justice policy lies outside this discussion (but see Pyle 1983). So far as the development and evaluation of more specific crime prevention and control policies in relation to particular offenders and offenses is concerned, however, it may be that this requires the investigation of actual decision processes rather than the further elaboration, in isolation, of a priori models. In this connection it is interesting to note that, as a result of their review of empirical economic studies using aggregate and individual-level data, Orsagh and Witte (1981) remarked that the relationship between economic viability and crime might vary with the type of crime and the individual involved. Such comments indicate the pressing need for further empirical data, such as those provided by Holzman's (1983) study of labor force participation among robbers and burglars, to clarify these issues and to encourage the construction of narrow-band empirically informed models.

D. Cognitive Psychology

With the few exceptions noted below, a considerable body of recent psychological research on information processing and decision making has passed largely unnoticed by criminologists. The impetus for this work, which itself contributed to criminological theory, should be briefly mentioned. During the 1960s, many psychologists were becoming disenchanted with the concepts of personality traits and predispositions as determinants of behavior; more attractive was the suggestion of radical behaviorism that the most important influences in relation to criminal behavior (reinforcements and punishments) lay outside the organism. This approach, which has some similarity to economic theories of crime, emphasized the importance not only of incentives and deterrents but also of current situational cues and opportunities. This latter emphasis became a primary influence on British studies of situational crime prevention (Mayhew et al. 1976), the further development of which drew attention to the need for a fuller understanding of criminal decisions (see Clarke and Cornish 1983).

Within academic psychology, the reaction during the last decade against the environmental determinism of radical behaviorism has led to an increasing recognition of the important role played by cognitive processes. This can be seen in the development of more sophisticated "social learning" theories (Bandura 1969, 1977) that stressed additional mechanisms of learning, such as imitation (which required the assumption of symbolic mediational cognitive processes), and reintroduced person variables in the guise of cognitive competencies and capacities (Mischel 1973, 1979). Several attempts to apply selected social learning concepts to an analysis of criminal behavior have been made (e.g., Akers 1977; Feldman 1977; Conger 1978).

It is not in respect of social learning theory alone, however, that developments of direct relevance to an understanding of criminal decision making have occurred. Studies of the professional judgments of clinicians and similar personnel concerning risky decision making, and of information-processing strategies in decision making, provide their relevant insights and analogies. The contributions itemized below relate as much to the methods and concepts as to substantive findings in this area:

i) Psychological studies of professional judgments made in clinical and similar settings have for a long while suggested that even experts often handle information in less than perfectly rational or efficient ways (Meehl 1954; Wilkins and Chandler 1965; Wiggins 1973).

ii) These findings received further support from early studies of risky decision making (see Kozielecki [1982] for a review) which suggested that people did not always behave in accordance with economic models of the rational, efficient decision maker—they frequently failed to make decisions that were objectively the "best" (Cornish 1978). An attempt to apply one such model (the subjective expected utility model) to an experimental study of the factors involved in juveniles' decisions about committing hypothetical crimes is reported by Cimler and Beach (1981).

iii) Some of the reasons for the failure of a priori models to explain decision making were identified by Slovic and Lichtenstein (1968). They suggested that real-life decision makers might be led to pay selective attention to certain risk dimensions over others by reason of their "importance-beliefs"—notions derived from past experience, logical analysis of the decision task, or even quite irrational fears and prejudices.

iv) These conclusions led naturally to an increased emphasis upon information-processing models and strategies in relation to real-life decision making (see Cornish [1978] on gambling; Carroll [1982] on criminal behavior). "Process tracing"—a technique for studying decision making as it actually occurs in natural settings by asking subjects to think aloud about the decision task (Kleinmuntz 1968)—has recently been applied to the investigation of offending decisions by Carroll and Herz (1981) and Bennett and Wright (1983).

v) Payne (1980) has suggested that more attention should be paid to the characteristics of the decision maker as information processor and their effect on the handling of choice problems. Warr and Knapper's (1968) model for person perception emphasizes the effects on information processing of the perceiver's stable personal characteristics, of ephemeral moods, previous experiences, and expectations, and of the decision rules employed by the decision maker's "processing centre." Crucial to the operations involved might be Slovic and Lichtenstein's "importance-beliefs," Cook's (1980) "standing decisions," and the wider concept of "knowledge structures" used by Nisbett and Ross (1980).

vi) An emphasis on decision rules suggested that inferential "rules-of-thumb" are universally employed in order to enable decision making to proceed rapidly and effectively. Some of these judgmental heuristics (Tversky and Kahneman 1974; Kahneman, Slovic, and Tversky 1982) can lead to error: for example, too much attention may be paid to information that is readily available or recently presented, and inductive rules may be too quickly formulated on the basis of unrepresentative data.

vii) Finally, it appears that the riskiness of an individual's decisions may vary according to whether the decision is made alone, or as a group member. Early studies had suggested that group decision making tended to be more "risky"; hence the phenomenon was termed "risky-shift" (Pruitt 1971). Recent reviews (Myers and Lamm 1976), however, suggest a more complex picture in which group decisions may also become more cautious under certain conditions.

The facts that people do not always make the most "rational" decisions, that they may pay undue attention to less important information, that they employ shortcuts in the processing of information, and that group decisions may be different from individual ones are all clearly relevant to an understanding of criminal decision making. But cognitive psychology is still at an early stage in its development and the topics studied so far are not necessarily those that best illuminate criminal decision making. For example, there has been perhaps too much concentration upon bias and error in information processing (see Nisbett and Ross 1980), whereas, in fact, the judgmental heuristics involved usually enable individuals to cope economically and swiftly with very complex tasks (Bruner, Goodnow, and Austin 1956)—a process Simon

(1983) has termed "bounded rationality." And there are some other basic issues, perhaps of particular relevance to crime control policies, which have scarcely been addressed by the discipline. These include the extent to which cognitive strategies are produced consciously or unconsciously, the degree to which they are under the individual's own control, whether they indicate a predisposition to process information in a certain manner or merely a preference for doing so, and the extent to which individuals differ in their information-processing capacities and competencies.

Finally, of special relevance to the present discussion, the question has not properly been considered whether those individuals who habitually make criminal decisions think in different ways from other people. This, in fact, is the claim made by Yochelson and Samenow (1976) on the basis of detailed clinical interviews with 240 criminals, most of whom had been detained in hospital as a result of being found guilty by reason of insanity. Yochelson and Samenow believe that criminals *choose* specific thinking patterns—of which they identify fifty-two characteristic modes including suspiciousness, self-seeking, manipulativeness, impulsiveness, concrete and compartmentalized thinking, and excitement or sensation seeking—which inevitably lead to crime. Such thought patterns, while internally logical, consistent, and hence "rational" to the offender, may be regarded as both irresponsible and irrational by the noncriminal.

Many methodological criticisms have been made of Yochelson and Samenow's work (e.g., Burchard 1977; Jacoby 1977; Nietzel 1979; Sarbin 1979; Vold 1979), but it remains true that the thinking patterns identified have much in common with many of the concepts reviewed above, that is, with individual information-processing styles and strategies and with motivational and cognitive biases. Moreover, they reflect themes commonly encountered in criminal life histories (Hampson 1982) such as the offender's preoccupation with maintaining "machismo" and with "techniques of neutralization." This further reinforces the point that a full (and policy-relevant) understanding of the processes of criminal decision making will not be gained through studies of "normal" decision making alone.

II. Models of Criminal Decision Making

Even allowing for some selective perception on our part, we believe that the material in Section I demonstrates that during the past decade there has been a notable confluence of interest in the rational choice, nondeterministic view of crime. This is a natural perspective for law and economics, but it has also achieved wide currency in criminology's other parent disciplines—sociology and psychology—as well as within the different schools of criminology itself. That the shift is part of a broader intellectual movement is suggested by the increasing popularity of economic and rational choice analyses of behaviors other than crime. Why there should be this movement at the present time and what social forces and events might be implicated is difficult to say, but cross-fertilization of ideas between different groups of people working on similar problems always occurs, and certain individuals have deliberately applied the same theoretical perspective to a variety of different problems. For instance, Gary Becker (1968) pioneered his economic analyses of crime when dealing with the economics of discrimination and has since extended his method to choice of marriage partner (Becker 1973, 1974).

Despite the shift of interest described above, there has been little attempt to construct a synthesis—within a rational choice framework—of the concepts and findings provided by the various approaches. As an illustration of the value of such a synthesis, it is worth making brief reference to the approach adopted by one of us in a review of the research on the determinants of gambling behavior (Cornish 1978). While not adopting so explicit a decision-making orientation, the review made similar use of concepts from sociology, psychology, and economics as a basis for analyzing existing control measures and for suggesting future directions for policy and research. It recognized, first, the importance of rational though not exclusively economic considerations when explaining a behavior commonly regarded as being pathologically motivated; second, the need to treat gambling, not as a unitary form of behavior, but as a collection of disparate behaviors each with their own distinctive features; third, and as a corollary, the need to pay close attention to situational factors relating to the gambling "event"; fourth, the need to develop explanations of gambling behavior which would make specific reference to factors determining, respectively, likelihood and degree of involvement; fifth, the role of learning in the development of heavy involvement in certain forms of gambling; and last, the scope for both exploiting and controlling gambling behavior through manipulation of people's information-processing activities.

The models of crime presented below also offer a way of synthesizing a diverse range of concepts and findings for the purpose of guiding policy and research, but they are developed within the context of much more explicit decision making. They are not models in which relationships are expressed either in mathematical terms (as in, e.g., economic models) or in the form of testable propositions (see, e.g., Brantingham and Brantingham's [1978] model of target selection). Nor are they even "decision trees" that attempt to model the successive steps in a complex decision process (see Walsh [1980] for an example relating to burglary). Rather, they are schematic representations of the key decision points in criminal behavior and of the various social, psychological, and environmental factors bearing on the decisions reached. Our models resemble most closely the kind of flow diagrams frequently employed to represent complex social processes—for example, the explanatory models for fear of crime developed by Skogan and Maxfield (1981) and for victimization proneness by Hindelang, Gottfredson, and Garofalo (1978).

The models, which need to be separately developed for each specific form of crime, are not theories in themselves but rather the blueprints for theory. They owe much to early attempts to model aspects of criminal decision making by Brantingham and Brantingham (1978), Brown and Altman (1981), and Walsh (1978, 1980). But these earlier models were largely confined to just one of the criminal decision processes—target selection—and they also depended upon a common-sense explication of the likely decision steps taken by the "rational" criminal. Our models are concerned not just with the decision to commit a particular crime, but also with decisions relating to criminal "readiness" or involvement in crime; and they also take some account of the recent psychological research on cognitive processing.

This research is still at a relatively early stage, and as yet there is only a comparatively small body of criminological data relevant to decision making upon which to draw. Any attempt to develop decision models of crime must at this stage be tentative. Thus our aim is only to provide models that are at present "good enough" to accommodate existing knowledge and to guide research and policy initiatives. Even such "good enough" models, however, have to meet the criticism that they assume too much rationality on the part of the offender. But as the review in Section I has indicated, rationality must be conceived of in broad terms. For instance, even if the choices made or the decision processes themselves are not optimal ones, they may make sense to the offender and represent his best efforts at optimizing outcomes. Moreover, expressive as well as economic goals can, of course, be characterized as rational. And lastly, even where the motivation appears to have a pathological component, many of the subsequent planning and decision-making activities (such as choice of victims or targets) may be rational.

A. *Modeling Criminal Involvement and Criminal Events*

There is a fundamental distinction to be made between explaining the involvement of particular individuals in crime and explaining the occurrence of criminal events. Most criminological theorists have been preoccupied with the former problem and have neglected the latter. They have sought to elucidate the social and psychological variables underlying criminal dispositions, on the apparent assumption that this is all that is needed to explain the commission of crime itself. But the existence of a suitably motivated individual goes only part of the way to explaining the occurrence of a criminal event—a host of immediately precipitating, situational factors must also be taken into account. And a further distinction that must be recognized by theorists concerns the various stages of criminal involvement—initial involvement, continuance, and desistance. That these separate stages of involvement may require different explanatory theories, employing a range of different variables, has been made clear by the findings of recent research into criminal careers (see Farrington 1979; Petersilia 1980).

The distinctions between event and involvement have to be maintained when translating traditional perspectives into decision terms. It may be that the concepts of choice or decision are more readily translatable and more fruitful in relation to continuance and desistance than to initial involvement, but to some extent this may depend on the particular offense under consideration. For some offenses, such as shoplifting or certain acts of vandalism, it might be easier to regard the first offense as determined by the multiplicity of factors identified in existing criminological theory and as committed more or less unthinkingly, that is, without a close knowledge or consideration of the implications. But however much people may be propelled by predisposing factors to the point where crime becomes a realistic course of action, it may still be legitimate (or, at least, useful) to see them as having a choice about whether to become involved. Once the offense is committed, however, the individual acquires direct knowledge about the consequences and implications of that behavior; and this knowledge becomes much more salient to future decisions about continuance or desistance. It may also provide the background of experience to render initial involvement in another crime a considered choice (see Walsh's [1980] discussion of burglary as a training ground for other crimes).

B. The Need for Models to Be Crime Specific

The discussion above has anticipated another important requirement of decision models of crime: whether of involvement or of event, these must be specific to particular kinds of crime. Recent preoccupation with offender pathology and the desire to construct general statements about crime, deviancy, and rule breaking have consistently diverted attention from the important differences between types of crime—the people committing them, the nature of the motivations involved, and the behaviors required. Whatever the purposes and merits of academic generalization, it is essential for policy goals that these important distinctions be maintained. And, moreover, it will usually be necessary to make even finer distinctions between crimes than those provided by legal categories. For instance, it will not usually be sufficient to develop models for a broad legal category such as burglary (Reppetto 1976). Rather it will be necessary to differentiate at least between commercial and residential burglary (as has already been done in a number of studies) and perhaps even between different kinds of residential and commercial burglaries. For example, burglary in public housing projects will be a quite different problem from burglary in affluent commuter areas, or from burglary in multioccupancy inner-city dwellings. And the same is obviously true of many other crimes, such as vandalism, robbery, rape, and fraud. The degree of specificity required will usually demand close attention to situational factors, especially in event models.

The emphasis on specificity, however, should not be taken as contradicting the fact, established in research on criminal careers, that particular individuals may be involved in a variety of criminal activities. But their involvement in separate activities does not necessarily derive from the same sources, though *in practice* the separate processes of involvement in different crimes may be interrelated. This means that in explaining a particular individual's pattern of criminal activity it may be necessary to draw upon a variety of specific models and perhaps to describe the links between them. However, this is a matter for those interested in the etiology of individual criminality and in related policies—such as rehabilitation and incapacitation—focused upon the individual offender. Whether they be specialists or generalists, our own interest in offenders is primarily restricted to occasions when they are involved in the offense under consideration. This is because each form of crime is likely to require specific remedies and, by shifting the focus from offender to offense, a range of neglected options is likely to be brought into the policy arena. All our models reflect this focus of interest and our purpose below is to lay out their formal requirements.

C. The Example of Residential Burglary

We have chosen below to illustrate the construction of decision models of crime through the example of residential burglary in a middle-class suburb. Although it might have made more interesting reading to have selected a less obviously instrumental offense, our choice in the end was made for reasons of convenience: knowledge about this offense is relatively well advanced and we have been involved in some of the recently completed research (Clarke and Hope, in press). This work suggests that the offenders involved are generally rather older and more experienced than those operating in public housing estates, but less sophisticated than those preying on much wealthier residences. Since decision models are for us primarily intended to make criminological theorizing of greater relevance to crime control policies, we believe that practical considerations should play a large part in determining the specificity of the model: the offense modeled should be as specific as current knowledge allows, while at the same time sufficiently common or serious to justify the development of special preventive policies.

In the following pages we will present four models—one concerned with the criminal event and the others with the three stages of criminal involvement—since the decision processes for each model are quite different. It may not always be necessary for policy purposes to model all four processes; indeed, as said above, decisions about which models to develop, and at what level of detail, ought to be governed by policy goals. Our present aim is primarily didactic: first, to set out the models in order to identify the links between them; second, to locate and to give some hint of the ways in which existing criminological data might be interpreted within a decision framework; and third, to illustrate how, through development and examination of the models, the most fruitful points of intervention in the criminal decision process might be identified. As our purpose is not to develop fully elaborated decision models of residential burglary, but only to demonstrate their feasibility, we shall not usually indicate where they draw upon empirical findings (which in any case have been mentioned above) and where they rely upon our own armchair theorizing.

One obvious implication of the need for specificity is that the configuration of the models may vary significantly among different kinds of crime. For instance, models involving offenses which appear to depend primarily upon "presented" opportunities (e.g., shoplifting, Carroll and Herz [1981]) will probably be simpler than those (such as residential burglary) involving opportunities that must be "sought" (see Maguire 1980). And these in turn will be simpler than those involving offenses where the opportunities are created or planned (e.g., bank robberies).

D. Initial Involvement

Figure 1 represents the process of initial involvement in residential burglary in a middle-class suburb. There are two important decision points: the first (box 7) is the individual's recognition of his "readiness" to commit this particular offense in order to satisfy certain of his needs for money, goods, or excitement. Readiness involves rather more than receptiveness: it implies that the individual has actually contemplated this form of crime as a solution to his needs and has decided that under the right circumstances he would commit the offense. In reaching this decision he will have evaluated other ways of satisfying his needs and this evaluation will naturally be heavily influenced by his previous learning and experience—his moral code, his view of the kind of person he is, his personal and vicarious experiences of crime, and the degree to which he can plan and exercise foresight. These variables in turn are related to various historical and contemporaneous background factors—psychological, familial, and sociodemographic (box 1). It is with the influence of these background factors that traditional criminology has been preoccupied; they have been seen to determine the values, attitudes, and personality traits that dispose the individual to crime. In a decision-making context, however, these background influences are less directly criminogenic; instead they have an orienting function—exposing people to particular problems and particular opportunities and leading them to perceive and evaluate these in particular (criminal) ways. Moreover, the contribution of background factors to the final decision to commit crime would be much moderated by situational and transitory influences; and for certain sorts of crime (e.g., computer fraud) the individual's background might be of much less relevance than his immediate situation.

The second decision (box 8), actually to commit a burglary, is precipitated by some chance event. The individual may suddenly need

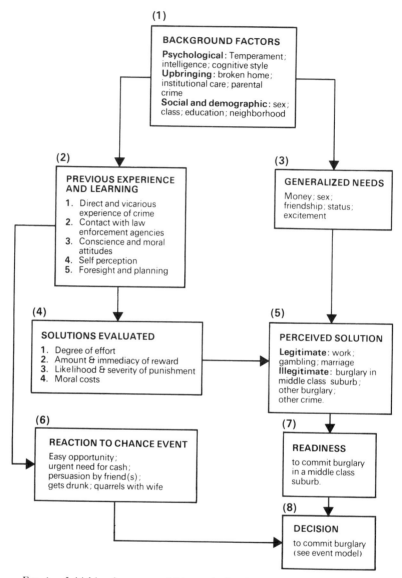

(1)

BACKGROUND FACTORS

Psychological: Temperament; intelligence; cognitive style
Upbringing: broken home; institutional care; parental crime
Social and demographic: sex; class; education; neighborhood

(2)

PREVIOUS EXPERIENCE AND LEARNING

1. Direct and vicarious experience of crime
2. Contact with law enforcement agencies
3. Conscience and moral attitudes
4. Self perception
5. Foresight and planning

(3)

GENERALIZED NEEDS

Money; sex; friendship; status; excitement

(4)

SOLUTIONS EVALUATED

1. Degree of effort
2. Amount & immediacy of reward
3. Likelihood & severity of punishment
4. Moral costs

(5)

PERCEIVED SOLUTION

Legitimate: work; gambling; marriage
Illegitimate: burglary in middle class suburb; other burglary; other crime.

(6)

REACTION TO CHANCE EVENT

Easy opportunity; urgent need for cash; persuasion by friend(s); gets drunk; quarrels with wife

(7)

READINESS

to commit burglary in a middle class suburb.

(8)

DECISION

to commit burglary (see event model)

Fɪɢ. 1.—Initial involvement model (example: burglary in a middle-class suburb)

money, he may have been drinking with associates who suggest committing a burglary (for many offenses, especially those committed by juveniles, immediate pressure from the peer group is important), or he may perceive an easy opportunity for the offense during the course of his routine activities. In real life, of course, the two decision points may

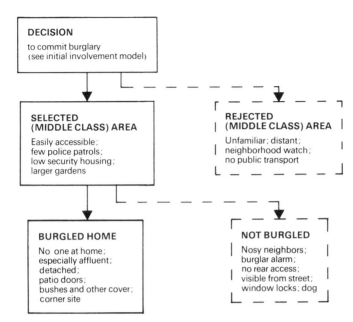

FIG. 2.—Event model (example: burglary in a middle-class suburb)

occur almost simultaneously and the chance event may not only pre-cipitate the decision to burgle, but may also play a part in the percep-tion and evaluation of solutions to generalized needs.

E. The Criminal Event

Figure 2 depicts the further sequence of decision making that leads to the burglar selecting a particular house. As mentioned above, for some other crimes the sequence will be much lengthier; and the less specific the offense being modeled, the more numerous the alternative choices. For example, should a more general model of burglary be required, a wider range of areas and housing types would have to be included (see Brantingham and Brantingham 1978). In the present case, however, there may be little choice of area in which to work, and in time this decision (and perhaps elements of later decisions) may become routine.

This is, of course, an idealized picture of the burglar's decision mak-ing. Where the formal complexity of the decision task is laid out in detail, as in Walsh's (1978, 1980) work, there may be a temptation to assume that it entails equally complex decision making. In real life, however, only patchy and inaccurate information will be available. Under these uncertain circumstances the offender's perceptions, his previous experience, his fund of criminal lore, and the characteristic features of his information processing become crucial to the decision reached. Moreover, the external situation itself may alter during the time span of the decision sequence. The result is that the decision process may be telescoped, planning may be rudimentary, and there may be last-minute (and perhaps ill-judged) changes of mind. Even this account may overemphasize the deliberative element, since alcohol may cloud judgment. Only research into these aspects of criminal decision making will provide event models sufficiently detailed and accurate to assist policy-making.

F. Continuance

Interviews with burglars have shown that in many cases they may commit hundreds of offenses (see, e.g., Maguire 1982); the process of continuing involvement in burglary is represented in figure 3. It is assumed here that, as a result of generally positive reinforcement, the frequency of offending increases until it reaches (or subsequently reduces to) some optimum level. But it is possible to conceive of more or less intermittent patterns of involvement for some individuals; and intermittent patterns may be more common for other types of offenses (e.g., those for which ready opportunities occur less frequently). It is unlikely that each time the offender sets out to commit an offense he will actively consider the alternatives, though this will sometimes be necessary as a result of a change in his circumstances or in the conditions under which his burglaries have to be committed. (These possibilities are discussed in more detail in regard to the "desistance" model of fig. 4.)

More important to represent in the continuing involvement model are the gradually changing conditions and personal circumstances that confirm the offender in his readiness to commit burglary. The diagram summarizes three categories of relevant variables. The first concerns an increase in professionalism: pride in improved skills and knowledge; successive reductions of risk and an improvement in haul through planning and careful selection of targets; and the acquisition of reliable fencing contacts. The second reflects some concomitant changes in lifestyle: a recognition of increased financial dependence on burglary; a choice of legitimate work to facilitate burglary; enjoyment of "life in the fast lane"; the devaluation of ordinary work; and the development of excuses and justifications for criminal behavior. Third, there will be changes in the offender's network of peers and associates and his rela-

Increasing frequency of burglary (due to success) till personal optimum selected

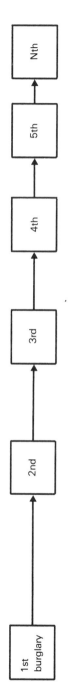

| 1st burglary | 2nd | 3rd | 4th | 5th | Nth |

INCREASED PROFESSIONALISM

Pride in improved skills and knowledge; successively reduces risk and increases haul through planning and careful selection of targets; acquires fencing contacts; develops skills in dealing with police and courts.

CHANGES IN LIFE STYLE AND VALUES

Recognition of financial dependence on burglary; chooses work to facilitate burglary; enjoys life in fast lane; devalues legitimate work; justifies criminality.

CHANGES IN PEER GROUP

Becomes friendly with other criminals and receiver; labeled as criminal; loses contact with straight friends; quarrels with relations.

FIG. 3.—Continuing involvement model (example: burglary in a middle-class suburb)

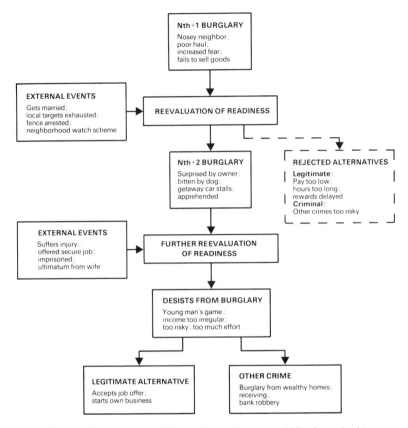

FIG. 4.—Desistance model (example: burglary in a middle-class suburb)

tionship to the "straight" world. These trends may be accelerated by criminal convictions as opportunities to obtain legitimate work decrease and as ties to family and relations are weakened.

This picture is premised upon a more open criminal self-identification. There will be, however, many other offenses (e.g., certain sexual crimes) that are more encapsulated and hidden by the offender from everyone he knows.

G. Desistance

It is in respect of the subject of figure 4 in particular—desistance from burglary—that paucity of relevant criminological information is especially evident. While the work of, for example, Parker (1974), Greenberg (1977), West (1978), Trasler (1979), Maguire (1982), and

West (1982) provides some understanding of the process of desistance, empirical data, whether relating to groups or individuals and in respect of particular sorts of crime, are very scanty. Nevertheless, there is sufficient information to provide in figure 4 an illustration of the offender's decision processes as he begins a renewed evaluation of alternatives to burglary. This follows aversive experiences during the course of offending and changes in his personal circumstances (age, marital status, financial requirements) and the neighborhood and community context in which he operates (changes of policing, depletion of potential targets). These result in his abandoning burglary in favor of some alternative solution either legitimate or criminal. While desistance may imply the cessation of all criminal activity, in other cases it may simply represent displacement to some other target (commercial premises rather than houses) or to another form of crime. Desistance is, in any case, not necessarily permanent and may simply be part of a continuing process of lulls in the offending of persistent criminals (West 1963) or even, perhaps, of a more casual drifting in and out of particular crimes.

H. Some General Observations

The decision models illustrated above should be seen as temporary, incomplete, and subject to continual revision as fresh research becomes available. Even now they could probably be improved by the explicit specification of linkages within and between models. Moreover, accepting the "good enough" criterion governing their development, they are still open to two general criticisms. On the one hand, it might be argued that the benefits of a decision approach have been oversold by selecting a crime such as burglary, which has clear instrumental goals and requires planning and foresight. However, the decision elements in many other forms of crime—such as fraud or traffic offenses (see Brown [1981] for the latter)—may be even more salient. And, as our earlier review suggests, a decision approach is applicable to all forms of crime, even apparently impulsive or irrational ones. On the other hand, considering the aptness of residential burglary for treatment in decision terms, one might have expected the resulting models to be better articulated and less dependent upon anecdotal evidence. Moreover, given the amount of further empirical data required to make even the burglary models adequate, can it be realistic to suggest that such models have to be developed for all the different kinds of crime? The answer must be that since the models are intended to assist policy-making, pragmatic considerations should be preeminent: the harm caused by the particular crime under consideration must be considered sufficient to justify the investment in research.

III. Conclusions

During the course of this discussion a number of deficiencies in current criminological theorizing have been identified. Many of these flow from two underlying assumptions: that offenders are different from other people and that crime is a unitary phenomenon. Hence, the preoccupation with the issue of initial involvement in crime and the failure to develop explanations for specific kinds of offending. Moreover, explanatory theories have characteristically been confined to a limited selection of variables derived from one or another of criminology's contributory disciplines; and none of the dominant theories has taken adequate account of situational variables. A decision-making approach, however, stresses the rational elements in criminal behavior and requires explanations to be specific to particular forms of crime. It also demands that attention be paid to the crucial distinction between criminal involvement (at its various stages) and criminal events. By doing so it provides a framework that can accommodate the full range of potentially relevant variables (including situational ones) and the various competing but partial theories.

A. Policy

These advantages for explanation also hold for analysis of policy. Instead of defining the search for effective policy in terms of coping with broad problems such as juvenile delinquency or the rise in crime, the decision models encourage a policy focus upon the specific crimes, such as school vandalism, joy riding, rape by strangers, and pub violence, which may be giving rise to the broader concerns. Breaking down larger problems into more clearly defined constituent parts usually affords a greater prospect of effective action. But the distinctions between crimes need to be finer, not only than those of existing theory (e.g., between instrumental and expressive offenses, or between predatory and violent offenses) but also than those provided by legal categories. In addition, the more comprehensive view of the determinants of crime provided by the interlocking decision models of involvement and event identifies a broader range of both policy options and possible points for intervention. Options can then be prioritized in relation to the specific offense under consideration in terms of practicality, immediacy of effect, and cost effectiveness. For example, the appropriate involvement and event models for joy riding (theft of vehicles for personal use) might suggest a variety of measures, including increased leisure provision for juveniles at risk, community service for convicted offenders, "lock-your-car" campaigns, and the provision of better public transport. The most cost-effective method might turn out to be the improvement of vehicle security, since the assumption of rationality underlying the decision perspective supports measures that either increase (or seem to the offender to increase) the costs and effort of offending or decrease the rewards. The costs of this improved security would need to be carefully assessed; they should be weighed against the costs of the offense—these latter being broadly defined to include personal inconvenience and waste of police time—and any possible costs incurred by displacement.

Both the crime-specific focus for policy and the decision perspective are likely to favor more narrowly defined situational or deterrent measures by, for example, enabling the limits of displacement to be more clearly specified. While there is much unrealized potential for such measures (see Clarke 1983), there are dangers in going too far down this road. For example, different crime problems are sometimes concentrated together in the same localities and this may suggest coordinated action. It may also be the case that the best chance of apprehending individuals involved in certain particularly vicious criminal behavior—multiple rapes, for instance—lies in crackdowns on certain other offenses such as "curb crawling" or "cruising" by men in automobiles looking for prostitutes.

This latter point relates directly to the issue how far offenders are generalists rather than specialists, which is at the heart of questions about the policy value of the decision models. There is certainly evidence from the criminal careers research cited above that many of the most recidivist offenders are generalists. But it is not entirely clear to what extent they may specialize in certain forms of crime at particular times. It seems likely that the more closely offenses are defined, the more they will be found to be committed by characteristic offender types. Thus children involved in vandalism of schools may be different from those who assault teachers or, indeed, who vandalize other targets. To the extent that their special characteristics, in particular the motives and reasons underlying their conduct, can be identified and described, it may be possible to suggest more carefully tailored forms of intervention. Catchall interventions for loosely defined offender groups are unlikely to achieve their objectives.

There are other ways in which the decision approach helps to account for the limited effectiveness of current treatment efforts. Programs tend to pay too much attention to modifying the influence of "disposing" variables and in doing so take too little account of the posttreatment environment, including the offender's current social and economic situation, the role of chance events, and the specific opportunities open to him for crime. To be successful, treatment must take more account of these contemporaneous influences. Where the pressures and inducements are primarily economic, the measures needed are ones likely to increase the attractions and possibilities of conformity, such as programs that give the offender new skills or ways of earning a living. These programs must be based not only on a more careful analysis of the particular needs and circumstances of the target group, but also of the market for labor: it may be, for example, that work programs are of limited effectiveness for those already in work or for those able to earn considerably more money by illegitimate means.

As for incapacitation, the relevance of decision models lies in the fact that they demand a detailed understanding of continuance and desistance. In particular more needs to be known about offenders' reasons for switching crimes or for engaging in a variety of different crimes at a particular time. Knowledge of this kind will help to determine the feasibility of identifying suitable target groups for containment.

B. Research

The decision approach suggests three important directions for research: the mounting of further crime-specific studies, the devotion of more attention to the offender's perspective when criminal careers are studied, and the elucidation of decision processes at the point of offending. Some notable examples of crime-specific research have been quoted in this essay. But there is much more scope for work of this kind, particularly if, as our analysis seems to require, finer distinctions between crimes are adopted. As for offenders' perspectives on their careers, examples of the sorts of information needed have already been given. A question of central importance concerns the part played in desistance by changes in personal circumstances as compared with being arrested and sentenced. For example, an understanding of the impact of law enforcement and criminal justice systems will require study of the offenders' sources of information and the way in which the information is evaluated. It cannot be assumed that offenders' views of the system and its measures bear a close relation to those of policymakers. It will be important to ask, for example, whether the official information is reaching its targets, whether the message is consistent, and whether it is believed. The need to understand the processing of information is also salient to modeling decision processes at the point of offending. More knowledge is needed, in particular, about the heuristic devices employed in assessing costs and payoffs, about how anxieties concerning the morality of the act and the risk of apprehension are dealt with (e.g., through shutoff mechanisms and techniques of neutralization) and about the effect of alcohol (see Bennett and Wright, in press), of anger, or, indeed, of other emotions.

Getting the questions right will help to determine the appropriate methodologies, and our preceding discussion has illustrated the wealth of available techniques to acquire the necessary information—participant observation, retrospective interviews, experimental studies of decision making, ecological mapping, crime site surveys, and "process tracing" in vivo or by using films and photographs. For some offenses, such as residential burglary, there may already be enough data to attempt a detailed simulation of the decision process.

Each of these methods makes certain theoretical assumptions and has its characteristic limitations. For example, the use of interviews and introspection to investigate criminal decision making may reveal more about people's post hoc commonsense or self-serving explanations for their behavior than about either the processes involved or the factors actually taken into account (Nisbett and Wilson 1977). Again, it should not be assumed that decision making in the real world can be easily simulated in the laboratory (see Ebbesen and Konecni 1980). Given the complexities of the issues and the dearth of information, triangulation of methods is essential, though any technique that enables criminal choices to be studied as they occur in naturalistic settings (see Payne's [1980] advocacy of process tracing) may be especially valuable.

The separation in the discussion above among theoretical formulations, policy, and research is, of course, artificial. In successful policy-relevant programs of research, there must be a dynamic interplay among theories, empirical studies, and policy implications. In particular, ongoing research should have a powerful feed-back effect upon the construction of models. And the impact of decision modeling on the structure of research is every bit as important as the policy applications discussed above.

C. Final Remarks

In conclusion, two general points seem worth emphasizing. First, the models have been developed primarily for the limited purposes of improving crime control policies and developing policy-relevant research. Such models have only to be "good enough"; they may not necessarily be the most appropriate or satisfactory for more comprehensive explanations of criminal behavior—though it seems likely that a decision approach might provide a useful starting point even for academic purposes. For example, Box (1981) has developed a sophisticated initial involvement model, based on control theory, which contains decision elements; while Glaser's (1979) more general "differential anticipation" theory incorporates elements of a decision approach within a hybrid involvement-event framework.

Second, decision models of crime might appear to imply the sort of "soft" determinism or modified classicism advocated by Matza (1964), namely, that while choices may be constrained, some leeway to choose still exists. And a criminology that makes use of such voluntaristic concepts might seem to have foresaken its traditional determinism.

A fuller discussion of this issue is beyond the scope of this essay (but see Glaser 1976; Schafer 1976). It is possible, however, to take a more pragmatic stance: while it is true that the concept of choice is likely to prove useful for generating and providing a framework for decision-making data, the resulting information supplies as many clues about determinants of behavior as it does about reasons and motives. This, in turn, enables both voluntaristic and deterministic models of offending to be elaborated further; it may be too soon, for example, to discount the sophisticated noncognitive accounts suggested by radical behaviorism (Skinner 1964, 1978). Perhaps, as Glaser (1976) implies, voluntaristic and deterministic assumptions are always best regarded as alternative heuristic devices for generating and organizing data. Under such circumstances it would not be surprising if the usefulness of their respective contributions to the task in hand—the more effective control of crime—appeared to vary from time to time. We believe, then, that decision-making concepts can be used for the purposes of constructing "good enough" theories without necessarily being firmly committed to a particular position in the free will/determinism debate—or to any consequential implications for crime control (Cressey 1979) or criminal justice (Norrie 1983). Indeed, the resulting policies remain, as before, the outcome of an uneasy blend of deterministic and neoclassical assumptions.

REFERENCES

Akers, Ronald L. 1977. *Deviant Behavior: A Social Learning Approach.* 2d ed. Belmont, Calif.: Wadsworth.

Åkerström, Malin. 1983. *Crooks and Squares.* Lund, Sweden: Studentlitteratur.

Athens, Lonnie. 1980. *Violent Criminal Acts and Actors: A Symbolic Interactionist Study.* London: Routledge & Kegan Paul.

Bandura, Albert. 1969. *Principles of Behavior Modification.* New York: Holt, Rinehart & Winston.

———. 1977. *Social Learning Theory.* Englewood Cliffs, N.J.: Prentice-Hall.

Becker, Gary S. 1968. "Crime and Punishment: An Economic Approach." *Journal of Political Economy* 76:169–217.

———. 1973. "A Theory of Marriage: Part One." *Journal of Political Economy* 81(4):813–46.

———. 1974. "A Theory of Marriage: Part Two." *Journal of Political Economy* 82(2):11–26.

Becker, Howard S. 1963. *Outsiders.* New York: Free Press.

Bennett, J. 1981. *Oral History and Delinquency.* Chicago: University of Chicago Press.

Bennett, Trevor H., and Richard Wright. 1983. *Constraints and Inducements to Crime: The Property Offender's Perspective.* Mimeographed. Cambridge: Cambridge University, Institute of Criminology.

———. 1984. "What the Burglar Saw." *New Society* (February 2), pp. 162–63.

———. In press. "The Relationship between Alcohol Use and Burglary." *British Journal of Addictions.*

Bevis, C., and J. B. Nutter. 1977. "Changing Street Layouts to Reduce Residential Burglary." Paper presented at the annual meeting of the American Society of Criminology, Atlanta, November.

Box, Stephen. 1981. *Deviance, Reality and Society.* London: Holt, Rinehart & Winston.

Brantingham, Paul J., and Patricia L. Brantingham. 1975. "The Spatial Patterning of Burglary." *Howard Journal of Penology and Crime Prevention* 14:11–24.

———. 1978. "A Theoretical Model of Crime Site Selection." In *Crime, Law and Sanctions,* edited by Marvin D. Krohn and Ronald L. Akers. Beverly Hills, Calif.: Sage.

Brown, B. B., and I. Altman. 1981. "Territoriality and Residential Crime: A Conceptual Framework." In *Environmental Criminology,* edited by Paul J. Brantingham and Patricia L. Brantingham. Beverly Hills, Calif.: Sage.

Brown, Ivan D. 1981. "The Traffic Offence as a Rational Decision." In *Psychology in Legal Contexts: Applications and Limitations,* edited by Sally M. A. Lloyd-Bostock. London: Macmillan.

Bruner, Jerome S., Jacqueline J. Goodnow, and George A. Austin. 1956. *A Study of Thinking.* New York: Wiley.

Burchard, John D. 1977. "Review of Yochelson and Samenow's *The Criminal Personality,* vol. 1." *Contemporary Psychology* 22(6):442–43.

Carroll, John S. 1982. "Committing a Crime: The Offender's Decision." In *The*

Criminal Justice System: A Social-psychological Analysis, edited by Vladimir J. Konecni and Ebbe B. Ebbesen. Oxford: Freeman.

Carroll, John S., and E. J. Herz. 1981. "Criminal Thought Processes in Shoplifting." Paper presented at the annual meeting of the American Society of Criminology, Washington, D.C., November.

Carter, Ronald L., and Kim Q. Hill. 1979. *The Criminal's Image of the City*. New York: Pergamon.

Cimler, Edward, and Lee Roy Beach. 1981. "Factors Involved in Juveniles' Decisions about Crime." *Criminal Justice and Behavior* 8:275–86.

Clarke, Ronald V., ed. 1978. *Tackling Vandalism*. Home Office Research Study, no. 47. London: HMSO.

———. 1983. "Situational Crime Prevention: Its Theoretical Basis and Practice Scope." In *Crime and Justice: An Annual Review of Research*, vol. 4, edited by Michael Tonry and Norval Morris. Chicago: University of Chicago Press.

Clarke, Ronald V., and Derek B. Cornish. 1983. *Crime Control in Britain: A Review of Policy Research*. Albany: State University of New York Press.

Clarke, Ronald V., and Tim Hope. In press. *Coping with Burglary: Research Perspectives on Policy*. Boston: Kluwer-Nijhoff.

Cohen, Lawrence E., and Marcus Felson. 1979. "Social Change and Crime Rates Trends: A Routine Activity Approach." *American Sociological Review* 44:588–608.

Cohen, Stan. 1972. *Folk Devils and Moral Panics: The Creation of the Mods and Rockers*. London: MacGibbon & Kee.

Conger, Rand D. 1978. "From Social Learning to Criminal Behavior." In *Crime, Law and Sanctions*, edited by Marvin D. Krohn and Ronald L. Akers. Beverly Hills, Calif.: Sage.

Cook, Philip J. 1980. "Research in Criminal Deterrence: Laying the Groundwork for the Second Decade." In *Crime and Justice: An Annual Review of Research*, vol. 2, edited by Norval Morris and Michael Tonry. Chicago: University of Chicago Press.

Cornish, Derek B. 1978. *Gambling: A Review of the Literature and Its Implications for Policy and Research*. Home Office Research Study, no. 42. London: HMSO.

Cressey, Donald R. 1979. "Criminological Theory, Social Science and the Repression of Crime." In *Criminology: New Concerns*, edited by Edward Sagarin. Beverly Hills, Calif.: Sage.

Decker, John F. 1972. "Curbside Deterrence: An Analysis of the Effect of a Slug Rejector Device, Coin View Window and Warning Labels on Slug Usage in New York City Parking Meters." *Criminology* (August), pp. 127–42.

Denzin, Norman K. 1977. "Notes on the Criminogenic Hypothesis: A Case Study of the American Liquor Industry." *American Sociological Review* 42:905–20.

Ditton, Jason. 1977. *Part-Time Crime: An Ethnography of Fiddling and Pilferage*. London: Macmillan.

Downes, David. 1966. *The Delinquent Solution*. London: Routledge & Kegan Paul.

Ebbesen, Ebbe B., and Vladimir J. Konecni. 1980. "On the External Validity of Decision-making Research: What Do We Know about Decisions in the Real World?" In *Cognitive Processes in Choice and Decision Behavior*, edited by Thomas S. Walsten. Hillside, N.J.: Erlbaum.

Ehrlich, Isaac. 1979. "The Economic Approach to Crime: A Preliminary Assessment." In *Criminology Review Yearbook*, vol. 1, edited by Sheldon L. Messinger and Egon Bittner. Beverly Hills, Calif.: Sage.

Farrington, David P. 1979. "Longitudinal Research on Crime and Delinquency." In *Crime and Justice: An Annual Review of Research*, vol. 1, edited by Norval Morris and Michael Tonry. Chicago: University of Chicago Press.

Feldman, M. Phillip. 1977. *Criminal Behaviour: A Psychological Analysis*. London and New York: Wiley.

Felson, Richard B., and Henry J. Steadman. 1983. "Situational Factors in Disputes Leading to Criminal Violence." *Criminology* 21:59–74.

Fink, G. 1969. "Einsbruchstatorte vornehmlich an Einfallstrassen?" *Kriminalistik* 23:358–60.

Freeman, Richard B. 1983. "Crime and Unemployment." In *Crime and Public Policy*, edited by James Q. Wilson. San Francisco: Institute of Contemporary Studies Press.

Furlong, W. J., and S. L. Mehay. 1981. "Urban Law Enforcement in Canada. An Empirical Analysis." *Canadian Journal of Economics* 14(1):44–57.

Garber, Steven, Steven Klepper, and David Nagin. 1983. "The Role of Extralegal Factors in Determining Criminal Case Disposition." In *Research on Sentencing: The Search for Reform*, vol. 2, edited by Alfred Blumstein, Jacqueline Cohen, Susan E. Martin, and Michael H. Tonry. Washington, D.C.: National Academy Press.

Ghali, Moheb A. 1982. "The Choice of Crime: An Empirical Analysis of Juveniles' Criminal Choice." *Journal of Criminal Justice* 10:433–42.

Gibbs, John J., and Peggy L. Shelly. 1982. "Life in the Fast Lane: A Retrospective View by Commercial Thieves." *Journal of Research in Crime and Delinquency* 19:299–330.

Glaser, Daniel. 1976. "The Compatibility of Free Will and Determinism in Criminology: Comments on an Alleged Problem." *Journal of Criminal Law and Criminology* 67:487–90.

———. 1979. "A Review of Crime-Causation Theory and Its Application." In *Crime and Justice: An Annual Review of Research*, vol. 1, edited by Norval Morris and Michael Tonry. Chicago: University of Chicago Press.

Gould, Leroy C. 1969. "The Changing Structure of Property Crime in an Affluent Society." *Social Forces* 48:50–59.

Greenberg, D. F. 1977. "Delinquency and the Age Structure of Society." *Contemporary Crises* 1:189–223.

Hampson, Sarah E. 1982. *The Construction of Personality: An Introduction*. London: Routledge & Kegan Paul.

Heineke, J. M. 1978. "Economic Models of Criminal Behaviour: An Overview." In *Economic Models of Criminal Behaviour*, edited by J. M. Heineke. New York: North-Holland.

Henry, Stuart. 1978. *The Hidden Economy*. London: Martin Robertson.

Hindelang, Michael J., Michael R. Gottfredson, and James Garofalo. 1978. *Victims of Personal Crime: An Empirical Foundation for a Theory of Personal Victimization.* Cambridge, Mass.: Ballinger.

Holzman, Harold R. 1983. "The Serious Habitual Property Offender as 'Moonlighter.' " *Journal of Criminal Law and Criminology* 73(4):1774–92.

Humphreys, Laud. 1970. *Tearoom Trade: Impersonal Sex in Public Places.* Chicago: Aldine.

Inciardi, James, A. 1975. *Careers in Crime.* Chicago: Rand McNally.

Jacoby, Joseph E. 1977. "Review of Yochelson and Samenow's *The Criminal Personality*, vol. 1." *Journal of Criminal Law and Criminology* 68:314–15.

Kahneman, Daniel, Paul Slovic, and Amos Tversky. 1982. *Judgment under Uncertainty: Heuristics and Biases.* New York: Cambridge University Press.

Kleinmuntz, Benjamin. 1968. "The Processing of Clinical Information by Man and Machine." In *Formal Representation of Human Judgment*, edited by Benjamin Kleinmuntz. New York: Wiley.

Klepper, Steven, Daniel Nagin, and Luke-Jon Tierney. 1983. "Discrimination in the Criminal Justice System: A Critical Appraisal of the Literature." In *Research on Sentencing: The Search for Reform*, vol. 2, edited by Alfred Blumstein, Jacqueline Cohen, Susan E. Martin, and Michael H. Tonry. Washington, D.C.: National Academy Press.

Klockars, Carl B. 1974. *The Professional Fence.* London: Tavistock.

Kozielecki, J. 1982. *Psychological Decision Theory.* Boston: Reidel.

Lejeune, Robert. 1977. "The Management of a Mugging." *Urban Life* 6(2):123–48.

Letkemann, P. 1973. *Crime as Work.* Englewood Cliffs, N.J.: Prentice-Hall.

Ley, David, and R. Cybrinwsky. 1974. "The Spatial Ecology of Stripped Cars." *Environment and Behaviour* 6:53–67.

Luedtke, Gerald, and Associates. 1970. *Crime and the Physical City: Neighborhood Design and Techniques for Crime Reduction.* Springfield, Va.: National Technical Information Service.

Maguire, Mike. 1980. "Burglary as Opportunity." *Research Bulletin* no. 10, pp. 6–9. London: Home Office Research Unit.

Maguire, Mike, in collaboration with Trevor Bennett. 1982. *Burglary in a Dwelling.* London: Heinemann.

Mansfield, Roger, Leroy C. Gould, and J. Zvi Namenwirth. 1974. "A Socioeconomic Model for the Prediction of Societal Rates of Property Theft." *Social Forces* 52:462–72.

Manski, Charles F. 1978. "Prospects for Inference on Deterrence through Empirical Analysis of Individual Criminal Behaviour." In *Economic Models of Criminal Behavior*, edited by J. M. Heineke. New York: North-Holland.

Mars, Gerald. 1974. "Dock Pilferage." In *Deviance and Social Control*, edited by Paul Rock and Mary McIntosh. London: Tavistock.

Marsh, Peter, Elizabeth Rosser, and Ron Harre. 1978. *The Rules of Disorder.* London: Routledge & Kegan Paul.

Matza, David. 1964. *Delinquency and Drift.* New York: Wiley.

Mayhew, Patricia M., Ronald V. G. Clarke, Andrew Sturman, and J. Michael Hough. 1976. *Crime as Opportunity.* Home Office Research Study no. 34. London: HMSO.

Meehl, Paul E. 1954. *Clinical versus Statistical Prediction: A Theoretical Analysis and a Review of the Evidence.* Minneapolis: University of Minnesota Press.

Mischel, Walter. 1973. "Toward a Cognitive Social Learning Reconceptualisation of Personality." *Psychological Review* 80:252–83.

————. 1979. "On the Interface of Cognition and Personality: Beyond the Person-Situation Debate." *American Psychologist* 34:740–54.

Myers, David G., and Helmut Lamm. 1976. "The Group Polarization Phenomenon." *Psychological Bulletin* 83:602–27.

Nietzel, Michael T. 1979. *Crime and Its Modification: A Social Learning Perspective.* New York: Pergamon.

Nisbett, Richard, and Lee Ross. 1980. *Human Inference: Strategies and Shortcomings of Social Judgment.* Englewood Cliffs, N.J.: Prentice-Hall.

Nisbett, R. E., and T. Wilson. 1977. "Telling More Than We Can Know: Verbal Reports on Mental Processes." *Psychological Review* 84:231–59.

Norrie, Alan. 1983. "Freewill, Determinism and Criminal Justice." *Legal Studies* 3(1):60–73.

Orsagh, Thomas. 1983. "Is There a Place for Economics in Criminology and Criminal Justice?" *Journal of Criminal Justice* 99(5):391–401.

Orsagh, Thomas, and Ann Dryden Witte. 1981. "Economic Status and Crime: Implications for Offender Rehabilitation." *Journal of Criminal Law and Criminology* 72(3):1055–71.

Palmer, J. 1977. "Economic Analyses of the Deterrent Effect of Punishment: A Review." *Journal of Research in Crime and Delinquency* 14:4–21.

Parker, Howard J. 1974. *View from the Boys: A Sociology of Down-Town Adolescents.* Newton Abbot, England: David & Charles.

Payne, J. 1980. "Information Processing Theory: Some Concepts and Methods Applied to Decision Research." In *Cognitive Processes in Choice and Decision Behavior*, edited by Thomas Wallsten. Hillsdale, N.J.: Erlbaum.

Petersilia, Joan. 1980. "Criminal Career Research: A Review of Recent Evidence." In *Crime and Justice: An Annual Review of Research*, vol. 2, edited by Michael Tonry and Norval Morris. Chicago: University of Chicago Press.

Pruitt, D. G. 1971. "Choice Shifts in Group Discussion: An Introductory Review." *Journal of Personality and Social Psychology* 20:339–60.

Prus, Robert C. and S. Irini. 1980. *Hookers, Rounders and Desk Clerks: The Social Organization of the Hotel Community.* Toronto: Sage.

Pyle, David J. 1983. *The Economics of Crime and Law Enforcement.* London: Macmillan.

Rengert, George F., and J. Wasilchick. 1980. "Residential Burglary: The Awareness and Use of Extended Space." Paper presented at the annual meeting of the American Society of Criminology, San Francisco, November.

Reppetto, Thomas A. 1974. *Residential Crime.* Cambridge, Mass.: Ballinger.

————. 1976. "Crime Prevention and the Displacement Phenomenon." *Crime and Delinquency* 22:166–77.

Samuel, Raphael. 1981. *East End Underworld: Chapters in the Life of Arthur Harding.* London: Routledge & Kegan Paul.

Sarbin, Theodore R. 1979. "Review of Yochelson and Samenow's *The Criminal Personality, vol. 1.*" *Crime and Delinquency* 25(3):392–96.

184   Ronald V. Clarke and Derek B. Cornish

Scarr, Harry A. 1973. *Patterns of Burglary*. For the U.S. Department of Justice. Washington, D.C.: Government Printing Office.

Schafer, Stephen. 1976. "The Problem of Free Will in Criminology." *Journal of Criminal Law and Criminology* 67:481–85.

Sheley, Joseph F. 1980. "Is Neutralisation Necessary for Criminal Behaviour?" *Deviant Behaviour* 2:49–72.

Shover, N. 1972. "Structures and Careers in Burglary." *Journal of Criminal Law, Criminology and Police Science* 63:540–49.

Simon, Herbert A. 1983. *Reasoning in Human Affairs*. Oxford: Blackwell.

Skinner, Frederick B. 1964. "Behaviorism at Fifty." In *Behaviorism and Phenomenology*, edited by T. W. Wann. Chicago: University of Chicago Press.

———. 1978. *Reflections on Behaviorism and Society*. Englewood Cliffs, N.J.: Prentice-Hall.

Skogan, Wesley G., and Michael G. Maxfield. 1981. *Coping with Crime: Individual and Neighborhood Reactions*. Beverly Hills, Calif.: Sage.

Slovic, P., and S. Lichtenstein. 1968. "The Relative Importance of Probabilities and Payoffs in Risk-Taking." *Journal of Experimental Psychology Monograph*, vol. 78, no. 3, pt. 2.

Sparks, Richard F. 1980. "A Critique of Marxist Criminology." In *Crime and Justice: An Annual Review of Research*, vol. 2, edited by Norval Morris and Michael Tonry. Chicago: University of Chicago Press.

Sturman, Andrew. 1978. "Measuring Vandalism in a City Suburb." In *Tackling Vandalism*, edited by Ronald V. G. Clarke. Home Office Research Study no. 47. London: HMSO.

Taylor, Ian, Paul Walton, and Jock Young. 1973. *The New Criminology*. London: Routledge & Kegan Paul.

Trasler, Gordon B. 1979. "Delinquency, Recidivism, and Desistance." *British Journal of Criminology* 19:314–22.

Tversky, A., and D. Kahneman. 1974. "Judgment under Uncertainty: Heuristics and Biases." *Science* 185:1124–31.

Vold, George B. 1979. *Theoretical Criminology*. 2d ed. New York: Oxford University Press.

Waldo, Gordon P., ed. 1983. *Career Criminals*. Beverly Hills, Calif.: Sage.

Waller, Irvin, and Norman Okihiro. 1978. *Burglary: The Victim and the Public*. Toronto: University of Toronto Press.

Walsh, Dermot P. 1978. *Shoplifting: Controlling a Major Crime*. London: Macmillan.

———. 1980. *Break-Ins: Burglary from Private Houses*. London: Constable.

Warr, P. B., and C. Knapper. 1968. *The Perception of People and Events*. Chichester: Wiley.

West, Donald J. 1963. *The Habitual Prisoner*. London: Macmillan.

———. 1982. *Delinquency: Its Roots, Careers and Prospects*. London: Heinemann.

West, W. Gordon. 1978. "The Short Term Careers of Serious Thieves." *Canadian Journal of Criminology* 20:169–90.

Wiggins, Jerry S. 1973. *Personality and Prediction: Principles of Personality Assessment*. Reading, Mass.: Addison-Wesley.

Wilcox, S. 1974. "The Geography of Robbery." In *The Pattern and Control of Robbery*, edited by Floyd Feeney and A. Weir. Davis: University of California Press.

Wilkins, Leslie T. 1964. *Social Deviance*. London: Tavistock.

Wilkins, Leslie T., and Ann Chandler. 1965. "Confidence and Competence in Decision Making." *British Journal of Criminology* 5:22–35.

Winchester, Stuart, and Hilary Jackson. 1982. *Residential Burglary: The Limits of Prevention*. Home Office Research Study no. 74. London: HMSO.

Witte, Ann Dryden. 1980. "Estimating the Economic Model of Crime with Individual Data." *Quarterly Journal of Economics* 94:57–84.

Wolfgang, Marvin E., Robert M. Figlio, and Thorsten Sellin. 1972. *Delinquency in a Birth Cohort*. Chicago: University of Chicago Press.

Yochelson, S., and S. E. Samenow. 1976. *The Criminal Personality*. 2 vols. New York: Aronson.

*Alfred Blumstein, David P. Farrington,
and Soumyo Moitra*

Delinquency Careers: Innocents, Desisters, and Persisters

ABSTRACT

The Philadelphia birth cohort study's finding that 6 percent of the boys born in Philadelphia in 1945 experienced 52 percent of the cohort's arrests stimulated a variety of research and policy initiatives including, recently, those relating to selective incapacitation. Results from three other longitudinal delinquency studies—from London; Racine, Wisconsin; and Marion County, Oregon—parallel those of the Philadelphia study. A high percentage, typically at least one-third, of cohort members are arrested or convicted. Of these, many have only one or a small number of official contacts with the criminal justice system. A small percentage have six or more contacts, and for these the probability of subsequent recidivism, after any contact, is approximately 80 percent. The prospective identification of these chronic offenders could have significant crime reduction impact. Most incapacitation research has, however, involved retrospective, not prospective, identification of chronic offenders and has been characterized by high false positive rates. The London study, by contrast, identified seven variables that are apparent by age ten (such as IQ, family background factors, and behavior problems in school) and that may permit prospective identification of a substantial number of chronic offenders. The prediction results closely match the results of predictions based on a theoretical model that uses aggregate recidivism data to partition a cohort into three groups: *innocents*, who have no offending record, *desisters*, who have a low recidivism probability, and *persisters*, who have a high recidivism probability. The results suggest the possibility of early discrimination between more and less serious offenders and also support the view that the rise in recidivism probability with increasing involvement in crime results from a changing mix of desisters and persisters among the offenders.

Alfred Blumstein is J. Erik Jonsson Professor and Director of the Urban Systems Institute, School of Urban and Public Affairs, Carnegie-Mellon University. David P. Farrington is University Lecturer in Criminology, Cambridge University. Soumyo Moitra is Assistant Professor, Bernard Baruch College, City University of New York.

I. A Tantalizing Finding

One of the most quoted findings in the recent history of criminology is the conclusion of Wolfgang, Figlio, and Sellin (1972) that only 6 percent of their cohort of 9,945 boys born in Philadelphia in 1945 accounted for 52 percent of the arrests recorded for these boys prior to their eighteenth birthdays.[1] These 6 percent, labeled the "chronic" offenders by Wolfgang et al. and defined to be those with five or more recorded arrests, are certainly the individuals of greatest interest for crime control. The results clearly hint that, if these individuals could only be identified and incarcerated, this could have a major impact on crime.

On closer examination, however, a number of problems emerge with this interpretation. First, if one were to ask an average Philadelphian what percentage of boys were ever arrested, the estimate might well be no higher than 6 percent. If that were the case, then those 6 percent would account for 100 percent of the arrests, and the results would appear far less tantalizing.

The shift in emphasis derives from the change in the base used to determine what percentage are the "chronics." Since an arrest experience is far from universal, it is more useful to think of the chronics who account for a disproportionate number of arrests in terms of their relationship to those who account for *any* of the arrests rather than in relation to the entire cohort. In such an accounting, the majority who contribute zero arrests are in a different category. Thus, the most relevant base is the population of boys who are *ever* arrested.

The prevalence of that population of ever-arrested boys turns out to be appreciably higher than our hypothetical Philadelphians might estimate. In the Philadelphia cohort of 9,945 boys, 3,475 (35 percent) had already been arrested by age eighteen, and had been arrested a total of 10,214 times. Thus, the 627 chronics (those with five or more arrests who accounted for 5,305 arrests, or 52 percent of the total) represented 18 percent of those ever arrested. Even though this is still an important disproportionality, it has far less dramatic appeal than the 6 percent figure.

More of the appeal disintegrates when one recognizes that the chronics were identified retrospectively rather than prospectively.

---

[1] Throughout their work, Wolfgang et al. (1972) use the term "offenses" to characterize the recorded contacts between the police and the boys in the cohort. These contacts are more properly treated as "arrests," which represent only a small subset of the offenses actually committed, and which may also include contacts in which no offense was actually committed. In this paper, we refer to these contacts as "arrests."

Even if all the arrested boys were truly homogeneous in their crime-committing propensity, chance factors alone would result in some of them having more arrests and others having fewer. Of course, those with the most arrests—those defined after the fact as the chronics who had five or more arrests—would account for a disproportionate fraction of the total number of arrests.

The possibility that the proportion of chronic offenders observed by Wolfgang et al. could have resulted from a homogeneous population of persisters was explored by Blumstein and Moitra (1980). After treating separately those with no arrests (the "innocents") and those with only one or two arrests (the "desisters"), they tested the hypothesis that all the others (the "persisters") could be viewed as having the same rearrest probability. If that were the case, then (denoting that recidivism probability as q) a fraction q of the persisters would have a fourth arrest while a fraction $(1 - q)$ would not. Of those with four arrests, the same fraction q would have a fifth arrest and a fraction $(1 - q)$ would stop at the fourth, and so on for each subsequent arrest number.

Such a model did indeed provide a reasonable fit to the distribution of the number of arrests reported by Wolfgang et al. In particular, it showed that those with five or more arrests accounted for the majority of the arrests among the persisters—but it highlighted the fact that this could occur even if all those with three or more arrests had identical recidivism probabilities. Therefore, the chronics (arbitrarily defined as those with five or more arrests) could have been indistinguishable from nonchronics with three or four arrests.

Even if the distribution of arrests could be explained with the assumption of a population with a homogeneous recidivism probability, it is not necessarily the case that the persisters *are* homogeneous. One would like to be able to distinguish *prospectively* the ones likely to accumulate the largest number of arrests. The tantalizing appeal of focusing on the chronic offenders was that it offered hope of finding discriminators that could distinguish in advance who was likely to emerge as a chronic offender (however defined) and who was likely to terminate criminal activity early. So far, however, no such discriminators have even been proposed for the Philadelphia chronics.

It was also disappointing that the model did not address the growth in recidivism probabilities between the first and third arrests; the recidivism probabilities were simply fitted to the data from the Philadelphia cohort. It would be desirable to formulate a model of the recidivism process that reflects that phenomenon more parsimoniously than has been done heretofore; it would also be desirable to test the results from the Philadelphia cohort on another population.

These are the issues we address here. First, we want to test whether the finding in Philadelphia that chronic offenders (those with more than some few offenses) all could have had reasonably similar recidivism probabilities can be generalized to other cohorts. In Section II, this question is addressed by examining the recidivism probabilities for cohort groups in London, Racine, Wisconsin, and Marion County, Oregon, as well as Philadelphia. Most of our comparative analyses use data collected in the Cambridge Study in Delinquent Development.[2]

Knowing retrospectively that some individuals are chronics is of little value unless one can identify them by characteristics which can be measured at a very early stage in an offending career. One of the disappointments in the frequent references to the Philadelphia chronics is the failure to indicate any way in which they can be identified in advance. Section III uses data collected in the Cambridge Study in Delinquent Development on a cohort of boys in London; data obtained at ages eight to ten are used to distinguish at their first conviction the chronics from the nonchronic offenders.

The use of such information for prediction offers some potential benefits, but also introduces some hazards associated with a mistaken prediction. Section IV presents a framework for developing decision rules based on benefits and costs associated with correct and incorrect predictions. The framework ascribes to each offender a score based on predictive attributes, and then establishes a cut-off point that separates predicted chronics from predicted nonchronics. The cut-off point is chosen to minimize the total costs associated with erroneous predictions.

The models discussed in Section II are not entirely satisfactory because they are based on retrospective identification of chronic offenders, and also because of a lack of a unifying perspective for explaining the growth of recidivism probabilities over the first few offenses. In Section V, we address this problem by dividing a cohort into three groups: innocents (those with no offenses), persisters (those with relatively high recidivism probabilities), and desisters (those with relatively low recidivism probabilities). The relative proportions of these groups in any cohort and their respective recidivism probabilities are estimated empirically. We also use the prediction methods developed in Section

---

[2] See West (1969, 1982) and West and Farrington (1973, 1977) for details of this study.

III to identify each of the offenders in the London cohort as a persister or a desister, thereby linking this analysis based on individuals to the model based on the cohort's aggregate data.

The approaches developed here provide a prospective prediction of subsequent serious offending. Perhaps even more important, they provide a way of incorporating prediction as a responsible policy tool in criminal justice decision making by explicitly taking account of the costs of incorrect predictions. They also highlight the differences between retrospective and prospective uses of prediction. In retrospective prediction, attention is focused on the discrepancy between the predicted and the actual outcome, which is characterized as a prediction error. In a dichotomous prediction (e.g., "chronics" vs. "nonchronics"), there are two kinds of errors, the familiar "false positives" and "false negatives." In prospective prediction, individuals are classified into groups based on their individual observable attributes, and to each group is ascribed a *probability* (either high or low) of a particular outcome (e.g., becoming a persistent offender by some criterion). Addressing the prediction issue in terms of probabilities recognizes explicitly that no prediction can be certain, but also that many chance events that occur after a prediction is made can exacerbate or moderate individual tendencies. Thus, prediction error can occur both because of the limitation of any predictor and because of unanticipated subsequent intervening events.

II. The Modified Geometric Model of Recidivism

Blumstein and Moitra fitted their model to the data on the number of arrests accumulated by the boys in the Philadelphia cohort by their eighteenth birthdays. Letting p_k represent the probability that an individual with $k - 1$ arrests experiences a kth arrest and q_i represent the homogeneous recidivism probability for all "persisters" (specified as those with at least $i - 1$ arrests), the parameters estimated by Blumstein and Moitra from the data in Wolfgang et al. were $p_1 = .35, p_2 = .54, p_3 = .65, q_4 = .72$.

One further partition of the persister population provides a still better fit to the Philadelphia data. If the "mild persisters" (those with three, four, or five arrests, who have a recidivism probability of .72) are distinguished from the "chronic persisters" (those with six or more arrests, who are assigned a recidivism probability of .80), the resulting model has $p_1 = .35, p_2 = .54, p_3 = .65, p_4 = p_5 = p_6 = .72$, and $q_7 = .80$. This model fits the arrest distribution in Wolfgang et al. very well,

1a. Philadelphia Cohort

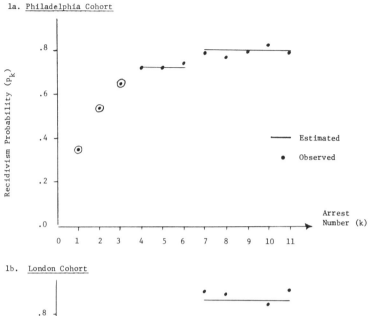

1b. London Cohort

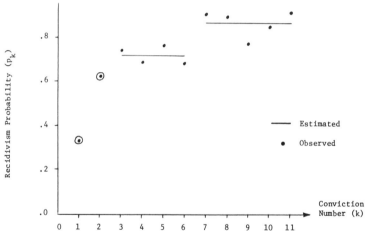

FIG. 1.—Recidivism probability (p_k) as a function of involvement number (k) for various cohorts.

with a χ^2 value of 5.52 for 6 degrees of freedom ($p > .10$) for recidivism events up to and including the eleventh arrest.

Figure 1*a* displays the actual recidivism probability as a function of the arrest number. It is clear from the figure that the recidivism rate increases through the first three arrests, that it is fairly stable at .72 through the next three, and that there is an increase to about .80 between the sixth and seventh arrest, visually confirming the benefit from partitioning the persister population.

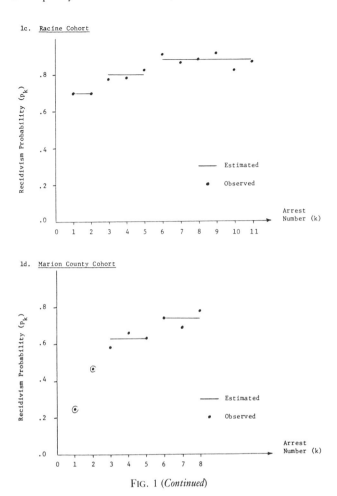

FIG. 1 (*Continued*)

The observed difference between a recidivism probability of .72 and .80 may appear small, but it can make an appreciable difference to the amount of subsequent offending. This effect is highlighted by a focus on the probability of *non*recidivism, which is reduced from .28 to .20. For the geometric distribution, the expected number of future arrests after any given arrest from the sixth onward is $q/(1 - q)$, so that if $q =$ .72, then each persister can expect to experience an additional 2.57 arrests; if the recidivism probability is .80, however, the expected number of future arrests is 4.00, which is 56 percent larger.

A similar model can be estimated for the distribution of *convictions* among the cohort of 396 boys from a working-class area of London who were followed up in the Cambridge Study in Delinquent Development.[3] These boys were all born between 1951 and 1954, somewhat later than the 1945 birth year of the Philadelphia cohort. Convictions (up to the twenty-fifth birthday) were used because official criminal statistics in England contain no record of arrests.[4] The offense types included are the indictable offenses, which are roughly comparable to index crimes in the United States. The shifted geometric model that best fitted the Cambridge data was one in which $p_1 = .33, p_2 = .63, p_3 = p_4 = p_5 = p_6 = .72$, and $q_7 = .87$. The χ^2 value here was 3.25 (7 df), reflecting a very good fit to the data. Figure 1b displays the data and fitted model for London.

This approach can be applied as well to other longitudinal cohort data, even where the prevalence of offending is markedly different from the one-third found in London and Philadelphia. We have examined data from Racine, Wisconsin, where 70 percent of the cohort was arrested, and from Marion County, Oregon, where only 25 percent had police contacts. Shannon (1981) reported on a cohort of 356 boys born in 1942 who were continuously resident in Racine from ages ten to eighteen. Focusing on the arrests for non–traffic offenses to age thirty-two, we fitted a model with $p_1 = p_2 = .70, p_3 = p_4 = p_5 = .80$, and $q_6 = .88$. The χ^2 value here was 5.08 (8 df), which also fitted the data quite well. Figure 1c displays these data and the fitted model.

Another major longitudinal data set was reported by Polk et al. (1981) showing police contacts for non–traffic offenses until age eighteen by males in Marion County. The model here results in $p_1 = .25, p_2 = .47, p_3 = p_4 = p_5 = .63$, and $q_6 = .74$. The χ^2 value here is 1.98 (5 df), a very good fit. Figure 1d presents these data and the fitted model.

The striking observation from all these analyses, based on different times and in different settings, with different cut-off ages, and the different criteria of involvement (arrest in the United States and conviction in London), is that very similar phenomena appear: (a) a very high prevalence of official involvement with law enforcement—over one-quarter in all cases, and as high as 70 percent in Racine; (b) a rapidly increasing probability of recidivism through the first few (three or four) involvements with the law; (c) high, stable recidivism rates through about the sixth involvement—at least 63 percent in all four cases; and

---

[3] Fifteen boys from the original sample of 411 were excluded because they had died or emigrated before the twenty-fifth birthday.
[4] Since conviction in London was very likely after arrest, the requirement of conviction in London does not represent a major distinction from the arrest data, which is more commonly available in the United States.

(*d*) a still higher but stable recidivism rate for subsequent involvements—at least 74 percent in all cases.

One implication of this analysis is that the arbitrary identification of chronic offenders in Philadelphia as those with five or more arrests is not the most appropriate dividing line. On the basis of transition probabilities, it would be reasonable to identify those with six or more arrests in Philadelphia as a relatively more homogeneous group of chronic offenders.

III. Attributes of the Chronics in London

The jump in recidivism probabilities suggests that it would be reasonable to identify the London youths with six or more convictions as the chronic offenders. That knowledge, however, is of little use until some predictive indicator is developed that can distinguish the chronics prospectively. In this section, we use data collected on the London cohort at age ten or younger to predict which of those convicted will become the chronics.

The twenty-three offenders with six or more convictions accounted for about half of all convictions recorded for the 132 youths ever convicted and for substantial proportions of the self-reported offenses.[5] When interviewed at age eighteen to nineteen, the youths were asked about offenses committed in the previous three years. The twenty-two chronic offenders interviewed at this age (5.7 percent of the total 389 interviewed and 17 percent of the 132 ever convicted) admitted 30.4 percent of all burglaries, 32.2 percent of all thefts of vehicles, 23.7 percent of all thefts from shops, and 20.8 percent of all thefts from vehicles.

If any preventive action was to be taken with these chronic offenders, the first realistic opportunity would be at the time of the first conviction. Therefore, it is important to investigate how well one could predict, out of all convicted youths, those who are destined to become the chronics. Included in this analysis were variables measured at age eight to ten, the seriousness of the first offense, and the age of the first conviction. The comparison was between the twenty-three youths with six or more convictions (defined here as the chronics) and the remaining

[5] See Farrington (1983). These figures differ from those in table 6*b* below (which shows twenty-two offenders with six or more convictions and 131 convicted) because one dead youth had seven convictions. He was included in this analysis because he clearly had six or more convictions, but he was not included in the analysis of transition probabilities because he was not at risk of reoffending up to his twenty-fifth birthday.

TABLE 1
Distinguishing Chronics among All Convicted
Offenders in the London Cohort

Variable (Age Measured)	Percent of 23 Chronics	Percent of 109 Nonchronics	Corrected χ^{2}*	Probability
Convicted early (10–13)	60.9	18.3	15.80	<.001
Low family income (8)	65.2	27.5	10.39	<.005
Troublesome (8–10)	69.6	33.0	9.14	<.005
Poor junior attainment (10)	66.7	30.4	8.38	<.005
Psychomotor clumsiness (8–10)	56.5	27.5	6.01	<.025
Low nonverbal IQ (8–10)	60.9	31.2	6.00	<.025
Convicted sibling (10)	39.1	14.7	5.89	<.025

NOTE.—Not knowns excluded from table.
*χ^{2} corrected for continuity (1 df).

109 convicted youths at risk up to the twenty-fifth birthday (defined here as the nonchronic offenders). Table 1 shows the only variables that discriminated significantly ($p < .025$) between these two groups. In comparison with the nonchronics, the chronics tended to be convicted at an early age, to come from low-income families, to be rated troublesome in their primary schools, to have low IQ and attainment, to be clumsy on psychomotor tests, and to have convicted older siblings.

The thirty-four youths who were legally children when first convicted (aged ten to thirteen) were significantly more likely to become chronics than the remaining ninety-eight.[6] In contrast, the type of offense committed on the first conviction did not seem to be predictive. Offenses were partitioned between (1) the more serious ones of burglary or violence and (2) the remainder (primarily theft, including motor vehicle theft). This analysis was restricted to individuals who suffered their first convictions as juveniles (under age seventeen) in order to give them ample time to accumulate six convictions by their twenty-fifth birthday. Of the seventeen youths whose first convictions were for the more serious offenses, six (35.3 percent) became chronics, in comparison with seventeen of the sixty-three (27.0 percent) whose first convictions were for less serious offenses ($\chi^{2} = .14$, 1 df, N.S.).

A logistic regression using the seven variables shown in table 1 was

[6] The minimum age for conviction in England and Wales is ten. Juveniles between the tenth and fourteenth birthday are referred to as "children" and those between the fourteenth and seventeenth birthday (the minimum age for adult court) are "young persons."

TABLE 2
Variables and Their Weights in Logistic Regressions for
Distinguishing Chronics and Convicted Offenders

Distinguishing Chronics from Nonchronic Offenders	Distinguishing Convicted Offenders from Nonconvicted Persons
Convicted 10–13 (1.70)	Troublesome 8–10 (.85)
Convicted sibling 10 (1.10)	Convicted parent 10 (.97)
Troublesome 8–10 (1.04)	Nervousness 8 (− .85)
Poor junior attainment 10 (.97)	Poor junior attainment 10 (.78)
	Daring 8–10 (.67)
	Separation from parent 10 (.70)

also used to distinguish the chronics from the nonchronic convicted offenders.[7] The results are shown in the first column of table 2. The strongest discriminator was the variable, conviction by age thirteen ($G^2 = 15.9$, 1 df, $p < .001$); the next most important indicator was having a convicted sibling ($G^2 = 7.0$, 1 df, $p < .01$). The other two significant variables were the ratings (by teachers and peers) of troublesomeness at ages eight to ten, and poor junior school attainment at age ten. The weights of the four variables when included in the logistic regression equation (also shown in table 2) indicate the relative influence of each of the variables.

There were fifteen convicted youths for whom, under this logistic regression model, the estimated probability of being a chronic exceeded 50 percent. Of these, eleven actually were chronics (with six or more convictions). Therefore, under this 50 percent criterion, about one in nine convicted offenders would have been identified as a probable chronic, this group consisting of three-quarters who *were* chronics and including about half of all the chronics. If the criterion of the predicted probability were lowered from 50 percent to 33 percent, more youths would be predicted to be chronics. That wider net would include an additional three actual chronics but an additional seven nonchronics.

---

[7] A logistic regression is similar in many respects to the more familiar multiple regression, where $Y = a_0 + a_1X_1 + \ldots + a_nX_n$, i.e., where a dependent variable (Y) is expressed as a weighted sum of independent variables (the X's). A logistic regression is often used when the dependent variable takes two values (here, every person is classified as either a chronic or a nonchronic offender). In a logistic regression, Y is the logarithm of the odds of having one of those values (i.e., the left-hand side of the equation becomes log $(P/(1 - P))$ where P is the probability of being a chronic offender).

When the fourteen chronics predicted under this broader criterion (out of twenty-five) were compared with the nine chronics who were not predicted, it was clear that the predicted chronics had a more extensive juvenile offending record: they had an average of 5.9 juvenile and 5.2 adult convictions, whereas the nonpredicted chronics averaged 2.9 juvenile and 6.0 adult convictions. Clearly, the persistent criminal activity of the nonpredicted chronics did not develop until later, and this later development distinguished them from the other chronics whose criminal involvement was predictable by age ten.

Table 2 also shows the variables (and their relative weights) in a logistic regression model that distinguished all the convicted youths from those who were never convicted.[8] The order of the variables in the table shows their order of entry into the logistic regression equation; the figures in parentheses show their weights in the final equation. The variables that serve both to distinguish the chronics from other convicted youths and to distinguish the convicted from not-convicted youths are "troublesomeness" and "poor junior attainment." Family criminality was also important in both cases, appearing as convicted siblings in the identification of chronics and as convicted parents in the identification of convictions. The other factors associated with conviction were nervousness of the youth (which was negatively related), daring, and separation from parents (for reasons other than death or hospitalization).

One problem with the first logistic regression model for distinguishing the chronics from all offenders is that it has not yet been validated on an independent sample of youths. In any prediction study, the prediction equation should be derived from one sample and then tested with another. Two independent samples are preferable to enhance generalizability, but this can be approached by dividing a single sample into two subsamples, one used for construction and the other for validation. The number of offenders here (132, including twenty-three chronics) was too small for even such split-half validation. However, some indication of the predictive efficiency which might be achieved in a validation sample was obtained by using another prediction index devised by a split-half method.

All the chronics were first convicted as juveniles, and so they might be regarded as extreme examples of juvenile official delinquents. Thus,

---

[8] This involved a comparison between 136 convicted youths and 265 not convicted and at risk of conviction (not dying or emigrating) up to the twenty-fifth birthday.

they would be expected to achieve the worst scores in any attempt to discriminate the convicted juveniles from the total group. One such prediction model has been developed using the Burgess method of assigning one point to each of a number of predictor variables. This method is simple, robust, and hence less likely than a regression model to suffer shrinkage when applied to another population. The weights in a regression model are finely tuned to the data in the construction sample, but the Burgess method has been shown by Gottfredson and Gottfredson (1980) to be no less efficient in a validation sample than any other method. Indeed, in Farrington (1985), the Burgess method has been shown to be more efficient in predicting the offenders in the London cohort than least squares multiple regression or logistic regression.

This analysis was based on seven predictor variables observed at ages eight to ten.[9] These seven variables were derived from a randomly chosen half of the London cohort designated as the construction sample and were validated on the other half.[10] Three of the variables were measures of bad behavior ("troublesomeness" rated by peers and teachers, "conduct disorder" rated by teachers and social workers, and "acting out," which included poor conduct, unpopularity, and a neurotic-extrovert personality), one variable reflected a deprived background ("social handicap," which was a combination of low income, low social class, poor housing, large family size, and physical neglect of the youth), and the other three variables were convicted parents, low nonverbal IQ, and poor parental child-rearing behavior (a combination of cruel or neglecting parental attitude, erratic parental discipline, and parental conflict).[11]

Table 3 shows the number of chronics (those with six or more convictions by their twenty-fifth birthday), nonchronic offenders, and unconvicted persons with each prediction score, Z, in the combined con-

---

[9] All the variables were dichotomized to contrast the worst quarter (given a score of one) with the remaining three-quarters (given a score of zero).

[10] The construction and validation samples each consisted of 204 youths, excluding three who emigrated before age fourteen, and the aim was to identify one-quarter of the youths as probable juvenile delinquents. Of the forty-nine youths in the construction sample with prediction scores of three or greater, 46.9 percent were convicted as juveniles, in comparison with 10.3 percent of the remainder ($\phi = .38$, $p < .001$). Of the 51 youths in the validation sample scoring three or greater, 45.1 percent were convicted as juveniles, in comparison with 14.4 percent of the remainder ($\phi = .31$, $p < .001$).

[11] Because our primary interest here is in prediction, no attempt was made to ensure that all variables were theoretically independent in these analyses.

TABLE 3
Prediction Scores on Seven-Point Scale for Chronics, Nonchronic Offenders, and Unconvicted Persons

Prediction Score* (Z)	Observed Chronics (6 or More Convictions)		Observed Non-chronic Offenders (1–5 Convictions)		Observed Unconvicted Persons (No Convictions)		Total	
	Number Scoring Z	Number Scoring Z or more	Number Scoring Z	Number Scoring Z or more	Number Scoring Z	Number Scoring Z or more	Number Scoring Z	Number Scoring Z or more
7	1	1	1	1	0	0	2	2
6	4	5	6	7	2	2	12	14
5	4	9	8	15	5	7	17	31
4	6	15	7	22	11	18	24	55
3	5	20	18	40	15	33	38	93
2	0	20	15	55	36	69	51	144
1	1	21	29	84	75	144	105	249
0	2	23	25	109	121	265	148	397

*The prediction score, Z, is the sum of the score at age ten on the following seven dichotomous items: troublesomeness, conduct disorder, acting out, social handicap, convicted parents, low nonverbal IQ, and poor parental child-rearing behavior. All boys were scored on all of the seven items except for fifteen out of 397, who were not scored on parental child-rearing behavior. In these fifteen cases, the boys' scores on the other six items were multiplied by 7/6 and rounded to the nearest integer.

struction and validation samples.[12] The fifty-five youths scoring four or more points out of seven included the majority of the chronics (fifteen out of twenty-three), twenty-two of the nonchronic offenders, and eighteen of those never convicted. These results suggest that, to a reasonable degree, many of the chronics can be identified at their first conviction on the basis of information available at age ten.

IV. Utilities Associated with a Prediction

The degree to which this or any other prediction rule is likely to be used depends strongly on the rates of correct and incorrect labeling of the individuals and on the benefits associated with correct labeling as well as the concern over mislabeling. A standard framework for addressing such issues is that of expected utility as formulated by von Neumann and Morgenstern (1944), and as applied by many others subsequently.[13] In this framework, positive utilities are the subjective benefits and negative utilities the subjective costs.[14]

These concerns can be reflected in a simple relationship that expresses the total utility of the labeling consequences associated with any labeling rule. The prediction score, Z, associated with each individual is the sum of his scores on each of the seven predictor variables. In using that score to identify the chronics, a cut-off point, Z^*, must be chosen. A high cut-off point will identify only a few of the actual chronics but would avoid incorrectly labeling too many nonchronics as probable chronics. Alternatively, a low cut-off point will capture more of the chronics, but also mislabel more nonchronics. Obviously, then, the choice of the cut-off point, Z^*, depends on the relative assessment of the utility of a correctly labeled chronic and the concern regarding

---

[12] The predictive efficiency in the validation sample was somewhat diminished, but still comparable to that in the construction sample. In the construction sample, thirty youths scored four or more, comprising eight of the ten chronics, eleven of the forty-seven nonchronics, and eleven of the 140 unconvicted. In the validation sample, twenty-five youths scored four or more, including seven of the thirteen chronics, eleven of the sixty-two nonchronics, and seven of the 125 unconvicted.

[13] For example, Loeber and Dishion (1983), in their review of delinquency predictors, use a standard expected-utility formulation presented earlier by Wiggins (1973). They treat all utility weights as -1, 0, or 1, a restriction that is not at all necessary.

[14] The concept of expected utility is reflected in the familiar lottery situation. If the chance of winning the lottery is p and the prize is V, then the expected benefit of a ticket is pV. If the cost of a ticket is C, then the expected net utility is $pV - C$. In Pennsylvania, a $1 lottery ticket pays $500 if it is drawn and has a 1/1000 chance of winning and so it has a net expected utility of $(1/1000) \times 500 - 1 = -\$.50$. The rational decision is to maximize the net utility (or to minimize the disutility). Here, since there is a net *dis*utility of 50 cents, it is rational not to play the lottery.

false positives (mislabeling a nonchronic as a probable chronic) compared to false negatives (failing to identify a true chronic as such).

We can formalize these considerations by a system of mathematical statements that express the benefits or net "utility" (or "disutility" in the case of negative benefits) associated with any cut-off point, Z^*, which depends on the number of errors of each type resulting from that cut-off point, and the relative concern over the two types of error. Then, any decision maker can choose the cut-off point, Z^*, to minimize the total expected disutility associated with a choice.

To address these issues, we define the following variables:

Z^* = the value of Z chosen so that anyone whose score is Z^* or greater is labeled as probable chronic;

U_c = positive utility associated with correctly identifying a chronic (true positive);

U_p = negative utility associated with mislabeling a nonchronic as a probable chronic (false positive);

U_n = negative utility associated with failing to identify a chronic as such (false negative);

$C(Z^*)$ = number of chronics scoring Z^* or above (and hence correctly labeled as chronics if Z^* is the cut-off point);

$P(Z^*)$ = number of false positives, that is, nonchronics scoring Z^* or above (and hence wrongly labeled as probable chronics if Z^* is the cut-off point);

$N(Z^*)$ = number of false negatives, that is, chronics who score below Z^* (and hence are not labeled as chronics if Z^* is the cut-off point);

$U(Z^*)$ = total utility associated with a cut-off point of Z^*, representing the sum of the positive and negative utilities associated with true positives, false positives, and false negatives.

Then, if we attach zero utility to a true negative identification (i.e., labeling an actual nonchronic as a predicted nonchronic), the following relationship linking these variables can be assumed to apply:

$$U(Z^*) = U_c C(Z^*) + U_p P(Z^*) + U_n N(Z^*).$$

We can now invoke the identity that $C(Z^*) + N(Z^*) = C =$ total number of chronics, so that

$$U(Z^*) = U_c C - U_c N(Z^*) + U_n N(Z^*) + U_p P(Z^*).$$

We can also assume, for reasons of symmetry, that the positive utility associated with making a correct identification of a chronic is the same magnitude as the negative utility associated with a failed identification (i.e., $U_c = -U_n$). Thus, our satisfaction in identifying a chronic is equal in magnitude to our disappointment at missing one. It follows that

$$U(Z^*) = U_c C + 2U_n N(Z^*) + U_p P(Z^*).$$

Since any utility scale is inherently arbitrary, and so is defined only to within any lateral translation or scale change, we can let

$$U'(Z^*) = \frac{U(Z^*) - U_c C}{2U_n}.$$

$U'(Z^*)$ is directly related to $U(Z^*)$, with the only modifications being those of the constants U_c, C, and U_n. However, since U_n is negative, maximization of $U(Z^*)$ requires minimization of $U'(Z^*)$, and so $U'(Z^*)$ represents a *dis*utility score.

It also follows that

$$U'(Z^*) = N(Z^*) + \frac{U_p}{2U_n} P(Z^*).$$

It is desirable to choose the optimal cut-off point, Z^*, that minimizes $U'(Z^*)$. The utility associated with any cut-off point Z^* depends on the numbers of false positives and false negatives and on the ratio of the utilities of false positives and false negatives.

We now consider the ratio U_p/U_n, which we label r. This ratio is a single index reflecting the relative concern about false positives compared to false negatives. A value of $r = 1$ implies equal concern about each person mislabeled. A value of $r = 10$ implies 10 times as much concern about mislabeling a nonchronic as about failing to identify a true chronic. If $r = .10$, then the reverse applies—the concern over missing a chronic is 10 times as great as the concern over mislabeling a nonchronic. Thus, the ratio r is a measure of intensity of civil-libertarian concerns. The value of r is a key consideration in any use of prediction. It will depend strongly on local estimates of subjective utilities, which will in turn be strongly influenced by the nature of the planned intervention with the labeled chronics. In particular, the more severe and more punitive the intervention, the higher should be the value of r imposed. Alternatively, if the intervention with the probable chronics involves providing various support services in a way that is

TABLE 4

Number of True Positives, False Negatives, and False Positives in
the London Cohort for Each Cut-off Point Z^*
for Labeling Probable Chronics

Z^*	True Positives $C(Z^*)$	False Negatives $N(Z^*)$	False Positives $P(Z^*)$
7	1	22	1
6	5	18	7
5	9	14	15
4	15	8	22
3	20	3	40
2	20	3	55
1	21	2	84
0	23	0	109

nonstigmatizing and possibly even attractive to those who are labeled, then a low value of r becomes appropriate.

We can use the data of table 3 to explore how the prediction decision rule varies for different values of r. Table 4 lists, for each value of Z^*, the number of chronics who score that value or higher, $C(Z^*)$, the number of chronics who fail to achieve that score, $N(Z^*)$, and the number of nonchronics who score Z^* or higher, $P(Z^*)$. These three columns are the true positives, false negatives, and false positives associated with each value of Z^* serving as the cut-off point for labeling an individual as a probable chronic.

This provides the basic information for the relationship

$$U'(Z^*) = N(Z^*) + (r/2) P(Z^*),$$

which enables us to examine how the civil-libertarian index, r, influences the choice of cut-off point, Z^*, for predicting the chronics among the London offenders at their first conviction. We can ignore $Z^* = 7$, since only two people had this score; we also ignore $Z^* = 2$ or less, since dropping Z^* from three to two finds no new chronics but mislabels an additional fifteen nonchronics. Figure 2 presents the graph of the disutility score as a function of r for the various values of Z^*. The optimal cut-off point, Z^*, that minimizes the disutility score $U'(Z^*)$ clearly depends on the value of the index r. As r increases, the optimal cut-off point also increases, and there are fewer labeled chronics.

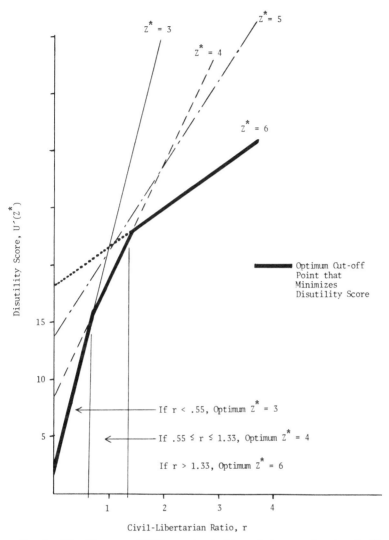

FIG. 2.—Disutility score, $U'(Z^*)$, associated with predictions as a function of utility ratio, r, for various values of cut-off point, Z^*, for labeling chronics.

For $r < .55$, the optimal cut-off point is $Z^* = 3$. The disutility score grows very quickly with r, however, and for $.55 < r < 1.33$, the disutility is minimized when $Z^* = 4$. Thus, the optimum cut-off point is four over the interval $.55 < r < 1.33$, where the concern about missing a chronic is comparable to—roughly within a factor of two—the concern about mislabeling a nonchronic. When $Z^* = 4$, fifteen chronics are correctly identified and eight are missed, but twenty-two nonchronics are mislabeled as chronics.

For higher values of r—above 1.33—reflecting a fairly strong concern about false positives, the identification of probable chronics is severely restricted, and the cut-off point is raised to six. It turns out that the disutility associated with $Z^* = 7$ is less than that for $Z^* = 6$ when $r > 1.33$, but a cut-off point of $Z^* = 7$ is of little use in this case. It is also interesting to note that $Z^* = 5$ is never an optimal cut-off point, since $Z^* = 4$ is preferable for $r < 1.33$ and $Z^* = 6$ is preferable above that value.

In addition to disutilities associated with prediction errors, it is necessary also to consider the choice of variables included in the predictor. Some variables, regardless of their predictive power, would be excluded from certain uses because they are inappropriately discriminatory (e.g., race) or outside the control of the subject (e.g., parental criminality). As with the consideration of the error disutilities, the restriction on certain variables would depend on the use to be made of the prediction. If the use is punitive, the restrictions should be severe, whereas the restrictions could be lessened if the subject views the intervention as beneficial.

V. A Three-Population Model of Recidivism: Innocents, Desisters, and Persisters

The analyses presented in the previous sections are less than fully satisfactory for two major reasons. First, they invoke a retrospective and arbitrary definition of chronic offenders as those with a specified number of involvements with the law and imply a sharp distinction between these and those nonchronics with even one less involvement. Second, the analyses are focused only on the chronic offenders after their recidivism probability has reached a stationary value, and the only attention directed to the first few arrests (when the group recidivism probability climbs to this value) is to fit these recidivism probabilities directly from the data. A model that accounted for the rising recidivism probability and that avoided the sharp chronic/nonchronic distinction would be both more parsimonious and more insightful.

It is possible that the growth in the recidivism probability following each of the first few involvements is a result of the labeling of the offender by the criminal justice system, thereby creating and reinforcing in the individual a self-identity of a criminal and amplifying any existing criminal tendencies. Some evidence that delinquent behavior increases after official processing has been provided by Farrington (1977).

It is also possible—and consistent with the findings of negligible success of the criminal justice system in improving the behavior of the individuals who come into contact with it[15]—that the observation more closely reflects selective filtering than behavior change. This would occur if the various individuals who do come into contact with the system differ in their prior propensity to engage in criminal activity. The rise in the recidivism probability could reflect the weeding out at the early stages of those individuals with a low propensity for involvement in crime, leaving a residue more richly populated by those with an appreciably higher crime-committing propensity.

If this were the case, then we could explain the rising recidivism probability by a simple model in which a cohort consists of three groups: (1) a nonoffending group, (2) a low-recidivism group that discontinues offending relatively quickly, and (3) a high-recidivism group that persists longer and increasingly predominates among the offenders. All members of a group are treated as having the same recidivism probability.

To convert this concept into technical terms, one could characterize any cohort as composed of the following three groups: (1) innocents, with no involvement with law enforcement and an associated probability of arrest of zero, who comprise a fraction β of the whole cohort; (2) desisters, with a low risk of arrest, p_a, who comprise a fraction α of the offenders; (3) persistent offenders, with a high risk of arrest, p_r, who comprise a fraction $(1 - \alpha)$ of the offenders. Under the assumptions of this model, in a cohort of N_0 persons, $N_1 = (1 - \beta)N_0$ will experience at least one arrest. This group of N_1 offenders includes $N_{a1} = \alpha N_1$ desisters and $N_{r1} = (1 - \alpha)N_1$ persisters, with α yet to be determined. A second arrest will be experienced by $N_{a2} = p_a N_{a1}$ of the desisters and by $N_{r2} = p_r N_{r1}$ of the persisters; a kth arrest will be experienced by

$$N_{ak} = p_a N_{a,k-1} = N_{a1} p_a^{k-1} = \alpha p_a^{k-1} N_1$$

and

$$N_{rk} = p_r N_{r,k-1} = N_{r1} p_r^{k-1} = (1 - \alpha) p_r^{k-1} N_1$$

of the desisters and of the persisters, respectively. At the kth arrest stage, the number of active offenders is $N_k = N_{ak} + N_{rk}$. Thus, the

---

[15] See Martinson (1974), Sechrest, White, and Brown (1979), and Martin, Sechrest, and Redner (1981) for a review of those findings.

TABLE 5

Parameter Estimates for the Three-Population Model for
Philadelphia, London, Racine, and Marion County

Parameter		Philadelphia ($N = 9,945$)	London ($N = 396$)	Racine ($N = 356$)	Marion County ($N = 1,227$)
β	(Fraction innocent)	.65	.67	.30	.75
p_r	(Recidivism probability for persisters)	.80	.87	.88	.74
p_a	(Recidivism probability for desisters)	.35	.57	.44	.29
α	(Fraction of first offenders who are desisters)	.56	.72	.41	.59

distinction between the persisters and the desisters is a distinction in initial (a priori) arrest probabilities rather than in later (a posteriori) actual arrests. There are persisters and desisters at each arrest stage, although the mix of the arrestees at each successive stage will increasingly be dominated by persisters.

This model requires estimates of the following four parameters: β = proportion of a cohort who are the innocents; p_r = arrest probability for the high-risk persistent offenders; p_a = arrest probability for the low-risk desisters; α = proportion of the offenders at the first arrest who are desisters. The four parameters can be estimated by first assigning β to be its observed value; there is little in the analysis of the recidivism process that can contribute to an estimate of β. Then, p_r was assigned its asymptotic value for those offenders with a large number of arrests.[16] A grid search technique was then used to estimate p_a and α, using the combination[17] that provides the best fit to the observed data (up to and including the eleventh arrest) in terms of minimizing the value of χ^2.

Using this procedure, the parameters for the Philadelphia, London, Racine, and Marion County cohorts were estimated to be the values shown in table 5. The fraction of "innocents" is consistent with those

[16] Other values of p_r can be tried, but in the estimation the best fit was obtained with p_r at the asymptotic value of the observed recidivism probabilities. Asymptotically, the arrestees will be composed almost entirely of persisters.

[17] A model with p_a varying with number of arrests, k, was tried, i.e., $p_a = b_0 + b_1 k^a$. The value of b_1 was not found to be significantly different from zero, and so the constant p_a was used.

shown earlier and reflects the substantial prevalence of involvement with law enforcement. The values of p_r reflect the high recidivism probability for those with the largest number of arrests. The values of p_a and α, which resulted from the grid search, were quite different for the two populations.[18]

In Philadelphia, the fraction of desisters was relatively low at the start, and their recidivism probability was much lower than that of the persisters. As a consequence, their numbers declined rapidly. The evolving composition of the population of offenders is displayed in table 6A. Thus, even though the desisters were a majority of the population of offenders at the first arrest, by the fourth arrest they comprised fewer than 10 percent. For comparison, the same parameters were estimated in Racine and Marion County. Table 5 shows that the Marion County figures are generally similar to those from Philadelphia. The figures from Racine show a very high prevalence, the lowest proportion of desisters, and the highest recidivism probability for the persisters. These values strongly suggest very active policing and a very low threshold of activity leading to a recording of a police contact.

In London, by contrast, the desisters comprised a larger fraction of the initial offending population (72 percent compared to 56 percent in Philadelphia) and their recidivism probability was much higher (.57 compared to .35 in Philadelphia). As a result, they continued to be an important part of the offending population much longer. As shown in table 6B, it was not until the ninth conviction that they shrank to less than 10 percent of the residual offending population.

Figures 3a and 3b depict the actual and the estimated recidivism probabilities for Philadelphia and London as a function of successive involvement. We notice that in Philadelphia the recidivism curve more rapidly rises to its asymptotic value. This results from the fact that the desisters comprise a smaller fraction of the initial population of offenders and also have an appreciably lower recidivism probability. These two factors result in the more rapid saturation of the recidivism probability in Philadelphia, as the few desisters drop out more rapidly, leaving only the persisters.

[18] In the grid search, a sensitivity analysis was conducted to assess the flatness of the χ^2 surface by identifying the contour (α, p_a) where the value of χ^2 exceeds the minimum by 10 percent. The surface is much sharper in Philadelphia than in London. In Philadelphia, the minimum χ^2 is 15.02 at $\alpha = .56$ and $p_a = .35$. The value of χ^2 reaches 16.50 at (.54, .32) and again at (.59, .37). In London, the minimum χ^2 is 6.606 at $\alpha = .72$ and $p_a = .57$, and χ^2 becomes 7.27 at (.60, .51) and again at (.90, .63).

TABLE 6

A. Philadelphia Cohort: Distributions of Arrests Observed and Estimated from Three-Population Model

Arrest Number (k)	Estimated Number of Persisters Still Active at k ($p_r = .80$)	Estimated Number of Desisters Still Active at k ($p_a = .35$)	Estimated Number of Offenders Still Active at k	Observed Number with k or More Arrests	Estimated Aggregate Recidivism Probability ($\hat{p}_k$)	Observed Recidivism Fraction (p_k)	Estimated Number with Exactly k Arrests	Observed Number with Exactly k Arrests
0	...	...	...	9,945	...	...	...	6,470
1	1,529	1,946	3,475	3,475	.349	.349	1,570.7	1,613
2	1,223.2	681.1	1,904.3	1,862	.548	.536	687.4	650
3	978.6	238.4	1,216.9	1,212	.639	.651	350.7	344
4	782.8	83.4	866.3	868	.712	.716	210.8	241
5	626.3	29.2	655.5	627	.757	.722	144.2	162
6	501.0	10.2	511.2	465	.780	.742	106.8	97
7	400.8	3.6	404.4	368	.791	.791	82.5	86
8	320.7	1.3	321.9	282	.796	.766	64.9	57
9	256.5	.4	257.0	225	.798	.798	51.6	39
10	205.2	.2	205.4	186	.799	.827	41.1	39
11	164.2	.1	164.2	147	.800	.790	...	...

B. London Cohort: Distributions of Convictions Observed and Estimated from Three-Population Model

Conviction Number (k)	Estimated Number of Persisters Still Active at k ($p_r = .87$)	Estimated Number of Desisters Still Active at k ($p_a = .57$)	Estimated Number of Offenders Still Active at k	Observed Number with k or More Convictions	Estimated Aggregate Recidivism Probability ($\hat{p}_k$)	Observed Recidivism Fraction (p_k)	Estimated Number with Exactly k Convictions	Observed Number with Exactly k Convictions
0	...	...	...	396	...	...	...	265
1	36.7	94.3	131	131	.331	.331	45.3	49
2	31.9	53.8	85.7	82	.654	.626	27.3	21
3	27.8	30.6	58.4	61	.682	.744	16.8	19
4	24.2	17.5	41.6	42	.713	.689	10.7	10
5	21.0	10.0	31.0	32	.744	.762	7.0	10
6	18.3	5.7	24.0	22	.774	.688	4.8	10
7	15.9	3.2	19.1	20	.799	.909	3.5	2
8	13.8	1.8	15.7	18	.819	.900	2.6	2
9	12.0	1.1	13.1	14	.835	.778	2.0	4
10	10.5	.6	11.1	12	.845	.857	1.6	2
11	9.1	.3	9.5	11	.854	.917	...	1
								...

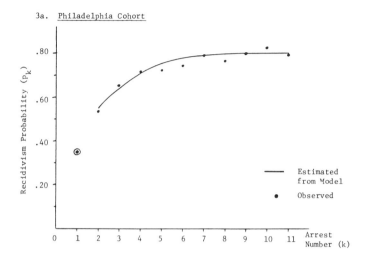

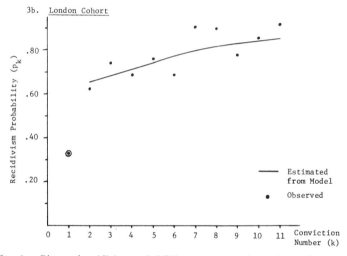

Fig. 3.—Observed recidivism probabilities (p_k) compared to estimates from a three-population model for Philadelphia and London cohorts.

The models proposed here are certainly more satisfactory than the shifted-geometric model and provide a reasonably good fit to the data from Philadelphia and from London. In London, the value of χ^2 was 6.61 for 7 degrees of freedom ($p > .10$), so that the model and the data were not significantly different. For the Philadelphia data, the fit was also very good, as reflected in figure 3a. The number of offenders (3,475) was over twenty-five times as large as in London, however. Therefore, any test of goodness of fit is bound to be excessively powerful—that is, the large sample makes the test excessively sensitive to small departures in the data from the postulated model. For Philadelphia, the value of χ^2 was 15.02 ($p < .05$), a reasonable fit to so large a population of observations.[19]

It should also be emphasized that the three-population model with internal homogeneity within each group is an abstraction that is formulated in those terms for reasons of analytical convenience in displaying the effect of differential drop-out. It is certainly true that there is more continuity between desisters and persisters than suggested by the two discrete populations of offenders. An increase of complexity of the model to take account of this continuity might improve the fit to the data but would contribute little to the insight to be derived from the model.

The critical problem, of course, is finding some means of identifying a priori (at the first encounter) those individuals who are the persisters (and more likely to recidivate) and to distinguish these from the desisters, some of whom will also recidivate, but who will desist much earlier. The seven-point prediction scale developed in the previous section can be used to identify the persisters in the London cohort at the first conviction. We will then be able to explore the consistency of recidivism results based on that identification in comparison with the recidivism behavior of the two groups implied by the persister/desister model.

For this purpose, we construct the cumulative joint Z-score and conviction distribution of table 7. The data for the table are the conviction records and the individual scores on the seven-point prediction scale of the 132 youths in the London cohort with at least one conviction. The first column of table 7 displays the number of youths with scores of Z or greater who have at least one conviction. The numbers in the successive columns decline with the number of youths who experienced at least the indicated number of convictions. Thus, for example, we note that thirty-seven of the convicted youths had scores of at least four, and that twenty-one of these youths had four or more convictions.[20]

---

[19] A four-population model (including a group of "weak persisters") would have provided a better fit but would have involved more elaboration than is warranted by the ten data points and by the basic concept.

[20] The data in table 7 are consistent, of course, with the data presented in table 4. Column 1 of table 7 is the sum of the "true positives" and the "false positives" of table 4, i.e., the total number scoring Z or greater. Column 6 shows the number of "true positives": i.e., the number of chronics with six or more convictions scoring Z or greater.

TABLE 7

Number of Youths in the London Cohort with Scores
of Z or More and with k or More Convictions

Score	(Z)	Number of Convictions (k)									
		1	2	3	4	5	6	7	8	9	10+
	7	2	2	2	1	1	1	1	1	1	0
	6	12	10	8	7	6	5	5	5	5	4
	5	24	20	17	13	11	9	8	8	5	4
Z*	4	37	31	26	21	19	15	14	14	11	10
	3	60	49	40	34	28	20	19	18	14	12
	2	75	57	45	36	30	20	19	18	14	12
	1	105	73	54	39	31	21	19	18	14	12
Total	0	132	83	62	43	33	23	21	18	14	12

The next task involves choice of a cut-off point, now to be used to distinguish the persisters from the desisters. We want to establish a score, Z^*, such that anyone scoring Z^* or above at the first conviction would be labeled a "persister" and anyone scoring below Z^* would be labeled a "desister." The previous analysis based on the model indicates that the fraction of persisters is 28 percent, and this can be used in the choice of the cut-off point, Z^*. As seen from table 7, the fraction scoring four or above is also 28 percent (37/132), so Z^* should be four.[21]

With the selection of the value of Z^*, we now have a way of identifying individuals at their first convictions as either persisters or desisters. We can now examine the drop-out process of the two groups so identified. Figure 4 displays the number of youths in each of the two groups with at least the specified number of convictions. It is clear that the individuals who were classified as persisters (because they scored $Z \geq 4$) have a much slower drop-out rate (i.e., a higher recidivism rate) than those classified as desisters (because they scored $Z < 4$). It is also interesting to compare these numbers based on individual recidivism experience with the aggregate numbers derived from the three-population model (with parameters $p_a = .57$, $p_r = .87$, and $\alpha = .72$). Figure 4 displays this comparison. The two processes—one based on aggregate analytical results from the model and one based on the assign-

[21] The importance of a score of four in this case is undoubtedly influenced by the six youths with this score who had ten or more convictions—a full half of the twelve most intense recidivists.

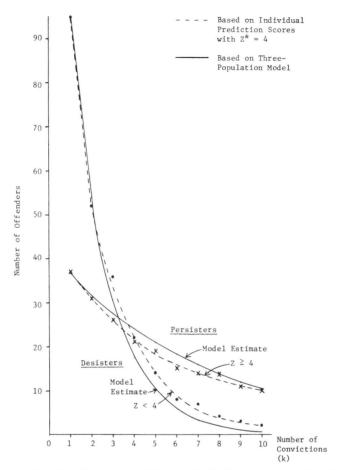

FIG. 4.—Number of persisters and desisters in the London cohort with at least *k* convictions.

ment of individuals based on their Z-scores—show high consistency. These results also highlight the usefulness of the seven-point Z score for distinguishing the persisters from the desisters, viewing those who score four or above on the prediction scale as persisters and those who score below four as desisters.

These results show the appropriateness of distinguishing individuals in terms of differential recidivism probabilities rather than in terms of realized convictions. That probabilistic characterization permits some persisters to drop out early (and so to be "nonchronics" in terms of number of convictions experienced) and some few desisters to accumulate a large number of convictions (and so to become chronics in a retrospective sense). At least in terms of prediction, this persister/desister characterization encourages thinking about populations of offenders in terms of probabilistic expectations rather than in terms of retrospective characterizations.

VI. Conclusions

We have here reviewed the recidivism experience documented within two major cohort studies of youthful offenders in Philadelphia and in London. Both groups displayed similar patterns of involvement with law enforcement. About one-third of each cohort was found to have some involvement: arrest for a broad range of offenses in Philadelphia, and conviction for indictable offenses in London. In both cases, the recidivism probability was found to be about 50–60 percent following the first involvement, to rise with successive involvements, and then to stabilize at a high level (about 80–90 percent) after the first few involvements. We have also analyzed data from two other major cohort studies—in Racine and Marion County—and have found a similar pattern of increasing recidivism, despite the very different prevalence rates (70 and 25 percent, respectively).

We analyzed this rising recidivism probability with a model that invokes three population groups: (1) a group of *innocents* never involved with law enforcement, (2) a group of *desisters* with a relatively low recidivism probability, and (3) a group of *persisters* with a relatively high recidivism probability. The rise in the observed aggregate recidivism probability then reflects the changing composition of the offenders at each stage of involvement; the desisters stop relatively early and so leave a residue composed increasingly of the high-recidivism persisters. This model is also consistent with the finding often reported of chronic offenders (who are always identified retrospectively as those with a large number of involvements) who account for a disproportionate fraction of the total involvements of a cohort of offenders.

The fundamental task in any policy use of this model involves finding a means of identifying the persisters early in the course of their criminal involvement. A scale comprising seven variables measured at ages eight to ten provided reasonably good discrimination between the offenders in the London cohort who had six or more convictions and those who had fewer than six.

There are two perspectives for considering the use of such a prediction scale. One involves an after-the-fact characterization as chronics of those offenders who displayed more than some arbitrarily specified degree of involvement. Then any predictor of the chronics generates an explicit false positive rate (those who were predicted to but did not pass that threshold) and false negative rate (those *not* predicted to pass but who did).

Another perspective suggests using a similar kind of predictor to identify the high-recidivism persisters at their first conviction. Under this perspective, since the persisters and desisters can both recidivate, but at different rates, it is to be expected that some few persisters will drop out early and also that some few desisters will continue to recidivate even after any arbitrary threshold. The two groups will differ markedly, however, in their respective fractions involved in large numbers of offenses. The seven-variable prediction scale was applied to the offenders within the London cohort to identify the persisters. *The dropout process of the persisters and desisters identified individually with this predictor very closely matched the aggregate dropout process for persisters and desisters based only on the theoretical model with parameters estimated from aggregate recidivism data.*

The strength of these results suggests the possibility of early discrimination between the more and the less serious offenders. It also endorses the appropriateness of representing the typical observation of growth in recidivism probability with successive involvements with law enforcement as a process involving a changing mix of a high- and low-recidivism group that is increasingly composed of the high-recidivism group.

Any use of predictors of offenders' subsequent criminal activity must take careful account of the competing concerns over the errors of falsely labeling a true desister as a persister (the false positive problem) or failing to identify a true persister (the false negative problem). The greater the concern over false positives compared to false negatives—the civil-libertarian index in our analysis—the more limited should be the population identified as persisters. Any reflection of that concern must take into account the nature of the intended intervention with those individuals who are labeled as persisters; the more severe the intervention, the greater should be the concern over false positives.

Almost certainly, convicted juvenile offenders will not be singled out for special penal treatment at an early age because they are behaving badly in school, come from poor families, have criminal parents or siblings, have low IQ and attainment, and are subject to poor parental child rearing. It is more likely that such results would inform the design of prevention efforts to be targeted at youths who are behaving badly and who matched the persister profile at their earlier ages. Efforts could then be made, using an experimental design, to counteract or alleviate some of the risk factors. Within that experiment, poorer families might be given income supplements or special help in achieving higher incomes and better living conditions; youths with poor scholastic achievement could be given special tutoring or enrichment programs designed to improve school performance; and parent training efforts could be pursued to improve unsatisfactory child-rearing techniques.

Of course, it would be desirable to try to avoid any stigmatizing effects of participating in the program; one approach to this problem would involve including within the treatment as well as the control group some youths *not* predicted to be delinquent. The treatment and control groups could then be followed up until at least age thirteen to investigate whether these programs have any effect on their behavior and the respective magnitudes of any effects.

If these small-scale experiments prove to be successful in indicating the validity of the predictors and in identifying effective interventions, then social programs based on those results could be formulated.

REFERENCES

Blumstein, A., and S. Moitra. 1980. "The Identification of 'Career Criminals' from 'Chronic Offenders' in a Cohort." *Law and Policy Quarterly* 2:321–34.
Farrington, D. P. 1977. "The Effects of Public Labeling." *British Journal of Criminology* 17:112–25.
———. 1983. "Offending from 10 to 25 Years of Age." In *Prospective Studies of Crime and Delinquency*, edited by K. Van Dusen and S. A. Mednick. Boston: Kluwer-Nijhoff.
———. 1985. "Predicting Self-reported and Official Delinquency." In *Prediction in Criminology*, edited by D. P. Farrington and R. Tarling. Albany, N.Y.: SUNY Press.
Gottfredson, D., and S. Gottfredson. 1980. "Screening for Risk." *Criminal Justice and Behavior* 7:315–30.
Loeber, R., and T. Dishion. 1983. "Early Predictors of Male Delinquency: A Review." *Psychological Bulletin* 94:68–99.
Martin, S. E., L. B. Sechrest, and R. Redner, eds. 1981. *New Directions in the Rehabilitation of Criminal Offenders*. Washington, D.C.: National Academy Press.
Martinson, R. M. 1974. "What Works? Questions and Answers about Prison Reform." *Public Interest* 35:22–54.

Polk, K., C. Alder, G. Bazemore, G. Blake, S. Cordroy, G. Coventry, J. Galvin, and M. Temple. 1981. *An Analysis of Maturational Development from Ages 16 to 30 of a Cohort of Young Men*. Eugene: University of Oregon, Department of Sociology.

Sechrest, L., S. O. White, and E. D. Brown, eds. 1979. *The Rehabilitation of Criminal Offenders: Problems and Prospects*. Washington, D.C.: National Academy Press.

Shannon, L. W. (1981). *Assessing the Relationship of Adult Criminal Careers to Juvenile Careers*. Iowa City: Iowa Urban Community Research Center, University of Iowa.

von Neumann, J., and O. Morgenstern. 1944. *Theory of Games and Economic Behavior*. Princeton, N.J.: Princeton University Press.

West, D. J. 1969. *Present Conduct and Future Delinquency*. London: Heinemann.

———. 1982. *Delinquency: Its Roots, Careers, and Prospects*. London: Heinemann.

West, D. J., and D. P. Farrington. 1973. *Who Becomes Delinquent?* London: Heinemann.

———. 1977. *The Delinquent Way of Life*. London: Heinemann.

Wiggins, J. S. 1973. *Personality and Prediction: Principles of Personality Assessment*. Reading, Mass.: Addison-Wesley.

Wolfgang, M. E., R. M. Figlio, and T. Sellin. 1972. *Delinquency in a Birth Cohort*. Chicago: University of Chicago Press.

Phillip E. Johnson

The Turnabout in the Insanity Defense

ABSTRACT

For over a century the dominant test of legal insanity in the United States was that set out by the English judges in Daniel M'Naghten's case in 1843, under which it must be "clearly proved that, at the time of the committing of the act, the party accused was laboring under such a defect of reason, from disease of the mind, as not to know the nature and quality of the act he was doing; or if he did know it, that he did not know he was doing what was wrong." In the 1950s, two competing formulas emerged: the "Durham" test—under which criminal conduct is excused when it is the "product" of mental disease or defect—and the American Law Institute's Model Penal Code. By the early 1980s, the Model Code formula, which excused a defendant if he lacked substantial capacity to control his own behavior, had been adopted in a majority of American jurisdictions. The case of John Hinckley, who attempted to assassinate President Reagan and who was acquitted on grounds of insanity, has precipitated calls for abolition or alteration of the insanity defense. The growing practice of deinstitutionalizing the mentally ill has cast doubt on the propriety of long term confinement of insanity acquittees. Several jurisdictions have adopted new approaches, including the defense of "guilty but insane." The major professional organizations—the American Psychiatric Association, the American Medical Association, and the American Bar Association—have repudiated the Model Penal Code approach. There is at present a near consensus that the insanity defense has become too broad and that it is a mistake to allow juries or expert witnesses to speculate about whether a defendant had free will at a given moment in the past. Medical and legal authorities are united in rejecting the notion of the previous generation of reformers that a broader insanity defense would make the criminal law more therapeutic and less punitive. Official positions adopted by the AMA, the ABA, and the APA signal these recent

Phillip E. Johnson is Professor of Law at the University of California, Berkeley.

© 1985 by The University of Chicago. All rights reserved.
0-226-80800-9/85/0006-0006$01.00

developments and illuminate the major differences among the approaches currently under discussion.

For over a century, the dominant test of legal insanity in the United States was that set out by the English judges in Daniel M'Naghten's case in 1843. The "M'Naghten rule" or "right-wrong test" allowed the defense only where it could be "clearly proved that, at the time of the committing of the act, the party accused was laboring under such a defect of reason, from disease of the mind, as not to know the nature and quality of the act he was doing; or if he did know it, that he did not know he was doing what was wrong" (Weinreb 1980, p. 452). Some jurisdictions supplemented this concept of "knowledge of wrong-fulness" with an additional "irresistible-impulse" test, which in extreme cases allowed the jury to acquit a defendant whose act resulted from a sudden and overpowering impulse (Weinreb 1980, pp. 459–60).

During the past twenty-five years, the insanity defense has been reshaped by the influential proposals of the American Law Institute's *Model Penal Code* (1955, 1962). The *Code* modified the traditional M'Naghten knowledge-of-wrongfulness test in a manner calculated to make it easier to demonstrate lack of criminal responsibility. There were two principal innovations. First, the new test excused anyone who lacked "substantial capacity to appreciate the criminality of his conduct." The purpose of using the terms "substantial capacity" and "appreciate" was to make it clear that a total lack of knowledge of the act's wrongfulness was not required, so that a defendant who "knew" only in some abstract sense that it was wrong to kill people or to steal might nonetheless be excused if his ability to understand or internalize that knowledge was seriously affected.

Second and more important, the *Code* introduced a volitional element to add to the solely cognitive test of the M'Naghten rule. The mentally ill defendant was to be excused, not only if he could not appreciate the criminality of his conduct, but also if he lacked "substantial capacity to conform his conduct to the requirements of law." The logic of excusing persons who cannot control their own conduct is straightforward: such persons ought not to be blamed, and in any event they cannot be deterred by the threat of punishment. If we assume that some criminal acts are directed by free will and others by psychological compulsion, and that juries guided by psychiatrists can accurately distinguish freely willed acts from psychologically compelled acts, then it follows that we should punish the former and not the latter. The *Code*'s drafters felt that the irresistible-impulse test was an inept formulation of this principle, because its wording implied a limitation to "sudden, spontaneous acts as opposed to propulsions that are accompanied by brooding or reflection" (American Law Institute 1955, p. 157).

The history of the insanity defense after 1962 was the history of gradual adoption of the *Model Penal Code*'s provision (commonly called the ALI [American Law Institute] test) in jurisdiction after jurisdiction. Even the United States Court of Appeals for the District of Columbia Circuit, which in 1954 had adopted the celebrated but unworkable "disease-product" rule that for a time seemed the wave of the future, acknowledged the superiority of the ALI formula in 1972 (*United States v. Brawner*, 471 F.2d 969 [D.C. Cir. 1972]). By 1982, every federal court of appeals and about half the states had adopted the ALI test. When the California supreme court belatedly adopted the ALI formulation in 1978, the court's opinion reflected an assumption that the step was nothing more than an acknowledgment of universally accepted scientific reality, much as if the court were to endorse the theory of relativity (*People v. Drew*, 22 Cal. 3d 333 [1978]). It seemed that the nearly impossible had been accomplished: a formulation of the insanity principle now existed that had the support of all except the most extreme determinists on one side and the most punitive reactionary elements on the other.

That complacency has been abruptly shattered. During 1982 and 1983, the American Psychiatric Association, the American Bar Association, and the American Medical Association announced official positions decisively repudiating the ALI test, and especially its crucial volitional element. The occasion for this shift of position was the notorious verdict in the case of John Hinckley, who wounded President Reagan and several other persons in an assassination attempt motivated by Hinckley's desire to impress a movie actress whom he had admired from a distance. Under federal law, the jury had to be instructed that they should acquit if there was a reasonable doubt about the defendant's sanity under the ALI test. If taken literally, that instruction amounted to a directed verdict of not guilty, given the fantastic motive and the fact that some distinguished psychiatrists had testified that Hinckley was insane. Frequently juries ignore the law in such cases and convict anyway, but the Hinckley jury surprised everyone by taking the instruction seriously and returning a not guilty verdict (Taylor 1982).

The resulting public outcry focused attention on the legal rules that seem to invite such a result. The *Hinckley* verdict was unquestionably the *occasion* for the reevaluation of the insanity defense by the major professional organizations, but it was no more the *cause* of their shift in position than the attack on Fort Sumter was the cause of the Civil War. Widespread intellectual discontent with psychiatric testimony and its accompanying ideology had existed well before the *Hinckley* case, and had already influenced a major law reform effort: the "deinstitutionalization" of the mentally ill.

Not very long ago, it was generally assumed that psychiatrists were capable of identifying dangerously mentally ill persons and predicting their future behavior. Society routinely locked such persons away in institutions until they should be "cured." Beginning in the 1960s, an unusual alliance of civil liberties lawyers, mental health professionals, and budget-cutting politicians cooperated to curtail drastically the practice of institutionalizing the mentally ill (Rhoden 1982). This change was made possible by a technological innovation: the development of new drug therapies that effectively control many of the destructive symptoms of mental illness. Deinstitutionalization also had its ideological side, however, and the ideology was one of pervasive distrust of psychiatric testimony. There was no lack of ammunition. Anyone with courtroom experience knows that psychiatric judgment is so extremely subjective that it is usually possible to retain a reputable psychiatrist to testify on either side of any controversial question. Diagnostic categories have changed enormously over the years, and on some topics (e.g., homosexuality) they have a political as well as a scientific dimension (Ennis and Littwack 1974).

The campaign to protect the liberties of the mentally ill particularly called into question the ability of psychiatrists to predict dangerous behavior. In this effect as in others, the opponents of psychiatric excess found that they had powerful allies within the psychiatric profession. Psychiatrists themselves were increasingly eager to disclaim omniscience. To their credit, genuine advances in knowledge inclined them to a greater humility in the face of what remained to be learned. Today, it is perfectly orthodox to say that psychiatrists have very little ability to predict behavior, and certainly their predictions are not sufficiently accurate to be relied upon as a justification for taking away a person's liberty (Diamond 1974).

There has been considerable difficulty over whether we can continue to justify routine confinement of the "criminally" insane in the light of the reforms in civil mental commitment law. Insanity acquittees are supposed to be not guilty, after all, and so they do not deserve to be punished. Furthermore, the verdict may mean only that there was a reasonable doubt as to the sanity of the accused at the time of the event, months or even years before the verdict. It would seem that a mental commitment order ought to be based on a determination that the former defendant is insane *and* dangerous at present, a conclusion that might be difficult to justify if we assume that there is no reliable method for determining dangerousness.

Judges have understandably been uncertain whether to accept a compelling line of argument that leads to outcomes—possibly including the outright release of such as John Hinckley—that society cannot accept. In *People v. McQuillan*, 392 Mich. 511, 221 N.W.2d 569 (1974), the supreme court of Michigan held that the State's insanity acquittees could be confined for evaluation only for sixty days, after which they were entitled to the same procedural protections as any other civilly committed patient. This decision led the Michigan legislature to pass the first law authorizing a verdict of "guilty but insane" (Stone 1982; see also *Benham v. Edwards*, 678 F.2d 511 [5th Cir. 1982]).

On the other hand, the United States Supreme Court recently upheld the constitutionality of the provisions of the District of Columbia Code which provide for automatic, indefinite commitment of defendants found not guilty by reason of insanity, with subsequent release only for those who can prove by a preponderance of the evidence that they are no longer insane or dangerous (*Jones v. United States*, 103 S. Ct. 3043 [1983]). The Supreme Court also held that the period of commitment was not limited by the maximum term of the criminal offense for which the accused might have been convicted. The *Jones* decision is highly questionable on its facts, since the only evidence of the acquittee's dangerousness was that he had committed an attempted petty theft, although he stipulated that he was insane at the time of the offense. It would be still more difficult for the courts to justify automatic commitment after a trial in which the acquittee had merely raised a reasonable doubt as to his sanity.

Although the customary practice of automatic commitment for insanity acquittees is not quite dead, its defenders are suffering from acute intellectual embarrassment. Dr. Alan Stone, a professor of law and psychiatry at Harvard University who was influential in formulating the American Psychiatric Association's statement on the insanity defense, commented that "the law created by the civil libertarians and the methods of treatment developed by psychiatrists now push in the same direction, and the traditional way of dealing with persons found not guilty by reason of insanity has been drastically transformed" (Stone 1982, p. 20).

The public reaction to the *Hinckley* verdict thus provided the occasion for a reevaluation of psychiatric defenses that was overdue and inevitable in any case. To guide the reader through the details of the three major reform proposals under consideration, following is an extremely condensed summary of each organization's institutional position:

1. The American Psychiatric Association's (APA) *Statement on the Insanity Defense* takes the position that the insanity defense should be retained but drastically narrowed. Because the criminal law presumes that punishment for wrongful deeds should be predicated on moral culpability, there must logically be a defense for defendants who do not possess free will and therefore cannot be said to have "chosen to do wrong" (APA 1982, p. 8). Although it assumes that lack of free will is the moral basis of the insanity defense, the APA nonetheless recommends eliminating the ALI test, with its controversial volitional element, in favor of a modernized wording of the M'Naghten formula drafted by Richard Bonnie (APA 1982, p. 12). This test excuses the defendant only if, as a result of mental disease or retardation, he was "unable to appreciate the wrongfulness of his conduct at the time of the offense." "Mental disease" is limited to conditions that "grossly and demonstrably impair a person's perception or understanding of reality": conditions such as "psychopathic personality disturbance" are emphatically excluded (APA 1982, p. 11).

Many lawyers and judges will be surprised to learn that psychiatrists no longer wish to testify as experts on the defendant's capacity to control his conduct and that they prefer a narrow definition of mental disease to an open-ended one. Expansion of the insanity defense in these respects was once thought to be necessary to permit psychiatrists to explain the defendant's condition without undue legalistic restrictions. Nonetheless, the APA *Statement* explains that psychiatric testimony about whether a defendant understood the wrongfulness of his act "is more reliable and has a stronger scientific basis" than does psychiatric testimony about whether a defendant could control his behavior. The APA acknowledges that "psychiatry is a deterministic discipline that views all human behavior as, to a good extent, 'caused.' " On the other hand, psychiatrists disagree about how this deterministic outlook should affect the moral and philosophical question of whether a person is responsible for his conduct. Expert psychiatric testimony about volition is therefore likely to be confusing to the jury (APA 1982, pp. 10–11).

The APA takes no position on whether the defense or prosecution should have the burden of proof, but does observe that psychiatric issues are usually not susceptible to proof "beyond a reasonable doubt." The APA does not oppose evidentiary rules that limit psychiatric testimony to description of the defendant's condition and bar any statement on the "ultimate issue" of sanity or insanity (APA 1982, pp. 12–13).

Finally, the APA argues that it is a mistake to treat persons acquitted of violent crimes on the grounds of insanity as if they were equivalent to mentally ill persons who have not attacked anyone. They should be confined in a secure facility and the decision to release should be made by a group similar in composition to a parole board (APA 1982, pp. 14–18). In other words, they should be treated much as they would be treated if they had been convicted. It is not clear that a defendant would receive any benefit from an acquittal under these circumstances, unless it be to escape a possible death sentence. Nonetheless, the APA *Statement* opposes allowing the jury to return a compromise verdict of "guilty but insane," on the ground that this too-easy alternative permits the jury to settle on a convenient label and thus avoid "grappling with the difficult moral issues inherent in adjudicating guilt or innocence," a task which serves an "important symbolic function" (APA 1982, p. 9).

2. The American Bar Association's (ABA) House of Delegates approved new standards for the insanity defense in February 1983. Like the APA, the ABA recommends dropping the volitional prong of the ALI test and excusing only persons who are "unable to appreciate the wrongfulness" of their criminal acts. The ABA does not limit the concept of mental disease to conditions producing a gross misperception of reality, however. Instead, it merely states that "mental disease or defect refers to impairments of mind, whether enduring or transitory, or to mental retardation which substantially affected the mental or emotional process of the defendant at the time of the alleged offense." The commentary states that this definition "attempts to clarify the meaning of the term 'mental disease or defect' " (ABA 1983, pp. 197–201). One wonders what the drafters would have written had their intent been to allow the term to remain obscure.

Otherwise, the ABA *Standards* provide that expert testimony about mental illness may be admissible where it is relevant to show that the defendant did not have the specific mental state required by the definition of the defense. (The APA did not address this question.) The defendant would be required to give advance notice of any defense based on mental condition and to submit to examination by court-appointed experts. The ABA would also restrict the psychiatrist from testifying on the ultimate issue of sanity and would place the burden of persuasion by a preponderance of the evidence on the prosecution. The ABA contemplates a civil commitment procedure following a verdict of not guilty by reason of insanity, but the sections of the *Standards* that deal with this subject have yet to be approved by the House of Delegates (ABA 1983, pp. 197–219).

3. The American Medical Association (AMA) approved a more radical change at its 1983 annual meeting. The AMA recommends that the defense of legal insanity be abolished outright and replaced by statutes providing for acquittal when a criminal defendant, as a result of mental disease or otherwise, lacks the state of mind or mens rea required as an element of the defense charged. Defendants found not guilty on this basis would be subject to civil commitment, with a presumption of continuing dangerousness for those acquitted of offenses involving violence. They would be released only on concurring medical certification and judicial determination that release poses no substantial public risk. Where mental illness does not serve as a defense (because it does not have the effect of causing the defendant to lack the culpability required by the definition of the offense), it could nonetheless be considered in mitigation of sentence (AMA 1983, p. 37).

The major disagreement, then, is that the organized medical profession wants to abolish the defense altogether, while the bar and psychiatric associations want to retain the defense but limit it fairly drastically. The AMA position explicitly endorses the reasoning of Norval Morris, whose book *Madness and the Criminal Law* (1982) argued for abolition of the special defense of legal insanity in favor of an approach directed solely to whether the defendant has satisfied the culpability requirements for the crime.

As applied to the *Hinckley* case, the AMA approach would mean that mental illness would be relevant only if it tended to show that Hinckley was incapable of forming an intent to kill anyone, which of course it would not. Hinckley's bizarre motive and history of irrational behavior would be considered only at sentencing, where such evidence might have a double effect. It would tend to lessen the defendant's blameworthiness, but at the same time it would tend to support confinement on the grounds of extraordinary dangerousness. Morris argues that psychiatric predictions of dangerousness are so fallible that courts should rarely rely on them as a basis for *increasing* a sentence (Morris 1982, pp. 171–72). Whether judges would respect that limitation in practice is doubtful.

The U.S. Department of Justice asked Congress to abolish the insanity defense during both the Nixon and Reagan administrations, although more recently it has supported the ABA-APA proposals to narrow the defense (Smith 1982). Now abolition has the support of the organized medical profession and one of our most prominent criminal justice scholars. The AMA report, relying heavily upon Morris, argues that it is arbitrary to single out mental illness from other factors that affect behavior. Why should mental illness be an excuse from criminal responsibility when "gross social adversity" (AMA 1983, pp. 30–31) is not? Morris wrote that because criminal behavior is less closely correlated with psychosis than with "being born to a one parent family living on welfare in a black inner-city area" (Morris 1982, pp. 62–63), it is irrational to allow a complete defense in one case and not the other (AMA 1983, pp. 30–31).

Moreover, according to Morris and the AMA Report, the special insanity defense does not even accomplish its stated purpose of shielding the mentally impaired from punishment. In practice it operates capriciously to exonerate a few mentally ill offenders who are either lucky or exceptionally well defended, while others with equally serious impairments go to prison. The AMA, quoting Morris, thus condemned the insanity defense as "an ornate rarity, a tribute to our capacity to pretend to a moral position while pursuing profoundly different practices" (AMA 1983, p. 30). This is a strong argument, particularly if one assumes that homicidal insanity acquittees are going to be locked away for at least as long as if they were convicted. How can the existence of such a defense be essential to the moral integrity of the criminal law if it makes so little tangible difference to the disposition of the offender?

Despite the strength of the argument, Morris's position is definitely a minority one among legal scholars. Most authorities would agree with the view of the APA and the ABA that recognition of an insanity defense is logically necessary to any criminal justice system based on a premise of moral accountability (Bonnie 1983). To understand the strength of this majority position, it is useful to compare the defense of insanity with the universally recognized and uncontroversial defense of infancy. The reason that we do not hold young children accountable under the criminal law is not that they are incapable of forming an intent. Even a dog knows the difference between being kicked and being stumbled over, and children know the difference between hurting other children accidentally and "on purpose." Although a child is capable of forming an intent, we do not consider small children to be sufficiently rational to hold them fully accountable for their behavior. Similarly, through the institution of the juvenile court we give adolescents something like a defense of "partial responsibility."

If this is uncontroversial with respect to actual children, then it ought to be equally acceptable when applied to the severely mentally retarded, and to psychotics who suffer a gross misperception of reality. The point is not that psychotics or the severely retarded are more likely than other people to commit crimes. On the contrary, it is probable that the more severely retarded or psychotic one is, the more likely it is that one will be incapable of complicated purposeful action of any kind, including criminal action. After all, six-year-old children hardly ever commit homicide, but when they do, they are excused. The insanity defense is a logical extension of the same principle. It divides those who are sufficiently rational to be held accountable for their actions from those who have not reached that level of understanding or maturity and perhaps never will (Johnson 1983).

The difference between children and psychotics, of course, is that psychotics are often extremely dangerous people, although it may be difficult to say exactly how dangerous a particular psychotic is. For this reason we confine psychotics who have committed violent acts, sometimes for a longer time than if they were found to be morally responsible. The AMA report cited this practice as evidence of social hypocrisy, and perhaps it is, but it is not illogical. The purpose of the insanity defense is not necessarily to benefit the insane offender, and it is certainly not to guarantee his liberty. On the contrary, a verdict of legal insanity (under a narrow definition such as that proposed by the APA) labels the individual as so thoroughly irrational that he cannot be trusted with liberty or expected to benefit from it. Perhaps the difference between convicting and committing a psychotic is largely a matter of symbolism (where the death penalty is not in the picture), but symbols are not necessarily unimportant.

An insanity defense of some kind therefore fits logically in a criminal justice system that holds most but not all human beings morally responsible for their actions. It does not follow, however, that we should have an insanity defense that is so broad as to exculpate persons whom the *community* considers morally responsible, regardless of whether a psychiatric diagnosis would appropriately include these persons within the category of the mentally ill. The ALI test contains the potential for extending the defense far beyond the limited number of persons whom the public does not in fact consider responsible for their actions. This is because the "substantial-capacity" test excuses persons who are not totally irrational, and especially because inability to control one's conduct is an open-ended, speculative concept. Our prisons are full of persons with damaged personalities and a long history of lack of success in controlling their impulses (Morris 1982).

The argument for adding a volitional element to the insanity defense was that it was thought to comport with the reality of mental illness, which may lead to a loss of behavioral control even where it does not affect the cognitive capacity to understand the wrongfulness of what one is doing (ALI 1955, p. 157). Progressive reformers in the early 1960s were not worried that the jury would fall under undue influence from psychiatrists, or be hopelessly confused by professional debate over the validity of untestable deterministic theories of human behavior. They thought that the problem was rather how to open up the trial process so that jurors could fully understand what the psychiatrists wanted to tell them about the psychological causes of the defendant's behavior. As the psychiatrists became more knowledgeable about the real causes of criminal conduct, they would succeed in persuading ordinary persons sitting as jurors to accept their theories. If increasing psychiatric knowledge led to an increasing number of insanity acquittals, then this would be because the community, acting through the jurors, willed it to be so. Increasingly accurate psychiatric diagnosis would also lead to increasingly effective cures, and the public's safety would be far more efficaciously protected by humane treatment of the offender than by a brutal prison system which embitters its inmates (see, e.g., *United States v. Wade*, 426 U.S. 64, 66–67, 72 [9th Cir. 1970]).

The dramatic turnabout that has occurred on this issue is best illustrated by the 1982 APA statement. Although lawyers who endorsed the ALI test thought that they were thereby permitting psychiatrists to testify more realistically to what they knew about the human personality and the causes of criminal behavior, the official voice of psychiatry now suggests that with all good intentions the lawyers were leading psychiatry into a quagmire. The familiar "battle of the experts" in insanity trials has embarrassed the profession enormously by giving the impression that psychiatrists are quacks or worse. But it is the question that the law asks, rather than the answers that the experts give, that is to blame for the situation. No one knows whether a criminal who has committed a crime for some bizarre motive could have acted otherwise if he had wished to do so. All three organizations agree on this point. In the words of Richard Bonnie, quoted with approval in both the ABA and the AMA reports: "[E]xperience confirms that there still is no accurate scientific basis for measuring one's capacity for self-control or for calibrating the impairment of such capacity. There is, in short, no objective basis for distinguishing between offenders who were undeterrable and those who were merely undeterred, between the impulse that was irresistible and the impulse not resisted, or between substantial impairment of capacity and some lesser impairment" (ABA 1983, p. 199; AMA 1983, p. 10; Bonnie 1983, p. 196).

It would be wrong to emphasize the disagreement over whether or not to abolish the insanity defense when there is so much on which all three organizations agree. All agree that the present law ought to be drastically changed, and all agree on the direction that the change ought to take. It is likely that Congress will legislate for the first time on this subject in the near future, and its task will be greatly assisted by the degree of consensus that exists among the three major professional organizations and the Department of Justice.

First, there is a general agreement that it is a mistake to allow either the jury or the expert witnesses to speculate about whether a particular defendant had free will at a particular moment in the past. In retrospect, it seems difficult to understand why the reformers of the previous generation were so confident that psychiatric testimony on this subject would be enlightening to the jury rather than confusing and contradictory. Perhaps the best explanation is that the reformers thought that no harm would be done by erroneous insanity acquittals, because confinement in a mental institution would adequately protect the security of the public and at the same time provide much more humane treatment to the offender than a term in prison. From this perspective, what needed to be done was to provide for as many insanity acquittals as public opinion would allow, the jury being seen as a surrogate for public opinion.

The reaction to the *Hinckley* verdict plainly belied the notion that the public regards the jury, particularly a jury subject to manipulation by lawyers and confused by incomprehensible legal standards, as an adequate safeguard for the public interest. It is also now clear that the psychiatric profession itself shares to some degree the general public's skepticism about the objectivity of psychiatric knowledge. Indeed, the APA *Statement* is so emphatic in denying that psychiatrists are experts about whether a particular individual had control over his behavior or not that the statement could be used in court to challenge the qualifications of a psychiatric expert even in the absence of any change in the law. If the organization best qualified to speak for the psychiatric profession considers free will to be a legal and moral concept whose existence cannot be proved or disproved by psychiatric methods, then no individual psychiatrist should be permitted to mislead a jury by offering "expert" testimony on this subject. Where a witness does so testify, the *Statement* should provide material for effective cross examination (see Johnson 1983).

The second major point of agreement is that persons found not guilty of a crime solely because of their mental illness should not be released outright but should be subject to civil commitment to protect the safety of the public. The *Statement* asserts that the dangerousness of insanity acquittees who have perpetrated violent acts can be assumed from the nature of those acts, without relying on psychiatric predictions. Release of violent mentally ill persons should be at the discretion of "an experienced body that is not naive about the nature of violent behavior committed by mental patients and that allows a quasi-criminal approach for managing such persons" (APA 1982, p. 17). In short, where confinement of the mentally ill beyond a reasonable period for treatment is necessary to protect the public safety or to satisfy public opinion, the psychiatrists would rather not be responsible for managing the institutions or setting the release date. The AMA report also contemplates civil commitment for defendants acquitted because a mental impairment prevented them from forming the required intent or mens rea. In such cases, the AMA recommends that there should be a "presumption of continuing dangerousness with respect to those acquitted of offenses involving violence." Release from custody "should be based on concurring medical certification and judicial determination that release poses no substantial public risk" (AMA 1983, p. 37). Probably the ABA position will be similar to the others, when the details of the civil commitment procedures have been officially approved.

It seems to be generally agreed that the difficulties of predicting dangerous conduct do not require that we release defendants who are found not morally responsible for violent actions solely because of their mental impairment. The APA and the AMA both reject the notion, popular with some lawyers and judges, that it is unfair to treat persons who have been found not guilty of a violent crime on insanity grounds differently from persons who have never attacked anyone. In fact, if we wish to preserve the liberties of mentally ill persons who do not commit serious criminal acts, it is essential to treat insanity acquittees as a separate legal category. The inevitable consequence of treating both groups alike is that society will demand broad civil commitment authority for all persons who are mentally ill, so it can be sure that homicidal psychotics will not be at liberty. The "criminally insane" ought to be treated separately from the harmlessly mentally ill, and the difference in treatment should be based on the actual commission of violent acts rather than on psychiatric prediction.

The difference between substantially narrowing the insanity defense and eliminating it altogether may not be very great in practical terms. Cases like *Hinckley*, where batteries of psychiatrists testify against each other in an all-out adversary battle, are the exception rather than the rule. Many insanity verdicts are by stipulation, with all parties agreed that a commitment for psychiatric treatment is a more appropriate disposition than a prison sentence. Presumably, some means would be found to divert most of these defendants from the criminal process even if they no longer had a defense. On the other hand, it is difficult to imagine that the prosecution would lose many contested insanity cases if the defense were limited to those defendants unable to understand the wrongfulness of their conduct, if the burden of proof were placed on the defense, and if psychiatrists were prevented from testifying about the ultimate issue of sanity. Under either proposal, few mental illness defenses would succeed in contested cases, and a successful defense would result in a civil commitment process fully adequate to protect the public interest. That this is the outcome desired by the leading professional organizations concerned with mental health is a striking change from the optimism and idealism of past years. We used to think that advancing psychiatric knowledge would make criminal punishment seem primitive and ineffective as a means of combating crime. Instead, we have learned how far we are from any ability to understand the mysteries of human freedom, evil, and moral responsibility.

Postscript
The reforms discussed in this article came to pass while this volume
was in press. On October 14, 1984, President Reagan signed the Comprehensive Crime Control Act of 1984, containing the "Insanity Defense Reform Act of 1984." This Act (codified as 18 U.S.C.A. § 20)
narrows the insanity defense in federal criminal cases to situations
where the defendant "as a result of a severe mental disease or defect,
was unable to appreciate the nature and quality or the wrongfulness of
his acts" at the time of the offense. The statute also provides that the
defendant has the burden of proving his insanity by clear and convincing evidence, and there are stringent civil commitment proceedings for
persons found not guilty by reason of insanity.

REFERENCES

American Bar Association. 1983. *Report on Standards for Criminal Justice: Nonre-
sponsibility for Crime.* Chicago: American Bar Association.
American Law Institute. 1955. *Model Penal Code.* Tentative Draft no. 4. Phila-
delphia: American Law Institute.
———. 1962. *Model Penal Code.* Proposed Official Draft. Philadelphia: Ameri-
can Law Institute.
American Medical Association. 1983. *Report of the Board of Trustees: The Insanity
Defense in Criminal Trials and Limitation of Psychiatric Testimony.* Chicago:
American Medical Association.
American Psychiatric Association. 1982. *Statement on the Insanity Defense.* Wash-
ington, D.C.: American Psychiatric Association.
Bonnie, Richard J. 1982. *A Model Statute on the Insanity Defense.* Charlottesville:
University of Virginia, Institute of Law, Psychiatry and Public Policy.
———. 1983. "The Moral Basis of the Insanity Defense." *American Bar Associa-
tion Journal* 69 :194–97.
Diamond, Bernard L. 1974. "The Psychiatric Prediction of Dangerousness."
University of Pennsylvania Law Review 123:439–52.
Ennis, Bruce J., and Thomas R. Littwack. 1974. "Psychiatry and the Presump-
tion of Expertise: Flipping Coins in the Courtroom." *California Law Review*
62:693–752.
Johnson, Phillip E. 1983. "Book Review." *University of Chicago Law Review*
50:1534–49.
Morris, Norval. 1982. *Madness and the Criminal Law.* Chicago: University of
Chicago Press.
Rhoden, Nancy K. 1982. "The Limits of Liberty: Deinstitutionalization,
Homelessness, and Libertarian Theory." *Emory Law Journal* 31:375–440.
Smith, William French. 1982. "Limiting the Insanity Defense: A Rational
Approach to Irrational Crimes." *University of Missouri Law Review* 47:605–19.

236   Phillip E. Johnson

Stone, Alan. 1982. "The Insanity Defense on Trial." *Harvard Law School Bulletin* 34(1):15–21.

Taylor, Stuart. 1982. "Too Much Justice." *Harper's* (September 1982), pp. 56–64.

Weinreb, Lloyd L. 1980. *Criminal Law: Cases, Comment, Questions.* Mineola, N.Y.: Foundation Press.

Annika Snare and Ulla Bondeson

Criminological Research in Scandinavia

EDITORS' NOTE.—Volume 5 included a collection of essays on the organization, funding, and orientation of criminological research in five countries—Australia, Canada, Great Britain, the Netherlands, and West Germany. This essay addresses criminological research in the five Scandinavian countries and considers both their common efforts under the auspices of the Scandinavian Research Council for Criminology and their separate national approaches. Although the Scandinavian countries are small in population, their contribution to criminological knowledge has been disproportionately large. The organization of research and teaching vary substantially from country to country, as do the research subjects that receive particular attention.

The Nordic community of criminological researchers defies categorization by country. The Finnish scholar Patrick Törnudd has observed: "When reading an anonymous piece of criminological research (to secure such anonymity would call for rather elaborate preparations!) the basic training, age and perhaps political orientation of the writer would, I think, generally be more easy to discern than the writer's country or employment by university/government" (1983, p. 7). This is true, but there are nonetheless substantial differences in national and political culture in the Scandinavian countries, and these are reflected in their approaches to criminological research. This essay reflects a tension between the cultural homogeneity that outsiders perceive to exist in Scandinavia and important national differences. We describe general trends that transcend national boundaries of criminological research, and we discuss the programs and emphases of the separate countries. Although Icelandic developments are mentioned briefly, primary emphasis is on the four larger countries—Denmark, Finland, Norway, and Sweden.

The first section discusses the Scandinavian Research Council for Criminology, established to build ties between the separate national

Annika Snare and Ulla Bondeson are, respectively, Senior Fellow and Professor of Criminology in the Institute of Criminal Science, University of Copenhagen.

efforts. The organization of research and teaching in the different countries is described in Section II. Section III explores the issue of government influence on research priorities, and Section IV offers an overview of recent research trends.

I. Scandinavian Research Council for Criminology

The Scandinavian Research Council for Criminology was established in 1962 to promote and coordinate criminological research within the member states. The national governments of Denmark, Finland, Iceland, Norway, and Sweden provide funding and appoint the thirteen members of the executive council. Iceland has only one delegate. The other countries each have three representatives, of whom two are acknowledged criminologists and a third represents the respective ministry of justice.

Day-to-day administration is handled by a secretariat based in the country of the chairman. The chairmanship rotates between countries with a term generally lasting three to four years. The first chairman, in 1962, was Professor Johs Andenæs, one of the founders of the council. The secretariat moved to Copenhagen in 1983 when Professor Ulla Bondeson became the current chairman. The annual budget is now equivalent to US$150,000 and is used to initiate and coordinate comparative research, to fund individual studies, to arrange and sponsor various seminars, and to disseminate reports and newsletters.

The council's limited resources do not permit full-scale support of major projects. Somewhat more than half of the annual budget is allocated for research grants—to sustain pilot projects or to help fund a limited part of a larger undertaking. The council has given particular emphasis to comparative studies and has initiated cross-national projects, for example, self-report studies and victim surveys.

Seven volumes of *Scandinavian Studies in Criminology* have been published under the council's auspices since 1965. These volumes, published in English, and two booklets prepared for the quadrennial U.N. world conferences on criminal policy (Aspelin et al. 1975; Bishop 1980), indicate the council's ambition to facilitate Nordic involvement in the international research community.

Since a major aim of the council is to enhance communication and cooperation among the five countries, a series of "contact seminars" are sponsored at which researchers and officials who share common interests in specific criminal justice subjects meet to discuss current research and policy issues.

The council also convenes an annual research seminar for criminologists from the five countries. About fifty people usually attend, representing the academic world, semigovernmental or governmental research institutions, the ministries of justice, and social work agencies. The twenty-fifth seminar was held in Finland in 1983. There were two themes: "environmental crimes" and Scandinavian criminology in a historical perspective. To give readers from other countries a sense of the issues that have been of particular interest in recent years, and perhaps to provide a basis for comparing Scandinavian trends with those in other countries, the subjects of the annual conferences since 1972 are listed in table 1.

The choice of subjects for the annual conference reflects changing research emphases and, to some extent, the preferences of the host nation. This last point should not be overstressed. Danish pragmatism, however, rests comfortably with a meeting focusing on the relevance of criminological findings to legislative or administrative policymaking. Likewise, it is not surprising that the formulation of a new criminal policy and the study of illegal economic activities have been debated on Finnish and Swedish soil and that meetings in Norway and Iceland have centered on such issues as alternatives to formalized means of social control and other instances of decentralization of power.

Although the Scandinavian Research Council for Criminology serves as a common ground for Scandinavian criminologists, most of their

TABLE 1
Scandinavian Research Council: Annual Meetings, 1972–82

Year and Host Country	Subjects
1982, Denmark	The impact of criminology on criminal policy
1981, Iceland	Municipal crime control
1980, Sweden	The macro perspective in criminology: societal development and control policy
1979, Norway	Conflict resolution
1978, Finland	Neoclassicism and criminology; way of life and criminality
1977, Denmark	The current situation of criminology and the role of criminologists
1976, Sweden	Alternatives to imprisonment; economic criminality; the police; institutions; sexual crimes
1975, Norway	Informal and formal social control; economic criminality
1974, Finland	Crime development and prognoses; alternatives to imprisonment; the police
1973, Denmark	Housing research; the police
1972, Sweden	Marxist research; police research

work takes place in institutions based in and funded by the separate national governments.

II. The Organization of Research in Different Countries

In Scandinavia, as in many European countries, criminology is a recently recognized university discipline. The first formal academic program was established in Norway thirty years ago. Denmark and Sweden followed. Finland today has no equivalent university-affiliated institution, although there are other major research facilities.

Of course, research on criminological subjects need not be conducted by criminologists. In all the Nordic countries, members of penal law faculties have long engaged in criminologically relevant research, as have the sociology of law institutes in Finland, Norway, and Sweden, and institutes of sociology and psychology. Researchers in departments of medicine, social work, anthropology, and history also contribute.

We have no basis for estimating the percentage of criminological writings produced by "criminologists," most of whom were trained in disciplines other than criminology. The important points are that there is substantial criminological research in Scandinavia and that most of the countries have created university-based research institutes.

Scientific endeavors are not, however, limited to the university. Government-sponsored organizations and research divisions of operating agencies have proliferated in recent years. In this section, we describe the major research facilities in the universities and outside.

A. Denmark

The principal criminological research program in Denmark is the Institute of Criminal Science in Copenhagen. It was established in 1957 as part of the law faculty. The late Professor Karl Otto Christiansen was the first holder of the institute's criminological chair. He was succeeded by Professor Ulla Bondeson, a Swedish sociologist. There are in addition in the criminology section of the institute two tenured lecturers and two persons with three-year faculty scholarships. Sociologists predominate, but by tradition psychology has been relatively more prominent in the Danish research than in the rest of Scandinavia.

Unlike Swedish and Norwegian universities, where doctoral level certificates in criminology are awarded, Danish universities do not award criminology degrees. Criminology is not recognized as a separate teaching discipline in Denmark, although optional courses are offered to law students. Criminological courses can also be found in departments of sociology and psychology and at social work schools. At the University of Århus, the Institute of Procedural and Criminal Science conducts criminological research.

Academic research profiles are more difficult to depict than those of semigovernmental or operating agencies. The subject matters of the former are diverse and their products are scattered, while the latter often set out their interests in published programs and annual reports. At the institute in Copenhagen, research topics range from pornography, rape, and crime development to studies of public perceptions of crime and punishment and evaluations of penal sanctions, sentencing processes, and police effectiveness. (Specific studies are discussed in Sec. IV.)

In 1971 the Danish national crime prevention council was established by the Ministry of Justice. Its work has a practical orientation and concentrates on such subjects as technical crime prevention and public information. Substantial resources have been allocated to municipalities to aid in preventing child and youth criminality. Funding is given to local projects and for organizing cooperation between social services, the schools, and the police. Scientific evaluations of some of these efforts have been initiated, but on the whole the council's research activity is limited.

The Danish Ministry of Justice has also appointed a permanent research committee with a mandate to initiate, support, and publish work of policy interest, including fact gathering and evaluations undertaken by the Department of Prison and Probation. The annual budget is quite small, equivalent to US$15,000, a sum which naturally does not allow for consistent support for larger research projects.

B. Finland

Criminological research in Finland largely takes place outside the universities. There are two major institutions, both semigovernmental in nature.

In 1974 the National Research Institute of Legal Policy in Helsinki replaced the former Institute of Criminology which had been in existence for about a decade. The institute is financially and administratively linked to the Ministry of Justice, but established legislation guarantees its independence. A governing board composed of scientific experts and senior civil servants takes care of appointments and makes major policy decisions. This semi-independent organization of nine permanent research officers consists of a criminology unit and a "general" sociolegal unit. Professor Inkeri Anttila was the first director, followed on her retirement in 1980 by Patrik Törnudd.

The institute's mandate is related to government information needs, as noted in a memorandum: "While the Research Institute is expected to sponsor and carry out research dealing with legal policy in general, the needs of the Ministry of Justice are given priority. The research program will thus favor research topics relevant to the legislative plans of the Ministry." Research initiatives, however, come from the research staff, and the institute determines both the choice of topics and the manner in which the studies are carried out. The former director has observed: "According to the present policy at the Research Institute, it intends to function midway between research carried out in the universities and research carried out by the administrative agencies. . . . However, attempts are made to relate all research activities in one way or another to decision-making" (Anttila 1978, p. 84).

The institute's long-term interests encompass projects dealing with crime causation and the quality of crime statistics. Examples of current interests are crime consequences and victimization, family violence and child abuse, urban crime, the ecological correlates of crime, and research relating to a proposed comprehensive reform of the penal code.

The other Finnish research entity, the Helsinki Institute for Crime Prevention and Control affiliated with the United Nations (HEUNI), was established at the end of 1982. It functions under the joint auspices of the United Nations and the government of Finland. Its position resembles that of the Research Institute of Legal Policy, with which it collaborates closely and from which came most of its research staff. Professor emeritus Inkeri Anttila was appointed the first director. The HEUNI's official purpose is "to provide for the regular exchange of information and expertise in crime prevention and control among various countries of Europe with different socio-economic systems," a task the institute pursues through conferences, coordination of materials, publications, and research.

Finland also has several small research units directly attached to the Ministry of Justice, working within the law and prison departments. Their work naturally is mostly applied research, as in the other Nordic countries. It is designed to have immediate practical relevance, and descriptive studies tend to rely on current data. Researchers in the Finnish penal administration have also undertaken historical investigations, the so-called VAHO-100 project, in connection with the one-hundredth anniversary of the central prison authority.

C. Norway

The Institute of Criminology and Criminal Law of the University of Oslo was founded within the Faculty of Law in 1954. The institute's initial function was to develop criminology as an auxiliary discipline to criminal law and criminal policy. Over time the focus of the institute's criminological section has shifted from this original task; its most characteristic trait today is the critical stance taken by much of its staff toward the functioning of the criminal justice system. Research projects center on the study of deviance and social control (Stang Dahl 1974; see also Olaussen and Sørensen 1980).

In the late 1960s this institute became the first in Scandinavia to offer graduate degrees in criminology. Enrollment increased steadily during the 1970s and has been particularly high in the last few years. As many as 200 social science students annually complete a year's study of criminology. A small number, typically ten to fifteen, continue for another semester. Fewer than a dozen students have finished full graduate training, complete with thesis. Teaching, including offering elective courses to law students, occupies a major portion of the staff's energies.

All but one of the current staff are sociologists by training. Since 1966 the criminology chair has been held by Professor Nils Christie. In addition, there are three tenured lecturers and one-and-a-half positions as scientific assistants, tenable for a maximum of six years. Two of the law faculty's five-year scholarships are currently held by criminologists. This gives the Oslo institute the largest university-based staff of any criminology program in the Nordic countries.

Affiliated penal jurists and researchers at the Institute of Sociology of Law, headed by Professor Thomas Mathiesen and earlier by Professor Vilhelm Aubert, have also contributed substantially to Norwegian criminology.

Direct governmental involvement in criminological research is limited. The Ministry of Justice operates a small research division, mostly doing prison surveys. Since 1981 Norway also has had a crime prevention council, but thus far its activities have not included research or funding of scientific projects.

D. Sweden

The Institute of Criminal Science/Department of Criminology in Stockholm has ties to both the law and social sciences faculties. Professor Knut Sveri, originally from Norway and the only lawyer among Nordic professors of criminology, has held the criminology chair since its creation in 1964. Formal teaching began in 1971, and since then five people have received doctorates. The staff consists of the professorship, three short-term positions for teaching, and research assistants. Researchers with outside grants are also affiliated with the institute.

The largest criminological research organization in Scandinavia is the Swedish National Council for Crime Prevention (NCCP), which was established in 1974. This agency is linked to the Ministry of Justice and is headed by a seventeen-member board appointed by the government. In addition to secretariats that handle administration and information, the organization includes a policy-planning unit and a research division. The latter, with its own seven-member advisory group, is, in a Nordic context, a giant among dwarfs. The permanent scientific staff in 1983 numbered more than ten. Relatively substantial funds are administered. In the fiscal year 1981–82 funding approached US$240,000 (1.9 million Swedish crowns), roughly split between intramural work at the research division and external studies. The budget for 1982–83 allows US$110,000 for outside research grants; these are generally made to university-based researchers.

The National Council for Crime Prevention functions on a much larger scale than do its counterparts in Denmark and Norway. Modern economic crimes and the relations between narcotics and crime are the NCCP's principal areas of interest for the current three-year period. Other focal subjects include general prevention and law obedience, youth and criminality, alcohol and criminality, preventive measures against crime, and institutional treatment of offenders.

Sweden's operating agencies also conduct criminological research. The National Police Board, the National Bureau of Statistics, and the city of Stockholm, for example, have recently conducted criminological studies. During the last decade, resources for intramural research on "social problems" have been created within the ministries of social affairs and justice.

More specifically, the Swedish National Prison and Probation Administration conducts investigations, supports outside studies of interest to the penal authorities, and acts as a "clearinghouse" for publication of results obtained in Sweden and abroad concerning correctional programs. Evaluation projects and systematic collection of statistical data receive high priority. The annual report for 1981, for example, presents data from a recidivism survey and discusses the use of prison population projections. It further describes evaluations of the new local penal institutions, prison medicine, new voluntary drug-free sections at certain prisons, and a pilot program for drug abusers who are placed in outside care during part of their sentence (see Bishop 1982). Various aspects of the drug situation in prison have generated a demand for more research. Supplementary funding amounting to 1.5 million crowns (approximately US$185,000) has been granted to the research and development unit for ongoing collection and analysis of information on prisoners' use of narcotics and on treatment programs.

Sweden is particularly known among the Nordic countries for its extensive official report writing. The documentation often contains large amounts of empirical material and related analyses. Noteworthy examples are the report *Prostitutionen i Sverige* (1980) and the national rape survey done for the Parliamentary Committee on Sexual Offences (Persson 1981).

This summary has a static quality that understates the interactions among researchers and policymakers in Scandinavia. These are countries with small populations, and people necessarily communicate across organizational boundaries. Experts from the universities are commonly consulted when policy reports or legislative reforms are under way. Criminologists work as committee members or scientific advisers, as in the case of the ongoing total revision of the Finnish penal code and the Norwegian governmental documents on criminal policy and on the role of the police in society.

III. Government Influence on Research

Nordic criminology includes a diverse body of academic, semi-independent, and administrative organizations. There is, however, a trend in the organization of criminological research toward greater reliance on state-affiliated establishments.

In the early 1970s students of criminology debated their role as experts on crime. To many the idea of becoming criminological technocrats had little appeal; some instead hoped to be transmitters of an antiestablishment ideology and expertise in shaping public opinion. Criminologists also wondered whether work opportunities would materialize and endure.

Professor Knut Sveri of Stockholm University has observed that criminological information is increasingly in demand "especially in the connection with new (or changed) legislation in the field of criminal law and penology." Sveri captures an ambivalence that many scholars feel about the acceptance and stature that criminology has achieved:

As a university professor I am both happy and unhappy about this development. I am happy because we are recognized, because our work counts and is considered to be important. I am unhappy because the state's university policy has been such that we have no resources to counter-balance the practical interests of the authorities with basic research within the universities. I am certainly unhappy because my best students are offered better research positions in governmental offices than at the university and that these offices steal my best students. I do not regret that they get better salaries and more secure positions than they can get at the university, but I do regret that their souls may be touched by the evil spirits of loyalties with the government and that they may lose their ability to be critical. [Sveri 1983]

The dilemmas of state-sponsored research in criminology are most apparent in Finland and Sweden, where the semigovernmental agencies dominate the field. Patrik Törnudd, the director of the Research Institute of Legal Policy in Helsinki, suggests that Swedish and Finnish governments have exercised less influence on research priorities than either advocates or critics of the government-affiliated programs had predicted (1983). Törnudd identifies two significant reasons for this. First, all criminologists share a common university background; the initial academic socialization of government agency researchers is reinforced by peer contacts and regular communications with university-affiliated colleagues. Some criminologists take temporary government assignments or switch between university and government employment. The ideal of the independent and critical scientist is reinforced, and academic research sets the prevailing methodological standards. Second, he suggests that government officials in Scandinavia do not necessarily perceive the proper role of science any differently than do scholars, and that the state-funded criminological research centers "are explicitly protected from overt pressures from above through various institutional arrangements" (p. 8).

By contrast, a former research worker at the Swedish NCCP, Henrik Tham, has argued that governmental influence both shapes and limits research at the government-affiliated institutions. In a review of published reports from 1974 to mid-1982, he points out that the reports are specialized, empirical, descriptive/evaluative, and largely oriented toward topical subjects (1983). Stated negatively, the research is characterized by its want of theory and a failure to locate research in historical and structural contexts. Tham further argues that the adoption of priorities and the NCCP board's veto power over suggested projects have had little controlling impact on the research program. This is partly because agency-employed criminologists tend to develop a narrow expertise and often choose research subjects that provoke little controversy. Moreover, as he explains it, the intramural researcher plays a waiting game vis-à-vis broad party-political solutions of social problems. Particularly if the problems are difficult to investigate, the researchers' special skepticism promotes a tendency to stay away from such politically "contaminated" areas. Last, Tham urges the need to focus on the consequences of intellectual co-optation—ministerial lawmaking opportunities can dictate the range of research activities. Pragmatism and technocratic viewpoints rule—the projects aimed at reducing criminality are the only ones to receive attention.

Nils Christie has characterized the criminologist's dilemma in terms of a choice between being technicians or poets. His idea of criminology "consists more of broad cultural views on society and its deviance, than of concrete applicable techniques" (Christie 1971, p. 145). In other words, he calls for humane generalists at a time when the market most highly values technical specialists. Although the criminologist as cultural worker is not likely to be valued by officials, Christie warns against taking their disparagement too seriously and claims that "our situation has a great resemblance to that of artists and men of letters." He believes that the independent researcher is needed, not to provide technical expertise, but to formulate alternative questions. He sees it as crucial for every society to make allowance for people who can roam in the frontiers, who are allowed to be impractical and to function as problem raisers rather than as problem solvers.

It is no coincidence that Nils Christie comes from Norway. The Norwegian social sciences are known for having "an outspoken critical outlook, primarily oriented towards public debate" while "in Sweden, on the other hand, the tradition of successful reform action initiated within the system is no less strong" (Törnudd 1983, p. 6).

Thus far we have described attitudes concerning government influence on research conducted within semigovernmental research institutions. Similar tensions beset the university-based researcher. Research institutions within the university, to an increasing extent, must rely on outside funds, particularly government funding. Research support is available from national foundations for the social sciences, scientific academies, bank trusts, private funds, and, in the case of Sweden, the NCCP. It would be an oversimplification to view the academic criminologist as beyond the influence of external priorities. It would also be an oversimplification to leave the impression that the

Nordic criminological research community and the criminal justice administration are fundamentally incompatible.

Researchers have long been closely connected with practice and practitioners. Small-scale nations cannot afford the luxury of inflexibility. The trademark of Scandinavian criminology has traditionally been its policy orientation, its empirical foundations, and its reliance on middle-range theories (Wolf 1976*a*). Abstract theorizing is not much to be found and "the younger generation of criminologists are predominantly empirically minded and/or oriented toward the practice of crime policy" (Wolf 1983, p. 166). This applies to all the Nordic countries. There is, however, an ever-present resistance among many criminologists to formulate their research questions mainly to fit the needs of the administration.

IV. Research Trends and Emphases

Nils Christie pointed out more than twenty years ago that Scandinavian criminology embodies a blend of a continental European scientific tradition based on law and medicine, and the sociologically oriented influences from the United States (Christie 1961). In the early 1970s, Inkeri Anttila noted: "A typical feature of Scandinavian criminology has throughout the last decade been a heavy orientation towards sociological research . . . and also psychologists and psychiatrists have accepted a fairly sociological outlook on crime and deviance" (1974, p. 5).

Anttila further observed a shift in emphasis from traditional survey studies to analyses of the crime control system, with emphasis on "how the system really operates and in the real consequences for the offender and for the society" (1974, p. 5). The shift of interest has unquestionably continued, and criminology today might be viewed as a science of deviance and a sociology of social control.

Attempts to explain the causes of crime have, of course, been made, but pragmatic Scandinavian criminologists have invested little energy in developing pure models or "schools" as have been developed on the Continent. Neither of two commonly used textbooks for students is highly abstract or theoretical. The Norwegian textbook (Christie 1975) discusses the structure of criminality in terms of industrialization and urbanization processes that weaken traditional social controls. The Finnish reader, also available in Swedish (Anttila and Törnudd 1973), is "functionalist" but shows the influence of both labeling and conflict approaches.

The book publishing market for criminological works has greatly expanded. Much research is disseminated in "publication series" connected to the university institutions, semi-independent organizations, or administrative agencies. For example, close to fifty documents have been put out by the Institute of Criminology and Criminal Law in Oslo and half that number by the Institute of Criminal Science in Copenhagen. The Finnish Research Institute of Legal Policy and its predecessor have since 1963 published sixty research reports. The National Council for Crime Prevention in Sweden has published more than fifty reports in the last ten years.

Criminological articles are sometimes published in national law journals and sociological periodicals. *Acta Sociologica*, published in English, works on a common Scandinavian basis. *Nordisk Tidsskrift for Kriminalvidenskab (NTfK)* (Nordic journal of criminal science) has since 1913 functioned as a forum for writing on penal law and criminology; prior to that, dating back to 1878, it was a journal for the prison services.

The *NTfK* holds a special position in being a cross-Scandinavian enterprise, although language barriers limit the number of Finnish readers and contributors. Its recent circulation approaches 2,000 subscribers.

The contents of *NTfK* over time may provide a general picture of evolving research interests. Preben Wolf (1976*a*) in a content analysis of *NTfK*, classified Scandinavian criminology into five categories: (1) the incidence and prevalence of crime, crime statistics, and dark numbers; (2) criminal populations; (3) specific types of crime; (4) sanctions and treatment; and (5) control systems (Wolf 1976*a*, p. 218). Wolf concluded that 85 percent of the articles appearing in *NTfK* during the years 1961–76 belonged to one of those five categories. The rest consisted mainly of general reviews, historical studies, biographies, policy suggestions and, in later years, a few victimization studies. The largest number of articles (35 percent) dealt with control systems, largely because writings by legal scholars or practitioners fell into this category.

Wolf's study looked at two subperiods with close to identical distributions. We have attempted a follow-up, but the depiction of the journal's contents from 1977 to 1983 suffers from several weaknesses, not least that the taxonomy employed leaves much discretion to the classifier. It appears that control systems remain the most favored research area. A category concerning "criminal policy" has to be added to Wolf's original list of major subjects. Writings in this group have primarily addressed modern penal legislation, the neoclassical tendency in penology, and criminal policy from an international viewpoint.

A qualitative look at the *NTfK* articles in later years suggests that certain new matters have gained prominent ground. They relate to research on narcotics, modern economic criminality, police behavior, immigrants and foreign workers, and women as offenders or victims. An outline of continuing and developing research emphases follows below, but first a cautionary note. We describe research *areas* that have received significant attention in the last fifteen years. Selected Nordic criminological projects carried out before 1970 are described elsewhere in some detail (Christie 1961, 1971; Crime and Industrialization 1974; Wolf 1976a). Works cited here are only illustrative, and the survey is neither exhaustive nor of direct bibliographical value. Our limited knowledge of Finnish (and Icelandic) literature poses a special obstacle in portraying all Scandinavian criminology.

A. *Crime, Criminals, and Victims*

The study of registered crimes and criminals has a long history in Scandinavia. Because Scandinavian populations are small and public records are good, scientists can study populations, not samples, and can follow up subjects in more than one respect. For example, records of criminal conduct and standards of living have been examined (Tham 1979).

The inter-Scandinavian "Project Metropolitan" that started in the mid-1960s continues its longitudinal study comparing life chances and educational and occupational careers, both conventional and criminal, for some 12,000 Danish boys and a cohort of 15,000 Swedish boys and girls born in 1953. The departments of sociology at the universities of Copenhagen and Stockholm carry out the two separate parts of the project. The Bank of Sweden Tercentenary Foundation primarily funds the Swedish study, while the Danish researchers carry on with little means of financial support (see further Høgh and Wolf 1981; Janson 1984).

Official crime statistics are the basic source for the annual descriptive analyses of crime trends and crime control developments produced by the NCCP in Sweden and by the Research Institute of Legal Policy in Finland. These data have also been used in analyzing broad-scale societal processes and historical changes (e.g., Christie 1975). Long-term efforts to compile comparable criminal statistics—using the official registrations—from Denmark, Finland, Norway, and Sweden have finally borne fruit. Thanks to the Swedish National Bureau of Statistics, researchers have been provided with a carefully documented sourcebook for the period 1950–80 (see von Hofer 1983 for an English summary). The sourcebook shows that the Scandinavian nations have high crime rates, with the Swedes and Danes at the top and the Norwegians at the bottom.

Unreported criminality is another subject in which a joint Nordic research effort has been attempted. The titles of the latest reports, "Criminality as Normality" and "Nuances in Gray" (Greve 1972; Stangeland and Hauge 1974), indicate the conclusions these authors reach on the basis of self-reported offenses. Special attention has been paid to the methodological and theoretical problems posed by such studies (Persson 1980).

Crime is not an uncommon activity in the general population, but neither is it evenly dispersed. Youth criminality is of prime criminological interest. Projects carried out in the 1970s often attempted close-up pictures of illegal juvenile deeds. Suburban communities in the neighborhood of Copenhagen and Stockholm were two sites of detailed investigations. Several reports on juvenile delinquency have been published under the auspices of the Danish and Swedish Councils for Crime Prevention.

Ongoing studies investigate the lives of today's young people, including their deviant acts. The concept of "life-style" may constitute a Scandinavian return to the "subcultures" research in classical criminological works. Subcultural milieus being studied include youths in "risk-zones," a group of "lawless" addicts (Kalderstam 1979), ordinary thieves and crooks (Åkerström 1983), and blood feuds among Finnish gypsies (Grönfors 1977).

Foreigners' criminality has lately become the target of much research, especially in Sweden.[1] One set of questions concerning the influx of foreign workers concerns the criminality of second-generation immigrants. The Nordic population is no longer as homogeneous as in the past. Criminologists' research findings from nations accustomed to racial, religious, and cultural heterogeneity will probably not provide an adequate basis for understanding Scandinavian problems.

Women's criminality has also received more attention recently. Al-

[1] The Swedish National Council for Crime Prevention has just published a report (available in Swedish only) that deals with foreigners and criminality (Eriksson and Tham 1983). The official statistics show that in 1981 foreign nationals represented only 13 percent of the total number of persons against whom legal actions had been taken and that Nordic citizens constitute more than half of all foreigners who had been subject to legal proceedings. However, immigrants get in trouble with the law twice as often as Swedes (taking the different age distributions into account), and foreign citizens constitute as much as one-fifth of the total number of persons admitted to correctional facilities.

though the female share of registered crimes remains low in the Nordic countries (about 10 percent for all offenses), the idea of "the new liberated criminal" motivated serious study of the criminality of women in the contexts of sex-role socialization, opportunity structures, and control theories. Researchers have examined female offenders in court and in prison, and quite a lot of research on prostitution has been done in Sweden and Norway. Women's experiences as victims have lately developed into a vital concern, both publicly and in the scientific community. A Nordic anthology in "women's criminology" has been published (Høigård and Snare 1983).

The first Scandinavian victimization study based on interviews with a representative sample of the population was conducted in Finland in 1970 (Aromaa 1971). Comparative victim surveys were later conducted as an inter-Nordic project (see Wolf and Hauge 1974; Wolf 1976b). As recently as 1981 one of these studies was nationally replicated to gain knowledge about changes over time (Olaussen 1982). Finnish researchers in particular have emphasized the importance of systematic information on the distribution of victimization and on the private and public costs of crimes. The Finnish National Research Institute of Legal Policy has published several reports, including English summaries (see also Lättila et al. 1983). Victimization research has broadened its focus from an original aim to supplement official crime statistics. The research efforts have helped make private and family violence a social policy issue. As in other parts of the world, the women's movement in Scandinavia has contributed to making battered women and children highly topical. Recent studies of rape and its handling have been influenced by a victim orientation (Lykkjen 1976; Carstensen et al. 1981; Persson 1981). Last, victimization research has stimulated inquiry into the fear of crime, including the detrimental social consequences that such anxiety entails for individuals or vulnerable groups (Balvig 1977). Notwithstanding these trends, victim studies have taken place within the context of traditional criminology. Victimology has not emerged as a discipline apart from criminology, as most Nordic criminologists would probably find a separation of the topics artificial.

B. Specific Types of Crime

Finnish researchers have paid special attention to public violence and its victims since the 1930s, presumably because Finland's violence rates have traditionally been higher than those of the other Nordic countries.

The Finnish criminological institute has included the study of family violence in its research program (e.g., Peltoniemi 1982). In the rest of Scandinavia, domestic violence is also receiving much attention.

Various researchers have studied long-term homicide trends, including Icelandic analyses (Gudjonsson and Petursson 1981). Researchers have also exhibited increased interest in urban violence. Except for Finland, the Nordic countries have long had low rates of violence, and recent increases in violent crime rates have catalyzed research initiatives.

Property offenses are the preponderance of registered crimes against the penal code but have received comparatively little specialized attention by researchers. Standard works in criminology do, however, discuss the increase in property offenses that accompanied rising living standards after the Second World War. One Danish study analyzes theft in the 1970s, including its prevalence, victimization risks, and its costs (Balvig 1980–83).

Modern economic offenses receive higher research priority than do the common-law property crimes. A common definition of this subject has proven difficult to achieve (see, e.g., Jepsen 1980). (A standard working definition is generally employed: that criminality which foremost entails economic profit as its direct motive, performed systematically within the frame of economic activity which, in itself, is not criminalized.) Special governmental committees, working bodies, and individual researchers have scrutinized fraudulent behavior in connection with bankruptcy, export-import business, tax regulations, the black or gray labor market, subsidies to enterprises, and environmental protection. A third of the individual research grants approved by the NCCP in 1983 concerned economic criminality.

Narcotics use and consequences is a newly important research subject. The involvement of young people with illegal drugs has in the last fifteen years become a major policy issue. Sweden and Norway lead the Nordic countries in drug-related crime prevention efforts and criminological research. The Finnish and Icelandic cultures have been less receptive to drugs, and the Danes' more "liberal" attitude toward the use of (at least) milder narcotics has produced less research and policy concern.

Drug incidence studies are yearly administered to representative samples of Norwegian and Swedish schoolchildren. The reliability of these self-report surveys has subsequently become the latest target of methodological debate among criminologists and social scientists. All the Nordic data point to a constant consumption level of illegal narcotic substances in recent years, or even a downward tendency in comparison with the early 1970s.

Trend analyses are also made of narcotic drug offenses and estimations are made as to these offenders' association with other types of crime. Researchers connected to the penal administrations have studied the control of narcotics inside the prison and the treatment of drug abusers (concerning Norwegian drug offenders, see Bödal [1982]).

This accumulation of drug-related research should be seen in the context of a shift toward harsher penal measures: large increases in maximum penalties provided by law, a judicial tendency to impose the maximum lawful sentence limit in narcotic cases, and a demand for coercive treatment of addicts.

The main point is that practically all areas of criminological research are now marked by the drug problem. It is a sign of the times that, in addition to the yearly crime survey, the Swedish NCCP in 1982 and 1983 prepared reports on drug developments (see, in English, Andersson and Solarz 1982), and that the Scandinavian Research Council's 1984 annual research seminar, to be held in Norway, is devoted to narcotics and control policies.

C. Studies in Social Control

If one were to pinpoint a single main theme of Nordic criminological research in recent decades, it would be social control systems. Interests have moved from lawbreakers to the law enforcement apparatus. Since the 1960s, this focus has taken the form of investigations of the limits of re-socialization efforts based on coercion. Researchers critically assessed the use of indeterminate sanctions: forced labor for alcoholic vagrants, youth imprisonment, and internment of "dangerous offenders" (see, e.g., Christie 1971, 1981).

Two major trends can be identified in Scandinavian prison research. First, correctional treatment studies have shown the detrimental effects of imprisonment in terms of prisonization and recidivism (see Bondeson [1974a] for a review). Other research has investigated the impacts of different styles of confinement (Christiansen, Moe, and Senholt 1972; Uusitalo 1972; Bondeson 1974b). These findings demonstrate that a treatment rationale for depriving people of their liberty is untenable.

A second brand of prison research is concerned with the Scandinavian prisoners' movement. Numerous critical writings on prison conditions and the operation of special preventative sanctions have appeared.

The prisoners' movements and their relation to "action research" have been analyzed in *Politics of Abolition* (Mathiesen 1974).

Penal measures other than prison use have been studied. The Nordic countries do not employ bail procedures, and legal scholars and government commissions have investigated the use of pretrial confinement, as have criminologists (see, e.g., Petersen et al. 1972; Finstad and Gjetvik 1980). Noncustodial sanctions, such as suspended sentences, probation, and parole, have been evaluated. Risking oversimplification, one could conclude that the less intrusive the punishment, the better the results as to recidivism (Bondeson 1977); that the mixture of service and control entails inherent contradictions (Hansen, Sørenson, and Trollvik 1980); and that allocation of more resources to this caretaking authority has little effect (Kühlhorn 1980).

Police research is common. For surveys, see Knutsson, Kühlhorn, and Reiss (1979) and Koch (1982). Swedish and Norwegian works on the police role in society were produced during the past decade (Cedermark and Klette 1973; Støkken 1974). *Policing Scandinavia* (Hauge 1980) contains a broad range of articles, including, among others, analyses of the reinforcement of the police force in recent years, a 1976 strike among uniformed policemen in Finland, recruits' adaptations to their profession, and the police role in labor conflicts. "Police violence and violence against the police" is a topic for the Ninth Nordic Criminal Science Meeting (in Helsinki in 1984).

Interest in the history of crime and crime control has increased. Studies investigate the institutionalization of imprisonment as a commonly imposed punishment and imprisonment trends in nineteenth-century Sweden (Snare 1977). Ericsson (1974) has studied the early institutionalization of the mentally ill in Norway, and Stang Dahl (1978) has studied the origins of Norway's child welfare system.

Proponents and critics disagree as to the real meaning or implications of the predominant modern penal philosophy, by some called "neoclassicism." It advocates that emphasis be placed on the offense, and not on the offender or individual need for treatment, and implies a strict proportionality between the gravity of the crime and the severity of the punishment. Whether such a philosophy will lead to a decrease or increase in the prison population, and whether it supports law-and-order dispositions or, instead, promotes a more just distribution of punishment has spurred much debate among criminologists. Deliberations on crime prevention ideologies that took place under the auspices of the Scandinavian Research Council for Criminology culminated in a

Nordic anthology on "Punishment and Justice" (Heckscher et al. [1980]; see also Anttila [1978] and Christie [1981] for a discussion of general deterrence).

In Scandinavia, as apparently in North America, a certain "moral climate" favors criminalization over decriminalization and punitive intervention over nonintervention. Most apparent are the prevailing attitudes concerning narcotics, tax evasion and other economic crimes, and the victimization of women. In the last two instances some regard stricter sanctions as means to promote "economic equality" and "sexual equality," respectively.

It remains in question whether criminological research on the public's general sense of justice will influence the direction of crime control in the 1980s (see, e.g., Kutchinsky 1972; Bondeson 1980; Linden and Similä 1982). It is, however, more likely that in the future, as in the past, studies dealing with the ideological backbone of society's control systems will characterize Scandinavian criminology.

REFERENCES

Åkerström, M. 1983. *Crooks and Squares: Lifestyles of Thieves and Addicts in Comparison to Conventional People.* Lund: Studentlitteratur.

Andersson, J., and A. Solarz. 1982. *Drug Criminality and Drug Abuse in Sweden, 1968–81.* National Council for Crime Prevention, Report no. 10. Stockholm: Liber.

Antilla, I. 1974. "Developments in Criminology and Criminal Policy in Scandinavia." In *Crime and Industrialization.* Scandinavian Research Council for Criminology.

———. 1978. *Papers on Crime Control.* Publication no. 26. Helsinki: Research Institute of Legal Policy.

Antilla, I., and P. Törnudd. 1973. *Kriminologi i kriminalpolitiskt perspektiv.* Stockholm: Norstedt. Revised Finnish edition. 1983. *Kriminologia ja kriminaalipolitiikka.* Helsinki: WSOY.

Aromaa, K. 1971. *Arkipäivan väkivaltaa Suomessa.* (Summary: Everyday violence in Finland.) Helsinki: Institute of Criminology.

Aspelin, E., N. Bishop, H. Thornstedt, and P. Törnudd. 1975. *Some Developments in Nordic Criminal Policy.* Scandinavian Research Council for Criminology.

Balvig, F. 1977. *Angst for kriminalitet.* Copenhagen: Gyldendal.

———. 1980–83. *Studier over tyveriforbrydelsen, I–V.* Research reports nos. 12, 13, 14, 20, and 22. Copenhagen: Ministry of Justice.

Bishop, N. 1982. "Prison and Probation Research in Sweden." Home Office Research Bulletin 14. London.

——, ed. 1980. *Crime and Crime Control in Scandinavia, 1976–80*. Scandinavian Research Council for Criminology.

Bondeson, U. 1974*a*. *Evaluation of Correctional Treatment: A Survey and Critical Interpretation of Correctional Treatment Studies in Scandinavia, 1945–1974*. University of Lund, Sweden.

——. 1974*b*. *Fången i fångsambället*. Stockholm: Norstedt.

——. 1977. *Kriminalvård i fribet: Intention och verklighet*. Stockholm: Liber.

——. 1980. "Rättsmedvetandet rörande brottens straffvärde och domarens straffmätning." In *Påföljdsval, straffmätning och straffvärde*. National Council for Crime Prevention, Report no. 1980:2. Stockholm: Liber.

Bödal, K. 1982. *350 narkoselgere*. Oslo: Universitetsforlaget.

Carstensen, G., A. Kongstad, S. Larsen, and N. Rasmussen. 1981. *Voldtægt— på vej mod belbedsforståelse*. Copenhagen: Delta.

Cedermark, G., and H. Klette. 1973. *Polis—myndighet—människa*. Lund: Studentlitteratur.

Christiansen, K. O., M. Moe, and L. Senholt. 1972. "Effektiviteten af forvaring og særfængsel m.v." Betænkning no. 644. Copenhagen: Ministry of Justice.

Christie, N. 1961. "Scandinavian Criminology." *Sociological Inquiry* 31(1):93–104.

——. 1971. "Scandinavian Criminology Facing the 1970's." In *Scandinavian Studies in Criminology*, vol. 3, edited by N. Christie. Oslo: Universitetsforlaget.

——. 1975. *Hvor tett et samfunn*. Rev. ed., 1982. Oslo: Universitetsforlaget.

——. 1981. *Limits to Pain*. Oslo: Universitetsforlaget.

Crime and Industrialization. 1974. First Seminar for Criminologists from Socialist and Scandinavian Countries, Helsinki, Finland, August 26–29, 1974. Scandinavian Research Council for Criminology.

Ericsson, K. 1974. *Den tvetydige omsorgen*. Oslo: Universitetsforlaget.

Eriksson, U., and H. Tham. 1983. *Utlänningarna och brottsligheten*. National Council for Crime Prevention, Report 1983:4. Stockholm: Liber.

Finstad, L., and A. L. Gjetvik. 1980. *Varetektsfanger forteller . . .* Oslo: Universitetsforlaget.

Greve, V. 1972. *Kriminalitet som normalitet*. Copenhagen: Juristforbundets forlag.

Grönfors, M. 1977. *Blood Feuding among Finnish Gypsies*. Research Report no. 213. Department of Sociology, University of Helsinki.

Gudjonsson, G. H., and H. Petursson. 1981. "Udviklingen i drabsforbrydelsen i Island, 1900–1979." *Nordisk Tidskrift for Kriminalvidenskab* 68(1):4–16.

Hansen, M. Wiil, A. Sørensen, and M. Trollvik. 1980. *Dømt til hjelp*. Oslo: Universitetsforlaget.

Hauge, R., ed. 1980. *Policing Scandinavia*. Scandinavian Studies in Criminology, vol. 7. Oslo: Universitetsforlaget.

Heckscher, S., A. Snare, H. Takala, and J. Vestergaard, eds. 1980. *Straff och rättfärdighet—ny nordisk debatt.* Stockholm: Norstedt.

Høgh, E., and P. Wolf. 1977. "Project Metropolitan: A Longitudinal Study of 12,270 Boys from the Metropolitan Area of Copenhagen, Denmark, 1953–77." In *Prospective Longitudinal Research in Europe,* edited by S. A. Mednick and A. E. Baert. London: Oxford University Press.

Høigård, C., and A. Snare, eds. 1983. *Kvinners skyld: Nordisk antologi i kriminologi.* Oslo: PAX.

Janson, C. G. 1984. *Project Metropolitan: A Presentation and Progress Report.* Department of Sociology, Research Report no. 21. University of Stockholm.

Jepsen, J., ed. 1980. *Økonomisk kriminalitet.* Copenhagen: Informations Forlag.

Kalderstam, J. 1979. *De laglösa.* Department of Sociology of Law, Report Series 3-79. University of Lund, Sweden.

Knutsson, J., E. Kühlhorn, and A. Reiss, Jr., eds. 1979. *Police and the Social Order: Contemporary Research Perspectives.* National Council for Crime Prevention, Report no. 6. Stockholm: Liber.

Koch, H. 1982. *Politiforskning i Norden.* Institute of Criminal Science, Stencil Series no. 17. University of Copenhagen.

Kühlhorn, E. 1980. *Non-institutional Treatment and Rehabilitation.* Shortened version. National Council for Crime Prevention, Report no. 7. Stockholm: Liber.

Kutchinsky, B. 1972. "Sociological Aspects of the Perception of Deviance and Criminality." In *Collected Studies of Criminological Research,* Vol. 9. Strasbourg: Council of Europe.

Lättila, R., M. Heiskanen, L. Komulainen, T. Niskanen, and R. Sirén. 1983. *Accidents and Violence: A Survey of the Incidence of Accidents, Criminal Violence and the Resulting Injuries.* Central Statistical Office of Finland, Study no. 80. Helsinki.

Linden, P. A., and M. Similä. 1982. *Rättsmedvetandet i Sverige.* National Council for Crime Prevention, Report 1982:1. Stockholm: Liber.

Lykkjen, A. M. 1976. *Voldtekt.* Oslo: PAX.

Mathiesen, T. 1974. "Politics of Abolition." In *Scandinavian Studies in Criminology,* vol. 4, edited by N. Christie. Oslo: Universitetsforlaget.

Olaussen, L. P. 1982. "Selvrapportert utsatthet for kriminalitet." *Nordisk Tidsskrift for Kriminalvidenskab* 68(4):178–97.

Olaussen, L. P., and R. Sørensen. 1980. *Norwegian Criminology and Changes in the Political and Ideological Structure in Norway.* Institute of Criminology and Criminal Law, Stencil no. 37. University of Oslo.

Persson, L. G. W. 1980. *Hidden Criminality.* Department of Sociology, University of Stockholm.

———. 1981. *Våldtäkt: En kriminologisk kartläggning av våldtäktsbrottet.* Stockholm: Liber.

Peltoniemi, T. 1982. *Perheväkivalta Suomessa ja Ruotsissa—yleisyys ja asenteet.* Publication no. 54. (Summary: Family violence in Finland and in Sweden—prevalence and attitudes.) Helsinki: Research Institute of Legal Policy.

Petersen, E., E. Dall, O. H. Nielsen, J. Rosenstock, and H. T. Truelsen. 1972. *I Varetægt—I Fængsel*. Mentalhygienjnisk Forskningsinstitut. Copenhagen.

Prostitutionen i Sverige. 1980. Ds S 1980:9. Stockholm: Ministry of Social Affairs.

Scandinavian Studies in Criminology. 1965–80. Vols. 1–7. Oslo: Universitetsforlaget.

Snare, A. 1977. "Work, War, Prison and Welfare: Control of the Laboring Poor in Sweden." D.Crim. dissertation, University of California, Berkeley.

Stang Dahl, T. 1974. "The State of Criminology in Norway: A Short Report." In *Deviance and Social Control in Europe*, edited by H. Bianchi, K. Schumann, and J. Young. London: Wiley.

———. 1978. *Barnevern og samfunnsvern*. Oslo: PAX. (English translation: *Child Welfare and Social Defense*. Oslo: Universitetsforlaget, 1985.)

Stangeland, P., and R. Hauge. 1974. *Nyanser i grått*. Oslo: Universitetsforlaget.

Støkken, A. M. 1974. *Politiet i det norske samfunn*. Oslo: Universitetsforlaget. Expanded ed., 1981.

Sveri, K. 1983. "The Usefulness of Concrete Criminological Research for Criminal Policy." Paper read at the Soviet-Scandinavian Seminar on Contemporary Crime Policy, Moscow, April 11–16, 1983.

Tham, H. 1979. *Brottslighet och levnadsnivå*. Stockholm: Liber.

———. 1983. "Kriminologin som inomverksforskning: Exemplet BRÅ." *Nordisk Tidsskrift for Kriminalvidenskab* 70(4):216–23.

Törnudd, P. 1983. "A More Sombre Mood: The Status and Roles of Criminology and Its Institutional Relations with Public Policy and Practice." Paper read at the Ninth International Congress in Criminology, Vienna, September 25–30, 1983.

Uusitalo, P. 1972. "Recidivism after Release from Closed and Open Institutions." *British Journal of Criminology* 12:211–29.

Wolf, P. 1976a. "Apparent Tendencies in Scandinavian Criminology during Recent Years." *Annales internationales de criminologie* 15(2):217–25.

———. 1976b. "On Individual Victims of Certain Crimes in Four Scandinavian Countries, 1970/1974: A Comparative Study." Paper read at the Second International Symposium on Victimology, Boston, September 5–11, 1976.

———. 1983. "Denmark." In *International Handbook of Contemporary Developments in Criminology*, edited by E. H. Johnson. Westport, Conn.: Greenwood Press.

Wolf, P., and R. Hauge. 1974. "Violence in Three Scandinavian Countries." In *Scandinavian Studies in Criminology*, vol. 5, edited by N. Christie. Oslo: Universitetsforlaget.

von Hofer, H., ed. 1983. *Nordic Criminal Statistics, 1950–1980(81)*. Statistics Sweden, Unit of Justice and Social Statistics, Promemoria 1983:8. Stockholm.